NO SAFE HAVEN:

HOMELAND INSECURITY

BY

ROBERT K. HUDNALL, JD
CAPTAIN (ret)

Omega Press
El Paso, Texas

2\ROBERT K. HUDNALL, JD

NO SAFE HAVEN: HOMELAND INSECURITY

OMEGA PRESS
An imprint of Omega Communications Group, Inc.

For Information Address:

Omega Press
5823 N. Mesa, #823
El Paso, Texas 79912

Or

http://www.kenhudnall.com

First Edition

Printed In The United States of America

OTHER WORKS BY THE SAME AUTHOR

UNDER THE NAME KEN HUDNALL

MANHATTAN CONSPIRACY SERIES
Blood on the Apple
Capital Crimes
Angel of Death
Confrontation

THE OCCULT CONNECTION SERIES:
UFOs, Secret Societies and Ancient Gods
The Hidden Race

WHEN DARKNESS FALLS

SPIRITS OF THE BORDER SERIES:
The History and Mystery of El Paso Del Norte
The History and Mystery of Fort Bliss, Texas

DEDICATION

As always, it is my long suffering, understanding wife, Sharon who has given me the encouragement and assistance to continue to produce books for my many readers in the face of active opposition by those unwilling or unable to get published. I owe all of my success to her.

6\ROBERT K. HUDNALL, JD

TABLE OF CONTENTS

EXCERPT FROM DEFENSIVE TATICS LESSON PLAN FOR INFANTRY OFFICER ADVANCED COURSE CLASS INSTRUCTED MARCH 1980

**DEFENSIVE TACTICS:
MILITARY OPERATIONS ON URBAN TERRAIN**

There are many who believe that the defender in an urban area has a massive advantage over an aggressor. In some respects this is certainly true, however, there are many other issues to consider and some very unique problems that arise in an urban environment.

CIVILIAN POPULATIONS

On the battlefield, there is generally not a very large civilian population for the defender to have to contend with. Anyone who can gets away from areas of combat as soon as possible. However, in an urban environment, the battle is fought among and around the domiciles of the civilian population that inhabit the city. The proposed battlefield is not some remote sparsely populated area, but rather the ground upon which their homes stand. Many will choose to remain in their homes to try and protect what they view as irreplaceable rather than flee from the advancing enemy. Therefore, there are issues that arise regarding the interactions between the defenders and the members of the civilian population that have chosen to remain in the city.

Troop commanders who are forced to dig in within the city proper will therefore, be faced with issues relating to law enforcement and crowd control in addition to preparing for a defense against an invading enemy force. A panicked civilian population can overwhelm the defending troops faster than any invading enemy force. Additionally, the panic demonstrated by the civilian crowds can spread to defending military personnel, causing desertions as soldiers scramble to evacuate or protect their families at a time when every soldier is needed in their defensive positions.

As an aggressor comes within range, there is also the very real possibility that there will be strikes directed against the civilian population in order distract the defenders from their primary mission.

CHAPTER ONE
TERRORISM 101

Our newspapers and the airwaves are filled with news about the current war on terror and the blitherings of the so-called 9/11 Commission. This supposedly bi-partisan commission is conducting some of the most gymnastic hearings, twisting words, creating new meanings for words and making public pronouncements that contain only partial truths. All this is being done in the name of the public's right to know and to "get to the bottom of things", while at the same time such commissions are used as forums in which to attack the administration.

With that said, I think it is time that the public was told the truth about terrorism and the threat that the American people face from these individuals determined to destroy our way of life. I will call this chapter, Terrorism 101 because it is necessary to go back to basics for the reader to really understand what is really taking place on the other side of the globe. However, the most important topic to be covered is the state of what I will call Homeland Security. We have been given many assurances, but it is sad to say that most are merely to pacify the public.

WHAT IS TERRORISM?

At its most basic, terrorism is the causing of intimidation through violence and fear. Now the law enforcement agencies dress up these basic concepts and create some really convoluted definitions such as the following:

DEFINITIONS

Of course, in order for the applicable laws regarding terrorism to apply to a act that we may all believe is a terrorist act, certain circumstances much apple. Like every profession, the law has its own language and sometimes even the definitions of words are different than the plain English definitions and sometimes based upon which law is applied, the meaning of the word terrorism, for example, can differ, reflecting the somewhat differing views of terrorism held by the creators of the definitions. Only by understanding the various definitions for terrorism is it possible to understand what acts are terroristic acts and which are not.

- The Federal Bureau of Investigation defines terrorism as the unlawful use of force or violence against persons or property to intimidate or coerce a government, the civilian population, or any segment thereof, in furtherance of political or social goals.

- The State Department defines terrorism as premeditated, politically motivated violence perpetrated against non-combatant targets by sub-national groups or clandestine agents, usually intended to influence an audience."

- The Department of Defense definition:

  "The calculated use of violence or threat of violence to inculcate fear, intended to coerce or to intimidate governments or societies in the pursuit of goals that are generally political, religious or ideological."

- The Department of Defense Directive 2000, 12H definition:

  "The calculated use of violence or the threat of violence to attain goals, whether political, religious or ideological in nature, by instilling fear or by using intimidation or coercion. Terrorism involved a criminal act, often symbolic in nature, intended to influence an audience beyond the immediate victims."

- The United States Code definition:

  "Premeditated, politically motivated violence perpetrated against non-combatant targets by sub-national groups or clandestine agents."

- The United Nations' definition:

"Terrorism is a unique form of crime. Terrorist acts often contain elements of warfare, politics, and propaganda. For security reasons and due to the lack of popular support, terrorist organizations are usually small, making detection and infiltration difficult. Although the goals of terrorists are sometimes shared by wider constituencies, their methods are generally abhorred."

When boiled down to their bare essentials, there are only four points to remember. First terrorism is a crime, and it is an attempt to intimidate a target population through fear and violence in furtherance of some political or social agenda. Everything else is simply window dressing. However, the unfortunate thing is that the goal of fighting terrorism has been used as a smoke screen to allow the removal of certain rights. With the passage of the Patriot Act in the aftermath of September 11, 2001, it now becomes a tug of war between what restrictions on our traditional liberties are needed to protect the public and what restrictions are placed on the American people simple to aid general law enforcement.

THE PURPOSE OF TERRORISM

Now that we have a basic idea of what terrorism is, why would anyone resort to such means in order to intimidate a target population? In order to understand this, it is necessary to add one or two other elements to our basic definition. Terrorism is a criminal act, that we have already established, but the purpose of this criminal act is to influence an audience much larger than the actual victims. Terrorism is actually a violent way to make a political statement.

A terrorist carries out his acts, not with the express purpose of killing a vast number of people, though this can be an effect f his actions, but to draw the attention of the local population, the government, and sometimes the entire world to their cause. A terrorist plans his attacks at a time and a place to drawn the maximum amount of publicity. The targets chosen are actually symbols of all that they oppose. Hence, the 9/11 terrorists chose the World Trade Center Buildings and the Pentagon as their targets as symbols of the United States military might and our financial dominance of the world. By damaging or destroying these symbols, they were symbolically damaging or destroying our military might or economic dominance.

The true success of a terrorist's acts is not how the victims or the authorities reacts but in how the population as a whole reacts to the terrorist acts. Did the 9/11 hijackers succeed? This is an important question that has really not been addressed in the news, per se. However, there is no doubt that the answer would be in the affirmative, because we changed so much of how we travel and do business as a direct result of their actions on that fateful day.

A group that turns to terrorism is one that feels that it has no chance of its own government dealing with the perceived problem. Thus it tries to lay its case before the court of world opinion by committing outrageous actions that garner maximum attention. Generally, the aims of these groups have dealt with politics, nationalism, religion, or some other special interest such as the right to life movement or the protect the environment movement or animal rights.

As part of their overall set of goals, the terrorist acts have an important pat to play. However, in the short term, terrorist acts are hoped to have the following effects:

- Produce fear in the civilian population, whether local, regional or national;

- Gain worldwide, national or local attention for their "cause" by attracting media attention;

- Harass or embarrass law enforcement or security forces in an attempt to cause an over reaction by the government which in turn will create either ill will toward the government or sympathy for the terrorist group;

- Steal or otherwise obtain money, arms and other equipment through the acts;

- Destroy facilities or otherwise disrupt communication or other infrastructure facilities in the hope of persuading the population that the government can't protect them;

- Discourage foreign investment, or tourism or other money making industries that support the existing power structure;

- Influence the government decision making process;

- Free imprisoned colleagues;

- Revenge;

- Force security or law enforcement forces to concentrate their forces leaving other area unprotected to a coordinated attack by other members of the terrorist organization or other allied terrorist organizations.

The ultimate goal of any terrorist act is to cause the government to crack down on the lawbreakers, at the expense of the rights of the majority and hopefully cause the governed to lose confidence in the government. Historically, terrorist groups carried out their programs using guns and bullets along with the occasional bombing. However with the ever-growing sophistication of civilization in general and in the United States in particular, there are a number of ways in which they can assault our society and cause a tremendous amount of damage to the existing social order in addition to using guns, bullets and bombs. These weapons are discussed below:

TYPES OF TERRORIST ATTACKS

Some of the terrorist groups operating in the world today have access to large amounts of funds similar to that possessed by small third world countries. An example of such a group would be the notorious Al-Qaeda group, a network of terrorist groups organized by Osama Bin Laden in the aftermath of the defeat of the Soviet Union in Afghanistan.

These well-funded groups can, naturally, indulge themselves in more sophisticated weapons than the less well endowed groups. In addition to conventional weapons, they can also make use of what I call unconventional weapons in their war against the western powers. In this particular section, however, I will discuss the various types of possible attacks commonly carried out by terrorists without specifying any particular group as being more or less likely to carry out the type of attack under discussion.

- Biological Warfare

Biological warfare is defined as the employment of biological agents to produce casualties in man or animals or damage to plants. Biological weapons include any organism or toxin found in nature that can be used to incapacitate, kill or otherwise impede an adversary. Biological weapons are characterized by low visibility, high potency, substantial accessibility and relatively easy to disperse to the enemy.

Attacks against enemy forces using biological agents are nothing new in warfare and launching such an attack against the civilian population of a combatant is also nothing new. The first recorded example of biological warfare that I can find in history took place when the Romans used dead animals to fouls the water supplies of their enemies.

The next was in 1346 at the Black Sea port of Kaffa[1] when rats and fleas from the city carried plague among the attacking Tartar soldiers. Angry, the Tartar's catapulted the bodies of dead Tartars into the emplacements of the defenders. The defenders, Genoese, in this case, contracted the plague and were forced to abandon Kaffa.

---

[1] Kaffa is now Feodossia, Ukraine.

In 1754 and 1767, the British Army attempted to use biological warfare against the American Indians by giving small pox infested blankets to the unsuspecting Indians during he French and Indian Wars. Shortly thereafter, outbreaks of small pox decimated the Indian tribes who had no immunity to this particular European disease.

In 2002, it was established by historical researchers in China that during World War II, the Japanese Biological Warfare program had killed almost 600,000 Chinese civilians in their campaign to destroy the Chinese people's will to resist their invaders[2].

This plague was inflicted upon the Chinese through the dropping of infected fleas and foodstuffs infected with cholera, typhoid, dysentery, anthrax, paratyphoid, glanders and other pestilences too numerous to mention.

The impetus for this diabolical program was a report written in 1925 reporting that over 1.3 million former soldiers and civilians still had health problems resulting from their exposure to poison gas during World War I. As a further reinforcement of how deadly biological warfare could be, there was also a reminder that in the middle ages, bubonic plague, also called the Black Death, had killed some 25 million people in Europe and there are some who maintain that the Tartar use of plague cadavers against the Genoese Kaffa was the start of the feared Black Death. When the Genoese returned to their home country, they carried the disease with them.

- Chemical Warfare

Chemical warfare is defined as tactical warfare using incendiary mixtures, smokes, or irritant, burning, poisonous or asphyxiating gasses[3]. The agents used in chemical warfare are normally divided into five categories: nerve agents, vesicants, choking agents, blood agents and incapacitants. The primary difference between a biological agent and a chemical agent is that the biological agent exists in nature and is developed for use as a weapon. A chemical agent, on the other hand, is something created, generally in the laboratory and does not usually exist in nature.

A chemical agent is normally defined as a chemical substance intended for use in military operations to kill, seriously injure or incapacitate humans or animals through its toxicological effects[4]. What we know as chemical warfare, as distinguished from biological warfare, has its beginnings with a German Scientists named Fritz Haber. He was the genius that developed poison gas for

---

[2] Barenblatt, Daniel, A Plague Upon Humanity: The Secret Genocide of Axis Japan's Germ Warfare Operation, HarperCollins, New York, New York. 2004.
[3] Webster's Ninth New Collegiate Dictionary.
[4] Medical Management of Chemical Casualties, published by the U.S. Army Medical Research Institute for Chemical Defense.

the German Empire during World War I. At the time of the First World War, Haber was already world famous, having developed a process for extracting nitrates from the atmosphere. These nitrates were, and are, used in fertilizer and gunpowder.

When war broke out in 1914, the German military was confident that it could easily defeat the British and the French forces, but their western movement was soon bogged down in the bloody trench warfare. As a result, Haber offered his discovery to the German High Command. He believed that poison gas would penetrate the strongest trenches and fortifications, incapacitating the defenders.

Poison gases of various sorts were already available as unwanted by-products of chemical processes. At his Berlin institute, founded by the Kaiser himself, Haber began experimenting with and refining such toxins to find those suitable for battlefield use. He initially focused on chlorine gas, the diatomic chlorine molecule, a highly reactive chemical that was used in the dye industry.

His home was on the grounds of the institute. While work and home life can clash, in the case of Haber the two quickly led to an outright war. His wife Clara was also a chemist, and was as strong-willed as he was. She believed that science should be used for constructive purposes, not to make weapons of mass destruction.

Fritz Haber tried to keep Clara in the dark about his work on poison gas. In December 1914, however, there was an explosion in the lab, and one of the workers, a Professor Sachur, was hurt. Clara rushed to Sachur, who was an old friend that in fact she had introduced to her husband. The man died. Clara made her objections to her husband's work plain, but Fritz continued his work on chemical weapons. Their marriage degenerated into warfare.

The startling thing about Haber's work on CW is that he did it on his own initiative. In fact, he approached the German military at the end of 1914 to sell them on poison gas, but the military had no great respect for scientists, and poison gases seemed unsporting anyway. Haber nonetheless convinced them to watch a demonstration, conducted at a military testing ground outside Cologne. Clara was present, and her loathing of her husband's activities increased.

With stalemate on the front, the German military could not be certain of victory. Defeat would be the greatest dishonor, so in early 1915 they decided to swallow their scruples and use Haber's poison gas. They gave him officer's rank, and he helped organize a chemical corps.

The Germans conducted the first chlorine gas attack on 22 April 1915, against French and Algerian troops facing them at Ypres in Belgium. The Germans set up 5,730 cylinders of chlorine gas and opened their valves. 180 tonnes (200 tons) of gas were released, forming a dense green cloud that smelled of bleach and rolled into Allied lines.

At 30 parts of chlorine to a million parts of air, chlorine gas is a nasty irritant that causes harsh coughing. At 1,000 parts per million, it is lethal, caustically stripping the lining from the lungs and causing victims to drown in their own fluids.

The results of the gas attack were devastating. The French and Algerian soldiers choked, their lungs burning, and slowly died. The gas cloud tinted everything a sickly green. Those who could escape the cloud fled in panic. Before dawn on 24 April, the Germans poured gas into Canadian lines, with similar results.

Allied casualties in the two days of gas attacks were estimated at 5,000 dead, with 10,000 more disabled, half of them permanently. Despite the fact that the French had captured a German soldier who was carrying a gas mask and who provided advance details of the attack when interrogated, the report was lost in the noise and the soldiers in the trenches had no warning.

The attack was unbelievably effective. Irritant chemicals, essentially tear gases, had already been fired in artillery shells by both the French and the Germans but they had not proven to be much more than a tactical nuisance. Even the German military was astonished by the results of Haber's chlorine gas. However, to Haber's fury, they were not prepared to exploit the breach they had made in Allied lines, and did not commit any serious force for a follow-up attack. This may have been partly because they didn't have the protective gear for large numbers of troops at the time.

The Germans launched a number of gas attacks during May 1915, with the last taking place on 24 May. The gas attacks then ceased. The prevailing winds over the lines had changed direction, and except for two small-scale attacks in October, the Germans did not return to gas attacks in earnest on the Western Front until December.

The attacks in April and May represented a squandered opportunity for the Germans. Had the gas attacks been performed on a larger scale and followed up, they could have decisively changed the course of the war. In practice, they just made the stalemate even more miserable.

That was not quite realized at the time, however. German newspapers were enthusiastic over the effectiveness of poison gas, and some even claimed that gas weapons were more humane than bullets and shells. Haber was promoted to captain. He threw a dinner party to celebrate. Clara Haber was not in a congratulatory mood. They had a furious argument that evening, with Clara accusing Fritz of perverting science. He called her a traitor to Germany.

Her verbal protests could not sway her husband. That night, she took his army pistol and shot herself through the heart. Fritz Haber left for the Eastern Front the next day, leaving his wife's funeral arrangements to others.

The change in prevailing winds allowed the Germans to use their new poison gases on the Russians. On 31 May 1915, Haber supervised the first chlorine gas attack on the Eastern Front. Gas proved extremely deadly against the poorly equipped Russians, though it was not very effective in winter cold, as it tended to freeze. The Russians ended up suffering more gas casualties than all the other combatants combined, and their attempts to retaliate in kind would often prove ineffective.

By the end of World War II, chemical weapons had proven themselves to be highly effective, though somewhat chancy to use if the conditions were not just right. However, as we shall see later on in this text, today's chemical weapons are much more effective.

There are, of course many and varied categories of chemical weapons, but they all have a few things in common that are still true today:

- o The delivery method of most chemical weapons is most always through inhalation, though on occasion there have been delivery through the contamination of food or water;

- o Many chemical agents are heavier than air and tend to hug the ground and tend to present an immediate noticeable effect on the person or persons infected;

- o Most chemical agents that infect through inhalation tend to break down when exposed to sun, if diluted by water or affected by high winds.

- Nuclear Warfare/Dirty Bomb

I have chosen to combine a discussion of nuclear warfare and the use of a dirty bomb together for somewhat obvious reasons. Nuclear warfare has been around since World War II, when the Manhattan Project created the first atomic bomb. The bombs dropped on Japan killed through a combination of explosive effects and lingering radiation. Due to the large support system needed to build and then launch a nuclear weapon, it would take a country to actually effectively utilize nuclear weapons. Of course, there are the fears of a "suitcase" nuke being detonated inside a large city, but the possibility is lower on the scale than a dirty bomb.

A dirty bomb, also called a Radiological Dispersal Device or RDD, is in its basic concept, a conventional explosive, such as dynamite, combined with radioactive material. The concept is that when the explosive goes off, those close by are killed or injured and the radioactive material contaminates surrounding areas.

In most cases, this is not the case at all. While the explosive certainly would be lethal, the probable sources of radioactive material available to a terrorist would not release enough radiation to either kill or cause severe illness. As an example, one source of radioactive material is normally though to be a hospital, however, the radioactive material used to treat cancer patients, for example, is sufficiently benign that about a 100,00 patients, national wide have this material injected into their bodies and then are released to go home.

However, there are also certain other elements that if released into the air as a result of the detonation of a dirty bomb could contaminate up to several city blocks.

A second type of RDD might involve a powerful radioactive source hidden in a public place, such as a trash receptacle in a busy train or subway station, where people passing close to the source might get a significant dose of radiation.

A dirty bomb is in no way similar to a nuclear weapon. The presumed purpose of its use would be therefore not as a Weapon of Mass Destruction but rather as a Weapon of Mass Disruption.

Impact of a Dirty Bomb

The extent of local contamination would depend on a number of factors, including the size of the explosive, the amount and type of radioactive material used, and weather conditions. Prompt detestability of the kind of radioactive material employed would greatly assist local authorities in advising the community on protective measures, such as quickly leaving the immediate area, or going inside until being further advised. Subsequent decontamination of the affected area could involve considerable time and expense.

Sources of Radioactive Material

Radioactive materials are widely used at hospitals, research facilities, industrial and construction sites. These radioactive materials are used for such purposes as in diagnosing and treating illnesses, sterilizing equipment, and inspecting welding seams. For example, the Nuclear Regulatory Commission, together with 32 states, which regulate radioactive material, has over 21,000 organizations licensed to use such materials. The vast majority of these sources are not useful for constructing an RDD.

Control of Radioactive Material

NRC and state regulations require licensees to secure radioactive material from theft and unauthorized access. These measures have been stiffened since the attacks of September 11, 2001. Licensees must promptly report lost or stolen material. Local authorities make a determined effort to find and retrieve such sources. Most reports of lost or stolen material involve small or short-lived radioactive sources not useful for an RDD. Past experience suggests there has not been a pattern of collecting such sources for the purpose of assembling a Dirty bomb. Only one high-risk radioactive source has not been recovered in the last five years in the United States. However, this source (Iridium-192) would no longer be considered a high-risk source because much of the radioactivity has decayed away since it was reported stolen in 1999. In fact, the combined total of all unrecovered sources over a 5-year time span would barely reach the threshold for one high-risk radioactive source. Unfortunately, the same cannot be said worldwide. The U.S. Government is working to strengthen controls on high-risk radioactive sources both at home and abroad. However, make no mistake, at this time there is sufficient radioactive material unaccounted for to make several dirty bombs.

- Bombings

Then of course, there are the more common terrorist bombings that we read about in the paper or see on the six o'clock news almost every night. Typically, these bombs are improvised devices that are inexpensive and easy to make. These devices are smaller, making them harder to detect, but in spite of their small size they are more dangerous than ever.

Terrorists also tend to use materials that are readily available to the average consumer to build their bombs. This using of common elements that might be found in any house in the country is another method of ensuring that law enforcement does not suspect that there is a bomb plot afoot[5]. The purchase of the nitrates and fertilizer used in this bomb, in a predominately farming area, would not excite undue excitement. Even something as common as aviation fuel would not excite the authorities, though we have seen the devastation that the use of aviation fuel can cause in the attacks on the World Trade Center on September 11, 2001.

Car bombings have been used by terrorist groups to spread terror and death for decades and are used commonly through the Middle East. However, bombings of this type do not cause widespread destruction or large numbers of casualties. As a result, their effectiveness as a weapon of terror is somewhat limited.

- Plane Hijackings

Hijacking, very simply, is the seizure by force of a vehicle, its passengers and/or its cargo. While there have been hijackings of almost every type of vessel used in the modern world, skyjacking, or the seizure of an aircraft, is generally thought of as the most common terrorist action. Primarily, this action has the most potential to gain the most advantage for the terrorist(s), gives them mobility and most importantly, national and sometimes international publicity.

---

[5] An example of the use of locally obtained materials to build powerful bombs is the fertilizer bomb that was used to allegedly destroy the Murrah Federal Building in Oklahoma City, Oklahoma.

- Arson

Arson is the intentional burning of a structure or other property, generally for profit. Many buildings are destroyed by alleged terrorism and the Insurance Companies pay the owners. The destruction of the World Trade Center in New York City in 2001 resulted in a massive insurance company payout. But the failure to pay, in this instance, by the insurance companies would have been considered nothing less than treason. Terrorists do, in fact, indulge in arson from time to time, but most often, they go for bigger crimes that can cause potentially more damage to the "system." However, in our rush to judgment, an accidental fire is often labeled as arson and innocent people convicted.

It is important, for a number of reasons to be able to determine if a fire is in fact arson or the result of mishap. There have, unfortunately, been many convictions for arsons that were actually manipulated by the Insurance Company in order to avoid paying the claim. If someone survives a fire, it is almost certain that the insurance company will prosecute them for insurance fraud and the authorities will prosecute for arson. However, the mere prosecution of someone as a suspected arsonist can send a shockwave of fear through the community that may often be unnecessary.

As an assist in understanding how someone can be falsely convicted of arson based on "scientific evidence" and as an aid to those who may want to be able to determine is a fire is arson, the following article is presented. I found Mr. Zeak's work outstanding and very thorough, so it is only just that I repeat it in its entirety.

The following are only a few of the common myths and false indicators that many fire investigators testify to be scientific evidence that an arson has occurred, when in fact many have been scientifically disproved. Some are also phenomena, which are regularly over-emphasized or misinterpreted to reach conclusions that are scientifically wrong. While the cause of some fires can clearly be determined, others cannot be determined. However, the causes of numerous fires are erroneously given for a variety of reasons.[6] Some are fraudulently misstated, but most wrong findings are just due to unsound teaching, ignorance, and an incredible campaign of false propaganda by the insurance industry. The following are a few of those reasons:

---

[6] Zeak, Tim, MYTHS AND OTHER FALSEHOODS ARE OFTEN PRESENTED AS SCIENTIFIC EVIDENCE: MANY RULINGS OF ARSON ARE NOT ARSON AT ALL. , http://www.publicadjustorsUSA.com, Public Adjustors USA, Inc.'s Insurance News/

- *Concrete spalling* is often given as evidence of arson when not too long ago, it was decided by most experts that it should be debunked. Numerous laboratory tests which saturated concrete with gasoline and other flammables (even torches were used on some) failed to produce the spalling. There are many reasons why concrete will spall, and arson is usually not one of them. Many consumers have lost everything to their insurance company because of this one faulty indicator alone.

- *Greasy windows* a couple of decades ago were at least an indicator to look at. However, with so many petroleum products now in the average home or business, greasy windows mean absolutely nothing. Yet in some circles, it is still seen as an indicator of arson.

- *Color of smoke* was often thought to be an indication of whether or not an accelerant was used. There are usually too many variables for this to be safely interpreted.

- *White ash* used to be a common theory until it was recently debunked. In fact, experiments have proven that the existence of white ash means exactly the opposite of what some "fire investigators" use to justify denials of claims.

- *Accelerants burn hotter* was disproved by none other than the National Fire Protection Association. In their guides section 921, 4-8.1 we read, "Wood and gasoline burn at essentially the same flame temperature." It is true that an accelerant fire gets hotter faster but not hotter overall. Still today, many consumers have their claims denied, and some even are convicted of arson because some ignorant or fraudulent "expert" convinced a jury that certain melted contents items proved accelerants were used.

- *Tripped circuit breakers* prove little. How often have you heard from some so-called expert that the power must have been on because it tripped? Not necessarily. Most all breakers' tripping action is spring loaded, so it can trip if the breaker gets hot enough even if it was off during the fire. If you don't believe us, try baking one in your kitchen oven. Put it in its OFF position, crank up the heat to 400°, and check it in about 20 minutes. While this is not a classic false arson indicator, it does show that many so-called "experts" don't even know or understand the basics. Yet they present long credentials to juries who assume they do.

- *Collapsed furniture springs*. NFPA 921,4-14 states, "The collapse of springs cannot be used to indicate exposure to a specific heat source such as "flaming accelerant or smoldering combustion." Another famous arson indicator is now debunked.

- **Fast fires** do not in themselves indicate an arson fire. There are many accidental fires that burn fast, too. Numerous variables must be considered, and this is another example of a "little knowledge" being dangerous. Captain Denny Smith ACFD recently wrote the following, "It is important to remember that an "accidental fire" can develop faster than an incendiary fire, and an incendiary fire can develop more slowly than an accidental fire. Basically, there is no relationship between speed of fire growth and any particular ignition scenario. Fire development scenarios (speed of fire growth) are contingent on many variables, such as HRR (heat release rates) of the initial fuel, geometry of the space (narrow rooms, wide rooms, high ceilings v. low ceilings), location of the fuel package within the space (in a corner, against a wall, near the center of the room), the lining materials, and the proximity of secondary fuels. These are some of the variables to be considered in a fire growth scenario. See NFPA 921, sections 3-4 and 3-5 for additional information. Also see section 17-2.8 which is a warning against using subjective observations and terms such as 'excessive,' 'unnatural,' or 'abnormal' fire growth as indicators of incendiary fire causes."

- **Burn patterns.** I have seen numerous "fire investigators" who read burn patterns less competently than someone would read tea leaves, and there is nothing about tea leaves that I believe. Some of these so-called "experts" will say that it is a definite sign of a liquid accelerant if they find the bottom of a door charred. Yet numerous tests have proven that that phenomenon generally occurs when a door is closed and hot gases (not accelerants) escape through the space at the top of the closed door. Cool air generally enters the compartment at the bottom of the door. The hot gases then escape under the door and cause charring under the door and possibly even through the threshold. In a recent test, accelerants were poured in a living room and set on fire. None was poured in the kitchen, yet holes were found in the kitchen floor but none in the living room (20 feet away). There are so many complex variables involved in studying fire behavior, which have caused many to call it "junk science." The fact of the matter is that many of these so-called "experts" are no more qualified to perform surgery on you than they are to look at a fire and determine its cause. Yet with refined speeches and designer suits, and with technical rhetoric that few judges and even fewer jurors can understand, they come across to most juries as "smooth as silk." While some burn patterns can be accurately interpreted, it is often forgotten that the more fire damage to the building, the less they can tell. One investigator pointed to a hole in the roof, which had collapsed and said that hole was evidence of a poured burn pattern. It's examples like this that are causing a growing number of people to call the field of fire investigation nothing but a "junk science." Is the risk of error too high and too common not to take drastic action?

- **Multiple origin fires**. While multiple origins are indeed a very good indicator of arson, it's down right sickening to see insurance companies' investigators and police authorities interpret drop fires as multiple origins. I was in a house once when a deputy fire marshal came in. He said he knew nothing about electricity or furnaces, but said he was going to find out "what the hell caused the fire." Within five minutes he thought he had it figured out. He saw what he said was a second fire in front of the living room window. When I asked him if it was possible for the heat from the utility room (clearly the point of origin) to have ignited the drapes, which then dropped to the floor and scorched it, he became mad and left. His report ruled that the cause of the fire was arson, when clearly it wasn't. The owner had recently moved (job transfer), so it was "obvious" to this "investigator" that the owner just had to have done it.

- **Unpredictability**: Honest experts who have conducted many tests will readily agree that fire sometimes does very mysterious things, which just cannot be explained. Some experiments come out totally inconsistent with what is generally normal. Many experiments produce results, which make no sense at all. The fact is, there are numerous variables (moisture content in wood, type of wood, drafts [many of which are unknown], vents, wind [and wind often shifts back and forth], humidity, oxygen, size of rooms, ceiling heights, seldom knowing for sure everything that burned (fuel), etc., etc....any one of which can make a fire behave unpredictably. Worse yet, after a fire does its damage, many possible variables are never even known to be considered. Lt. Steckmeister recently wrote, "One of the many problems in fire investigation is that no single indicator can be taken at face value without considering other factors."

EDITOR'S NOTE TO ARTICLE: Because the industry is wrong so many times and has failed to adequately police itself, more and more people have been raising the argument that fire investigation is nothing but a "junk science" or some kind of voodoo. It appears that some courts may be agreeing. The U.S. Supreme Court Case of Daubert v. Merrill Dow Pharmaceuticals ruled that expert testimony in areas of untested scientific theory (junk science) requires the proving the scientific reliability of every aspect of the analysis used to reach a *final opinion. While the Daubert case was not about a fire investigation, nevertheless, The U.S. Court of Appeals has applied it to one in Michigan Miller's Mutual v. Benfield, U.S.C.A.No.97-9138. Because so many innocent people are being jailed and wrongfully losing their homes and businesses to insurance companies, it is probably wise if Courts would declare it a "junk science" until a system with scientific integrity can be put in place. We profusely apologize to the many fire investigators who are honest and competent, but there are just too many who are not which puts the public at too great of a risk. We need to catch arsonists. That is a good thing to do, but we cannot allow the "lynching" of numerous innocent people by fraudulent and ignorant witch hunters. A couple of years ago, a mother was not only charged with arson, but also charged with the murder of her children who died in the fire. When testimony of the deputy fire marshal during the criminal trial didn't "gel" the prosecutor became very suspicious. Other fire experts were able to show that the investigation was not conducted or processed in accordance with professional standards. The criminal charges were dropped against the mother and the deputy charged with perjury. He was later ordered to pay the mother $500,000 in damages. If the deputy didn't trip himself up, the likelihood of a different verdict would have been quite great. Our hat goes off to this prosecutor who did not allow the adversarial process of our judicial system nor the fact that he originally believed the deputy to be credible to cloud his thinking.*

So while arson is certainly a tool in the bag of tricks of all terrorists, it is also a crime that can easily be laid at the doorstep of the innocent property owner or fire survivor by law enforcement that wants a quick clean end to an investigation. It is a crime that is normally carried out in stealth and secrecy and so no one really knows the identity of the culprit.

- Armed Attacks and Assassinations

When I talk of armed attacks, I include raids and ambushes. The attacks on several European Airports several years ago and other gathering locations are certainly terrorist type actions. Assassinations are merely armed attacks designed to target specific individuals. In the Iraq armed attacks and assassinations have been used together in the attacks on convoys that have been used to kill senior members of the newly appointed Iraqi ruling council. Historically, terrorists have assassinated leaders to for shock value or to cause disruption in government programs.

- Kidnappings and Hostage Takings

Terrorists indulge in the risks associated with kidnapping and hostage taking to establish bargaining positions and to gain national or international publicity. A completely successful kidnapping is a very difficult act to accomplish, but if they are successful, the terrorists can gain a great deal of money in the form of ransom as well as the accomplishment of certain goals such as the release of comrades jailed by the authorities.

Hostage taking involves the seizure of some facility or location and the capturing of personnel within the facility or location. While a kidnapping results in very careful actions on the part of the authorities, hostage taking can result in an actual confrontation between the terrorists and the authorities. Once again, the actual targets of the terrorists' message in a hostage scenario are not the hostages, but the worldwide audience watching the drama play itself out in the media.

- Robberies/Extortion

Terrorists will many times resort to outright robberies or extortion in order to gain the capital to undertake larger operations. If they are forced to take hostages in order to accomplish their goals, it is continually stressed to the media that the terrorists are not criminals, but rather freedom fighters.

- Cyber terrorism

This is a new area of attack for terrorist groups made possible by the broad expansion of the Internet and the spread of Internet connection and coordination of various parts of the western infrastructure. Cyber terrorism allows the terrorists to carry out their operations without ever leaving their homes. As technology becomes more sophisticated, so do the weapons at the disposal of the terrorists groups.

Later on in this text, we will discuss the attacks in detail, but for now let us examine other related areas.

32\ROBERT K. HUDNALL, JD

CHAPTER TWO

MY CREDENTIALS
AND
THE PROBLEM WITH GENERALS

A terrorist act is not an act of war, but rather a rather vehement political expression!

As I sit and write these words, this country is in a war. Unlike past wars, this one is completely different in almost every respect, as we are not fighting against another country, but against an idea. Such a war can be far more bloody and deadly than conventional warfare. As I shall show, the mere fact that we have become so technologically advanced is in actuality a serious Achilles heel that will very shortly be used against us in ways that we can only contemplate.

As I think back over the years, and watch the war in the middle east unfold on my television each day, there is no doubt in my mind that in spite of being the last remaining super power, that this country is woefully unprepared for this new type of warfare. I firmly believe that the worst is yet to come in regard to the damage that the terrorists will ultimately inflict on the totally defenseless American people. I should know, I taught the principles of urban warfare to some of those who are now among those that we call the terrorists.

There is a tendency among the American public to assume that anyone who has written a book on some particular topic is an automatic expert on the subject. Unfortunately, this is not always the case. In fact, in regard to the current war in the Middle East, there have been a large number of books written by individuals who have never left their air conditioned offices or spent a night in the bush sweating out a counterterrorist operation, but they still call themselves counterterrorism experts and the government offers them high level jobs and fat salaries for their so-called knowledge.

In this new information age, someone on the National Security Council (NSC) who spent his entire career sitting at a desk shuffling papers and then writes a tell all book about his heroics protecting the American people from enemies foreign or domestic at the risk of serious paper cuts is an expert. Or someone who has never served a day in the military but who has chaired a Congressional Committee on the topic of terrorism is now looked at, and holds himself out, as an expert on the deadly art of counterterrorism. Or lastly, and my personal favorite, someone who never served a day in the field but worked for the government's "point man[7]" on counterterrorism and who has been chosen to advise a Presidential candidate on how to combat terrorism is now an expert assigned to make the rounds of the Sunday morning talk shows.

Since my service connected injuries were incurred over twenty years ago, I have read a great number of medical books and had numerous conversations with practicing physicians about my conditions, so according to this same yard stick I would suppose that I am now an expert on the topic of internal medicine. I have decided to set the record straight in so far as who is an expert in these matters. However, unlike the former government officials who are now self-appointed experts in terrorism and urban warfare, but who spent their careers behind the desk, I trained many of those individuals that we now call terrorists. I will leave it to you, the reader, to decide if I have the background to know what I am talking about.

At the same time, I hope to be able to show very clearly the doctrinal problems that develop with an advance force, such as our own military, goes up against a smaller force. When a military is focused on a particular type of war, it is not always easy to make the transition to another type. During the Cold War, doctrine ruled the day, but we are now engaged in an asymmetric type of warfare. For the first time we are outclassed by an enemy. We are now playing catch up.

THE FIRST STEP

The first important consideration for the reader to be aware of is that under both the laws of the United States as well as International Law, a terrorist act is a violation of criminal law[8]. Less it be assumed that the only credentials that I bring to this effort are in the area of military small unit tactics, I might

---

[7] In military parlance, a point man is the first one of a unit to enter an area, however, in the language of the bureaucrats, a point man is the lead paper shuffler.

[8] Of course, then come the problems of determining what part of the criminal code was violated, who has jurisdiction to prosecute and apprehending the perpetrators.

point out that I hold a Bachelor of Science Degree (BS) in Criminal Justice[9] and a Master of Science Degree (MS) in Criminal Justice Administration[10] and a Juris Doctorate (JD) in Law[11]. Prior to becoming totally disabled as a direct result of my military service, I also spent several years as a practicing criminal defense attorney and also handled several cases as a special prosecutor.

I would submit that my legal training coupled with my military experience gives me a firm foundation for understanding and discussing terrorism in all of its many facets. I believe that my military training is especially important to the understanding of such an endeavor. In 1975 I was commissioned as a Second Lieutenant in the United States Army directly out of college. I had become involved in the Reserve Officers Training Corp (ROTC) my senior year in high school and as a result of my involvement in the program and the superior instruction I received, I was awarded the distinction of being named a Superior Military Cadet and was awarded a four year scholarship from the United States Army to attend the school of my choice. I enjoyed military training and showed a distinct bent for small unit tactics. Even then, I knew instinctively that the days of massed battalions and divisions moving across the battlefield against an equally arrayed enemy were numbered.

In 1974, as a junior in college, I transferred to Columbus College, a small university located in Columbus, Georgia, that was part of the University of Georgia System. The ROTC was just getting started and it had the extra-added benefit of being close to home. I had married during my time at Auburn University and, naturally, money was in somewhat short supply. Additionally, the newly appointed Professor of Military Science at my new school and the staff of instructors were fresh from service in Vietnam and understood not only doctrinal issues, but the conduct of small unit operations as well. Not only could I get first hand information on conditions in that small Southeast Asian country that it appeared I would soon visit, but also they had a positive opinion of small unit tactics and counter insurgency operations. With the full support of the Department, I, with a senior by the name of John P. Hodge, started an extra curricular unit that was named Counter Insurgency Group, Raiders. The mission statement of this small group was to teach, and learn, counter insurgency warfare from the inside out.

The training program designed for this small group of enthusiastic cadets was very heavy in the same type of training that an insurgent would receive before being sent into battle and it was matched with counter insurgency training on how to best negate the effectiveness of the insurgents. Basically this training program consisted of how to use a small number of people to carry out operations

---

[9] My Bachelors Degree came from Columbus College, Columbus, Georgia.

[10] My Masters Degree came from Troy State University, Phoenix City, Alabama.

[11] My Juris Doctorate was awarded by Walter F. Georgia School of Law, Mercer University, Macon, Georgia.

designed to cause mass confusion, panic, and casualties among, both the military, as well as the civilian population of a target country. After having mastered the basics of military training, training such as this was not only a lot of fun, but it gave all of us a real grounding in the type of operations that are now being carried out against the citizens of the United States by the middle eastern terrorists.

The Assistant Professors of Military Science that devised the training program and served as advisors for the group recognized that this type of operation was something that I seemed to have a natural talent for, not only in the devising, but also in carrying out the operations phase. More than one of them made the comment that I had a totally bizarre mind and a unique way of looking at things that served me well in the unconventional warfare arena. I was quickly made an instructor, teaching younger members of the cadet corps that joined the Raiders the basics of counter insurgency operations. Without knowing it, I had dived into the deep end of the pool in regard to what are now known as special operations and loved it.

I was not aware at the time that most career minded officers stayed as far away from special operations as possible. The only career path for a career officer during the 1970s, was very clearly, Platoon Leader, Company Commander, Battalion Commander and then, with luck, and a mentor, promotion to General. The problem is that these officers, while perhaps experts on accepted doctrine, marching and all of the other things that a soldier must master, are about as up to date in the tactics of combating terrorism, and as useful, as the dinosaur. Most of them are so afraid of offending the powers that be that they would not dare throw the book away and meet the terrorists with the same type of do or die fanaticism that the terrorists direct at us. This attitude on the part of our military would not be considered politically correct and unfortunately, even the military fell victim to this way crazy way of looking at things foisted on this country by the Clinton's. The current uproar over the so-called torture of Iraqi prisoners is a classic example of the microscope that our military must operate under. No officer that valued his career would dare take the battle to the enemy in a 9/11-type scenario.

I was proud to be commissioned and wear my country's uniform, but as an ROTC commissioned officer, I quickly learned that as far as the powers that be were concerned, I had two strikes against me when I entered the service. First, I was not a "ring knocker[12]", in other words I had not gone to West Point, though I had received an appointment to this service academy my senior year in high school. Second, I made it a point to think for myself and looked for "better" ways to do things. I reasoned that if I conducted my field operations by the book, and

---

[12] People that believe that the Freemasons are a tight band that look out and help promote each other have never dealt with the cult of the West Pointer. A West Point ring is an automatic cure for complete and utter stupidity on the part of the wearer.

rigidly stuck to established doctrine, that the potential enemy had probably read the same book as well. Thus, my opponent would have access to what was essentially my game plan. To me, this seemed crazy. Unfortunately, my superiors were not enthusiastic about a Lieutenant who disagreed on tactical maneuvers. Thus, I was not considered a team player, a label that in another day would have been heresy. General Officers did not like those who were not team players.

However, after some operations where my platoon was pitted against several Special Forces A Teams in the jungles of Panama, the staff of the Special Forces unit stationed at Fort Sherman, Panama Canal Zone was impressed enough with my somewhat unorthodox field performance to offer me the opportunity to transfer into their unit and be sent to the Special Warfare School at the JFK Center, for advanced training in special operations. I thought this was a great idea and was shocked at the vehement negative reactions of my chain of command[13]. As an example, I had my Brigade Commander, a two star general, threaten me with bodily harm if I accepted the offered transfer to the Special Forces. He very clearly stated in ponderous terms that the day of Special Operations was over and no officer under his command would join the Special Operations Group.

Military tactics during Vietnam had become very free and easy; doctrine went out the window in favor of what worked. Due to the jungle environment, savvy commanders had leaned toward special operations type insertions. This was a hard lesson to learn for many conventional doctrine trained officers and led to the massacre of more than one U.S. military unit by smaller, highly mobile insurgent units of Viet Cong. However, as Vietnam began to wind down, the military turned its eyes toward the obvious future enemy, the Soviet Union. Vietnam, and the need for special operations units was an aberration; conventional tactics was where the future lay. Frankly, the senior commanders made no secret about the fact that, in their considered opinions, Special Operations officers were useless on the modern battlefield. The era of Combined Arms had arrived.

AN OBSOLETE IDEA BECOMES THE LAW

When I entered the service, the big push had begun for a return to conventional combined arms forces. The concept of combined arms is a military doctrine[14] that called for several distinct types of soldiers and/or weapon systems to be coordinated operationally and tactically in order to provide maximum flexibility and cooperation during military operations. Theoretically, this concept

---

[13] I had expected my Company Commander, a Ranger School graduate to support my request, but he was quick to point out that getting a Ranger tab was just getting your ticket punched, no one in his right mind would want to be in a Ranger unit.

[14] From Wikipedia, the free encyclopedia.

allows for a quick massing of firepower against enemy positions or units in a relatively short period of time.

Though the lower-echelon units of a combined arms team may consist of homogeneous forces, a balanced mixture of such units are combined into an effective higher-echelon unit, whether formally in a table of organization or informally in an *ad hoc* solution to a battlefield problem. A good example of this concept would be a typical armored division, the poster child, if you will excuse the metaphor, of modern combined arms doctrine, which normally consists of a mixture of infantry, tank, artillery[15], reconnaissance, and perhaps even helicopter units, all coordinated and directed by a unified command structure.

The mixing of arms is sometimes pushed down below the level where homogeneity ordinarily prevails, for example by temporarily attaching a tank company to an infantry battalion. Combined arms doctrine contrasts with segregated arms where each unit is composed of only one type of soldier or weapon system as to provide maximum cohesion and concentration of force in a given weapon.

NOTHING IS NEW

We are in the first decade of the 21st century and yet the basic idea of combined arms operations dates back to antiquity, where ancient armies would usually field a screen of skirmishers to protect their spearmen during the approach to contact. In more elaborate situations the armies of various nationalities fielded different combinations of light, medium, or heavy infantry, cavalry, chariot units, men mounted on camels or elephants, and artillery (mechanical weapons), with the cooperating units variously armed with side-arms, spears, or missile weapons in order to coordinate an attack in time and space that would best disrupt and then destroy the enemy forces arrayed against them.

For example, the classical basic unit of the Roman legion was a unit of heavy infantrymen, but it was normally fielded with integral or attached skirmishers, and some legions even incorporated a small cavalry unit, used primarily for attacks on isolated small units of the enemy or for scouting forays. The legion was sometimes also incorporated into a higher-echelon combined arms unit, for example, in one period it was customary for a general to command two legions plus two similarly sized units of auxiliaries, lighter units useful as screens or for combat in rough terrain.

However, when Sparticus, the Roman slave and gladiator, led the slave revolt against the Roman Empire, he trained his followers in the use of unorthodox tactics that took into account the weaknesses inherent in the Roman

---

[15] Artillery as used here refers to both indirect fire weapons as well as Air Defense Artillery.

field tactics. His newly organized army, though smaller in size, devastated several experienced Roman Legions before his force was weakened by attrition and then simply overwhelmed by numbers. My point is that against the standard doctrine of the Roman Legions, the Army that dominated the known world, the rebel forces under the command of Sparticus, a Roman slave, using what were basically the tactics used by insurgent forces throughout history, was incredibly successful against conventional tactics.

MODERN COMBINED ARMS DOCTRINE

Before moving on, I think at this point, we should look at the standard U.S. doctrine in use as I write these words. Operational level combined arms operations in modern warfare normally proceed by securing logistic paths first, and then using these paths to deliver maximum firepower and damage to the enemy. This method of warfare proceeds in very clearly defined stages that are easily discernible by anyone that cares to follow the conflict in question.

The first stage in any overall battle strategy is to control space, a recent addition to the ancient concept of combined arms. It is thought that from space, one then controls the sea and air. From the sea and air, one can control the land. With control of the land, the battle and the war are as good as over. While this strategy is not as simple as it sounds, it does allow for the ultimate victory.

In U.S. doctrine, the control of space is secured by the expedient of just simply outspending other countries in research and development and in fielding new weapons systems as well as by using diplomatic efforts to control the development of anti-satellite and antiballistic weapons by other potentially hostile countries. Historically, war has long been the ultimate way that one country can influence another, however, in this new era, war has become big business where only the very wealthy countries can hope to compete in the modern arms race with any chance of victory.

America has long been the leader in the utilization of electronic and scientific advances for military purposes As a result, today, there is no country that can field an army that has any chance of success against the forces and weapons systems of the last remaining super power. To insure that the United States maintains its superiority in space technology, it is possible that the U.S. military covertly opposes inexpensive civilian access to space because it could permit a less-wealthy opponent to gain military access to space. Such uncontrolled military access to space could feasibly tip the balance of power.

The U.S. also controls the oceans using naval warfare, especially using carrier-based aircraft and nuclear attack submarines to interdict undesired foreign naval and ship traffic anywhere in the world. Our large fleet also allows the rapid deployment of combat units to any place on the globe.

With the control of space assured, the second stage of a normal military campaign is an extended intelligence-gathering phase, at least several weeks long. This intelligence gathering attempts to identify command and control nexus, the enemy's assets and order of battle, significant enemy personnel, their habits, radio traffic, telephone systems, cable traffic, decryption, and any other information thought to be beneficial to US forces. A clear understanding the enemy and his military capabilities is a major advantage on the modern battlefield. No less a military leader than General George S. Patton commented that if he could get inside his enemy's head, he could beat him.

The U.S. uses significant space and human intelligence gathering assets in this phase of the operation. There are satellites orbiting the planet that are designed for multi-spectral imaging, and the collection and decryption of radio signals. The U.S. also has high-resolution radar mounted in aircraft, to detect land warfare assets and aircraft. These are crucial to the military commanders for maintaining battlefield situational awareness.

Because of range limitations of chemically powered aircraft, modern air power is generally concentrated in the particular local area that is the immediate goal of the advancing forces. When the U.S. military desires to achieve air superiority, it follows a standard plan to accomplish this goal. A portion of the plan involves what I call smoke and mirrors.

In peacetime, airmen take part in realistic air combat training designed to flex our military muscles for all of those foreign intelligence assets that are watching the exercises. This is somewhat like psyching out an enemy with the demonstration of the sheer air power available to US ground forces. In wartime situations, the U.S. first acquires one or more local bases suitable for supporting the available air assets, or, in the alternative, concentrates one or more aircraft carriers that operate as mobile air bases. Obtaining forward airbases allows the concentration of aircraft and support units as close to the front lines as possible and cuts down the amount of airtime lost as aircraft return to their bases for re-arming or refueling.

Next, enemy anti-aircraft defenses are systematically attacked from both the air as well as the ground. Removing these potential barriers to air attacks leaves the enemy forces vulnerable to air attacks or the air insertion of combat ground troops. Anti-air defense attacks use stealth aircraft and precision-guided bombs and cruise missiles to damage control centers, search radars and air-defense missile systems.

Next, enemy command and control centers are systematically and persistently attacked to hinder the formation and coordination of enemy forces. Unlike earlier doctrines, major civilian airports are not intentionally damaged during this phase of the operation, because once they come under our operational control, they provide logistical beachheads that can be used by our forces after the area defenses are destroyed. Enemy aircraft on the ground are still attacked at outlying military airports, however.

During the period of the air war, psychological warfare efforts begin that are designed to reduce civilian and paramilitary resistance to U.S. forces. An essential component of this activity are efforts focused on minimizing civilian casualties, and giving the indigenous population reassurances that the U.S. forces will respect their property rights. It is also essential to a successful psychological warfare campaign that ground combat troops be disciplined to prevent looting and raping of the local population. A failure in this area can totally negate the effectiveness of the psychological warfare operations. The backlash that can result of this segment of the operation failing can be judged from the international uproar over the alleged torture of Iraqi prisoners by members of the US Military.

The next phase of the war is to infiltrate target-location soldiers[16], and begin to use helicopters and ground attack aircraft to destroy the enemy's land-warfare assets, such as command and control nexi, tanks and troop concentrations. The attacking aircraft of this phase are slower, less-agile aircraft designed to deliver maximum firepower on enemy positions, rather than the faster hit and run type aircraft. These aircraft also have limited air time and do not normally "stooge around" over enemy territory waiting for targets of opportunity, but need to be sent directly to their target and then return to their bases for refueling and re-arming. They would be in more danger if enemy air-defense assets had not first been removed.

After maximum destruction is inflicted on enemy land warfare assets, the next phase according to U.S. doctrine is to begin a sweep of enemy territory using tanks, supported by troops mounted in armored personnel carriers, and supported by air power. The goal of these forces is to destroy any remaining troop concentrations and pacify areas overrun during the advancement of the U.S. forces.

A textbook example of such a sweep would be the amazing "Thunder Run[17]" of the Spartan Division in the capture of Baghdad. On April 7, 2003, three battalions[18] of the Second Brigade of the Third Infantry Division punched a hole through the ring of steel that Saddam Hussein had placed around his capital and raced for the Presidential Palace.

Although the above is the "by the book" description of U.S. tactics, some changes to standard doctrine have occurred in other conflicts as will be seen below. I would also point out that in this instance doctrine was effective as we were engaged in combat with one of the world's largest standing armies that was also trained to fight according to their doctrine. I would also point out that we had trained a substantial portion of their combat leaders so it was a relatively

---

[16] An example of target location soldiers might be infiltrating of special operations troops who are trained to call in air attacks and indirect fire on hidden enemy assets.

[17] Zucchino, David, Thunder Run: The Armored Strike To Capture Baghdad, Atlantic Monthly Press. New York. 2004

[18] This Brigade consisted of fewer than 1,000 combat effectives.

level playing field from the standpoint of leadership training. However, when it came to combat effectiveness, we literally ran over the Iraqi army.

AIR MOBILE

Airborne troops have been part of the United States Military since prior to World War II and have proven quiet useful in historical combat. However, even more effective than the use of airborne troops, the helicopter has had profound influences on modern warfare. In the Vietnam War, troops were deployed in large part by helicopters. For this reason, U.S. troops in Vietnam saw more than six times as much combat as in any preceding war, because so much less time was spent on logistic delays. The result was that the infantry units became at least four times as effective for their size, when supported with fuel, ammunition and helicopters. This force multiplier effect allowed by rapid deployment and re-supply assets has become a standard part of war-gaming exercises in determining the ability of units to hold their positions or advance against the enemy.

In the Soviet war in Afghanistan, the Soviet military planers treated the helicopters much like flying light tanks. These heavily armed aircraft were almost always the first assault element to make contact in a battle, and often the most effective. Titanium and composite armor used in their construction made them invulnerable to fire from light arms. However, when the Afghanis were furnished with Stingers and other light anti-aircraft weapons by the Central Intelligence Agency the feared Soviet helicopters quickly became flying death traps for the Soviet military.

In the 1991 Gulf War at times the line of battle moved at more than 50kph, and tank commanders were literally *unable to keep up with the speed of the battle.* It rapidly became clear to the Iraqi commanders that defensive positions could not long be held against U.S. forces when U.S. combat troops were being landed in their rear areas. Chinese authorities have said that the U.S. attacks in that war were primarily helicopter-borne, and the tanks were used merely to consolidate areas already reduced by air attacks, including especially close helicopter attack.

In 2000, the U.S. Army began developing a new set of doctrines intended to capitalize on our advanced electronic capabilities so that we could use information superiority to wage warfare. Six pieces of equipment were crucial for this: AWACS, an air-borne lookdown radar; JSTARS, GPS, SINCGARS VHF digital radio, and field adaptable personal computers. The mix of advanced electronic components were then supplemented by satellite photos and passive reception of enemy radio emissions, forward observers with digital target designations, specialized scouting aircraft, anti-artillery radars and gun-laying software for artillery. Everything feeds the information network. Such a clear and complete picture of the battlefield turned prepared defensive positions into virtual deathtraps for enemy forces.

The coordination software for this massive effort was based in large part on software originally debugged as part of large-scale war-games with data distributed over the Internet to all forces. Basically, every item on the battlefield was identified by its location, direction, and speed to every other vehicle in the network. The actual position of each item on the battlefield was then recalculated in real time in every local computer on the network. Thus, in theory, every local computer knew the position of every vehicle in a theatre of battle. When a vehicle changed course, the new course was distributed to each computer on the network. When the view on a local computer's screen was "pulled back" more vehicles were included in the calculation. Unfriendly vehicles were identified by the air-defense and lookdown radars and then targeted for destruction.

The "god's eye view" that these electronic marvels can allow field commanders severely reduces the fog of war, though it does not eliminate such things as wrong turns on the battlefield and ambushes such as happened to the 509th Maintenance Company from Fort Bliss. A typical example is that ammunition trucks can always find their battalion artillery and re-supply it – an operation that historically was not so easy when the artillery was forced to shoot and scoot to avoid enemy artillery fire.

In the invasion of Iraq, U.S. forces used these assets to support what was called "swarm" tactics. For the first time, U.S. forces did not have to be organized in lines of advance to avoid friendly fire. Instead, every friendly vehicle was identified by GPS coordinates transmitted through the digital network to all units on the network. Any other military vehicle not identified by the network could be identified as hostile and engaged. Therefore, many U.S. ground vehicles moved across the landscape alone. If they encountered an enemy troop or vehicle concentration, they would hunker down; lay down as much covering fire as they could, designate targets over the network and call for help. Within a few minutes, loitering aircraft would be able to concentrate fire to cover the ground vehicle and engage the enemy elements. Within a half hour or so, heavy attack forces would concentrate to relieve the isolated vehicle. In an hour and a half, the relived vehicle would be re-supplied. While very frightening for the troops in the isolated vehicle, this technique moved the battle very fast, and rapidly located and destroyed enemy assets.

The above scenario sounds frighteningly effective. However, in war games and even on the ground, opposing forces have found the system vulnerable to deception and asymmetric attack. One of the most disruptive actions of simulated opponents was to substitute motorcycle couriers for electronic communications. This effectively made the location of enemy command and control centers invisible to radio-surveillance satellites.

Another significantly disruptive activity was to move assets and use decoys. Relatively simple decoys fooled aircraft ground-search radars and satellite scanning.

Many U.S. doctrines assume naval and space superiority at the beginning of a conflict. In simulated conflicts, massed torpedo attacks by enemy controlled fast attack boats on offshore U.S. naval assets were extremely disruptive to the U.S. order of battle. It would appear that another crucial asymmetric weapon would be a fast, stealthy torpedo boat to attack U.S. naval forces, especially aircraft carriers and transports. Another would be an effective anti-satellite missile to knock down the eye in the sky.

According to doctrine, once an area is pacified, and civil populations become docile, achieving political goals is usually possible. This is standard doctrine and all of the good little West Pointers expect things to go according to standard doctrine. Unfortunately, someone forgot to tell the enemy and the current war in Iraq is proof that standard doctrine is not always effective. Granted we overran the country in record time, but now we are losing the peace because the uprising of the Iraqi forces in the cities are keeping our hand full. This is happening because our military is not really geared toward urban warfare or nondoctrinal conflicts. Why? – Because it is not part of our standard doctrine and the U.S. Army has traditionally abandoned asymmetrical methods of combat. One example is the discontinuing of the "unnecessary Jungle Combat Courses."

CHAPTER THREE

JUNGLE WARFARE

I had the advantage of being in the military during the period of time when doctrine Generals won the battle over the special operations Generals so I was able to see first hand the how and the why of the specialization of the military. In many cases this happened because the doctrine Generals were politically connected and the concept of conducting battles according to doctrine made the General the most important cog in the wheel. Grand battle plans devised by doctrine generals that resulted in victories made for promotions to the Olympian level of the Joint Chiefs of Staff. A battle fought according to doctrine is almost a set piece affair, with the General making the master plans, handing down the plans to subordinates and then the plan being executed. Special Operations on the other hand made the junior officers who must make decisions on the fly in the field, as important if not more so than the General that devised the initial plan. To a West Pointer, this was heresy[19].

It was also a major factor that entire careers had been built based upon the premise that Russia would be our next enemy and eastern Europe would be the next battlefield. This mantra was hammered into those of us chosen to instruct our fellow officers. Training for any other type of warfare became targeted for elimination as a waste of resources. Everything else became of

---

[19] I was at a briefing when I heard a Major General make the comment that he looked at Special Forces Officers the same way he did Blacks in the military. They were a necessary evil, but you wouldn't want your sister to marry one.

secondary importance to getting ready to fight the "Red Menace" that was just waiting for the opportunity to overrun West Germany and devour those countries unlucky enough to be in its path.

There was also the implicit belief that the next war could quickly go nuclear and therefore, there was no real need for Special Operations units since there would not be enough time to get them into the action before everything was lit by a large red glow and turned into fused slag. For this reason, the lessons of Vietnam were discarded as so much useless baggage as we returned to contemplating battalions and brigades moving to contact with an equally mobile enemy on the broad plains of Europe.

When the paperwork was prepared for my commissioning, Vietnam was still a viable option as an assignment and to "teach me a lesson" on how to be a team player my Professor of Military Science pulled strings to arrange my tour of Southeast Asia. So I received my orders to go to Southeast Asia[20] a few days after I received my notification that I would be commissioned at Graduation. However, even the best-laid plans of the Pentagon can go awry; by my commissioning date, we were not sending lambs to the slaughter in that particular theater of war any longer. Saigon had fallen to the North Vietnamese and we ran for cover rather than prop up our ally once again. So as the next best thing, my orders were changed directing that I join the 193rd Infantry Brigade in the Panama Canal Zone. I was assigned to the 4th Battalion, 10th Infantry, a straight leg (non-airborne) Battalion to be educated in the proper manner befitting a career Regular Army (RA) Officer.

However, before I could go off to save the free world from the evil Red Hordes, I first had to attend the Infantry Officer Basic Course (IOBC) at Fort Benning, Georgia. This course was designed to give the newly commissioned second lieutenant a solid grounding in regard to conventional tactics and to instill all of the things that an officer should know to survive his first assignment. Throughout the entire period of instruction, I continually heard that Special Operations was not the bread and butter of an officer and that conventional tactics was where it was at! Every time a potential enemy was mentioned, the discussion would always turn to the Russian Army, the power of their T-62 tanks, and their massive waves of assault vehicles. They were bigger, so we had to be better. However, in the continuing barrage of instruction, one thing that I noticed was that there was very little instruction in unconventional weapons such as chemical, biological, or radiological weapons and virtually none in counter

---

[20] This brilliant idea was that of my Professor of Military Science who did not approve of my choice of wives. He felt that sending me so far away and to this particular country would end any chance of my marrying the woman who became my second wife. As the Sergeant Major of the ROTC unit, CSM Virgil Greene, used to say to me, if the "Army wanted you to have a wife they would issue you one". My Professor of Military Science was adamant that I needed to be single during my first assignment and then marry a General's daughter. I am sorry to say, in hindsight, that I now believe he was correct.

insurgency operations. Granted we were required to go out to one of the ranges and sit inside a gas chamber, then remove our masks and breathe CS gas[21], but there was no real detailed instruction in regard to these potential weapons and how devastating they could be.

Finally, I made it through all of this preliminary instruction and I was assigned to the Airborne School and it was scheduled that when I finished Airborne School, then I would enter Ranger School prior to going to my unit for "a rest". Like most gung ho Second Lieutenants, I thought that I was supposed to be Ranger/Airborne (and Special Forces was a glimmering dream in the back of my mind) in order to be the best that I can be[22]. So with boundless enthusiasm, I reported to Airborne School.

Airborne is a very unique school where instructors who are all muscle run you until you drop in order to prepare you to jump out of perfectly good airplanes so that in many cases the enemy sitting comfortably on the ground can shoot you full of holes while you gracefully float down into his lap. The theory for the running is that you will be in such tip top physical condition that hitting the ground will not injure you. Unfortunately, I made the mistake of landing wrong and felt something snap in one knee. The Physicians Assistant assigned to the Airborne School diagnosed it as "Airborne Knee", gave me two aspirin and sent me back to duty. I was never allowed to see the Orthopedic Surgeon at Martin Army Hospital at Fort Benning. I was an officer and sick call was a waste of time, I had to get ready for Ranger School.

When I reported for Ranger School, my left knee was the size of a small grape fruit and movement was painful. After a preliminary examination, the instructing staff, with the concurrence of the Department of the Army, sent me to the Orthopedic Department at Martin Army Hospital at Fort Benning for evaluation. After an examination that consisted of asking me where it hurt, it was decided that I actually did have a serious case of "Airborne knee" and needed time to heal before undertaking something as strenuous as Ranger School. So I was sent to the Panama Canal Zone to join my unit and my Ranger School orders were tabled until my next tour of duty at Fort Benning. So I was finally entering the "real" army.

MY FIRST UNIT

The Panama Canal Zone was an American enclave in those days before Reverend Carter gave it back to Panama as a gift of "love and peace." The mere fact that this agreement displaced American families what had worked for the PanCanal Company and had lived in the Canal Zone for two or three generations

---

[21] Also referred to in civilian life as tear gas.

[22] This was the U. S. Army's advertising slogan before someone with too much time on his or her hands came up with that goofy slogan "An Army of One!"

was small price to pay to make Panama happy, since Mr. Carter did not have to pay the price. According to some banker friends of mine, Omar Torrijos, the then Panamanian strongman and government head wanted to pull off a major coup to increase his status among world leaders so he threatened to default on loans Chase Manhattan and other world class banks had made to Panama unless the Canal Zone was returned to Panama forthwith. Mr. Carter, that brilliant politician and leader of the free world caved in almost at once[23].

The Panama Canal Zone was a 553 square mile strip of territory consisting of the Panama Canal and an area extending five miles on either side of the canal. The Zone, as it was called by the Americans living there spanned three of Panama's provinces and was an autonomous area within the confines of Panama's borders. The United States and the country of Panama had never signed a status of forces agreement, so this led to some very unusual legal events. It was actually legal for a U.S. soldier to marry a Panamanian woman in the country of Panama while stationed in the Canal Zone and also be married to a woman within the Zone. Under certain circumstances, the Army would not recognize the marriage within the country of Panama and the country of Panama would not recognize the marriage within the zone.

The Zone was created in November of 1903 with the signing of the Hay-Bunau-Varilla Treaty and this Zone was administered by the United States until 1977. In an effort to improve the United States' relationship with Latin America, U.S. President Jimmy Carter, as part of his program to get people to like him at the expense of the U.S., negotiated a 1977 treaty with Panamanian leader Omar Torrijos arranging for the gradual handover of the canal and the military bases.

Even though General Torrijos was a murderer and a thug, he was a truly brilliant man and a superb actor. One example of his brilliance can be seen from his use of carefully staged media events as part of his campaign to get the U.S. to turn the Canal Zone back over to his government. He saw control of the Zone as a major source of revenue for his government[24] and missed no chance to press his case to the world media. A world media, I might add, that after Vietnam rarely found anything good to say about the United States.

There was a residential area of the city of Panama City that bordered on the fence that separated the U.S. controlled Zone from the city, and country, of Panama. This area was one of the worst slums that I have ever seen and I have traveled many places in this world. I once made some comment to the Battalion Adjutant about the appearance of this slum and he told me a story. It seems that this area was called Hollywood by the U.S. forces. Several years earlier, this area had burned down and the U.S. Army went in and rebuilt the area for the

---

[23] Omar Torrijos was killed in a helicopter crash alleged engineered by his able lieutenant, Manuel Norriega.

[24] And according to all the stories that I heard, a lot of the money went into his own pockets as well.

Panamanians that lived in that neighborhood, building homes comparable to those given to enlisted personnel within the Zone.

Instead of being grateful for this assistance, General Torrijos had been enraged at this benevolent action on the part of the U.s. Army. Hollywood had been his showpiece to the world media where he would conduct interviews standing with his back to the chain link fence separating Hollywood from the Canal Zone. Against this backdrop, he would compare the slums that his people had to live in with the nice housing of the Americans just across the fence. I was told that within the space of six months Hollywood looked even worse than it had before the fire.

Even so, Reverend Jimmy Carter[25] was bullied into returning the Canal Zone to the Panamanian Government. His justification for this was that by returning the Canal to Panamanian control, that the countries of South America would like us better. Frankly, most of those countries thought we were the biggest sucker to come to town and stepped up their requests for the same type of assistance, which he was happy to give. After all, the money wasn't coming out of his pocket, but that of the American Tax Payer.

Under the terms of the treaty, from 1977 until 1999, the Zone was under joint United States-Panamanian control. In 1999, the Panama Canal was turned completely over to Panamanian control and our ability to move naval assets from ocean to ocean now depended to the efficiency of the corrupt Panamanian government.

The United States maintained a constant military presence in Panama between 1903 and 1999. The 193rd Infantry Brigade was activated on 8 August 1962 at Fort Kobbe, Canal Zone as a mobile force for swift intervention in case of trouble in Latin America. The brigade consisted of two infantry battalions (one company of one battalion remaining airborne), a field artillery battalion and a support battalion. Brigade headquarters was at Fort Clayton, Panama Canal Zone.

A 5,196-acre army base on the Pacific side of the Panama Canal, Fort Kobbe hosted three units of U.S. Army South (USARSO), the army component of the U.S. Southern Command. These were the U.S. Army's 536th Engineer Combat Battalion (Heavy), the 228th Aviation Regiment, and the 87th Infantry.

---

[25] Even though Jimmy Carter was the President of the United States at this time, he looked, sounded and acted like every Southern Baptist Minister that I have ever known. I grew up in the South and had learned that most of those who felt the calling to ascend to the pulpit, lacked a firm grip on the realities of the real world and that they could be depended upon to try to better everyone else's life at the expense of the members of the Congregation. In this case the America people were his congregation. He single handedly placed US readiness capability vis a vis movement of naval assets in the hands of the Panamanians who in turned made a large number of deals with the Chinese Communists for their assistance in the operation the Canal. As I said earlier, there was a lack of a firm grip on the realities of the world to be found in most ministers and Reverend Carter tried to better everyone else's life at our expense.

In September 1997 the U.S. Southern Command (SOUTHCOM), the military body responsible for Latin America and the Caribbean, moved its headquarters from Quarry Heights, atop Ancon Hill near downtown Panama City, to a new facility in Miami, Florida. The American Canal Zone government ceased to exist in 1979. The U.S. Military turned over control of the territory (but not the canal or some of the bases) to Panama in 1990. All bases are now closed (as of August 1, 1999), and the official transfer of the canal occurred on December 31, 1999.

In anticipation of the Panamanian government's taking over complete control of the Canal Zone in 1999, the 193d Infantry Brigade was deactivated in 1994. On December 31, 1999, the last U.S. military personnel left Panama in compliance with the 1977 Accords. The last U.S. facilities in Panama to close were Fort Clayton, Fort Kobbe, Howard Air Force Base, Fort Sherman, Rodman Naval Station, Galeta Island, and three firing ranges.

I was originally slated to be assigned as a Platoon leader with the 4th Battalion, 10th Infantry, headquartered at Fort William D. Davis on the Atlantic side of the Canal Zone. However, upon landing at Howard Air Force Base, my military sponsor, an officer within the 4th of the 10th could not be found. At the same time, the 4th Battalion (M) 20th Infantry stationed at Fort Clayton on the Pacific side of the Isthmus had just lost an officer due to unspecified causes and needed a replacement. So my orders were changed and I was sent to Fort Clayton; within a few days, I was a rifle platoon leader for 3rd platoon, A Company, 4th Battalion (M) 20th Infantry. After all of the training in how things worked in the Army, boy was I in for a shock.

EVEN A LIEUTENANT CAN DIE

I had been in command of my platoon for less than a week when I found out two things that gave me pause for reflection. The first week had been an education in and of itself with me finding out a great many things that the instructors at the Infantry Officer Basic Course had never even dreamed of talking about.

First, the Lieutenant that I replaced as platoon leader, who I had been led to believe went AWOL[26], was actually murdered. The ensuing investigation by the Military Police and the Criminal Investigation Command failed to turn up the specific culprit or culprits. It was only some time later, after my platoon learned that I was really trying to look out for their best interests that my Platoon Sergeant, SFC Hill, told me the story of what had really happened. It was an open secret so to speak, but no one wanted to talk about it.

It seems that the dead Lieutenant had been the type who yearned to make a big drug bust so that he could get a medal from the General and so he actually

---

[26] AWOL is military slang for being absent without leave.

stalked his subordinates waiting for them to smuggle drugs into the barracks so that he could arrest them and be a hero[27]. It should be understood that the Canal Zone in those days was like living in Happy Days. You could really believe that you had stepped back into the 1950s. There were third generation American families living their as many PanCanal[28] employees had returned in the zone. There was not a heck of a lot to do unless you liked to go into Panama City, chase women, drink, and gamble. So a lot of troops turned to drugs, which were easy to obtain.

One night the Lieutenant that I replaced had actually caught some of the troops under his command having a pot party in one of the barrack rooms in his platoon area. The problem was that in his enthusiasm to be a great crime buster, he had neglected to check behind the door when he burst into the room, waving a .45 and demanding that they surrender or else. One of his own men hit him in the head with a table lamp and killed him. The death happened to quickly that no one really knew what to do. Lacking any better ideas, the Lieutenant's body was stuffed inside a wall locker, which was then thrown out of the window[29]. I was told that no one bothered to look inside the battered locker until the tropical heat caused the body to begin to stink. So it was a tad unnerving to know that I had a murderer under my command. The culprit was never caught to my knowledge, but, luckily, no one tried to kill me. However, in the field I always carried a loaded .45 and I never tried to make drug busts unless someone was stupid enough to light up or shoot up in front of me.

COUNTER-INSURGENT ACTION

The second eye-opening event took place on the fourth day that I was in charge of the platoon. Military intelligence had picked up a rumor that there was going to be an attempt to damage the Mira Flores Locks, the last set of giant locks that a ship had to pass through before a west bound ship through the Canal reached the Pacific side of the isthmus. If the Locks were damaged, then the losses could run millions of dollars, as ships would be unable to use the Canal until the Locks were repaired. The Mira Flores Locks was very close to Fort Clayton and was normally protected only by the PanCanal[30] Security Forces.

---

[27] During the mid 1970s drugs were a major problem in many military units and the 193rd was no exception. In fact, it was easier to get the drugs in the Panama Canal Zone due to the close proximity to the major drug chains in South America.

[28] The PanCanal Company was a US Government Agency charged with operating the Panama Canal Zone.

[29] The room in question was located on the 3rd floor of the tropical billets, which meant that the room was actually on the 4th floor as the first floor consisted of the entry and storage.

[30] The U.S. Government Agency that operated the Panama Canal was referred to as PanCanal. This United States Government Agency maintained stores of all types for

So on a Thursday night, I found myself being briefed by the Battalion Operations Officer[31], Major Nicholas J. Turciano, on the threat to the Locks from some terrorist group. Then I, and my platoon were trucked over to the Mira Flores Locks and I was told to post my men. This may sound like an easy assignment, but in Panama there were no easy assignments. The Mira Flores Locks were surrounded on both landward sides by what was called Elephant Grass. This grass, which could cut like a razor if you were not careful, sometimes grew over 6 feet tall and was too thick to even see movement unless you were above the tops of the stalks of grass and then you could only see the grass wave gently. So I had my first practical lesson in counter insurgency operations that long, hot, lonely night. I posted lookouts on top of the Locks and I prowled the hot Elephant Grass with one or more roving patrols ensuring that no naughty terrorists attacked the Locks.

Though the 4th Battalion (Mechanized) 20th Infantry was a mechanized battalion and my platoon owned four Armored Personnel Carriers (APCs), we spent much more time on the ground that we did riding in our carriers. This was not the conventional tactics that the instructors at the Infantry Officer Basic Course in their starched, tailored Battle Dress Uniforms had spent countless hours talking about. I do not think that we ever took part in a mass movement against a mechanized enemy, such as the Russians were rumored to be.

No, this was down and dirty, slip through the tall grass looking for the bad guy one on one anti-terrorist operations. Luckily for me, the insurgents either decided it was too hot to set off bombs on this particular night or it was a Battalion training exercise and there was no actual threat or we scared the insurgents away, because nothing happened. However, this would a continuing part of my life in the Canal Zone.

We would get such warnings a couple of times a month and you never knew if it was a training exercise or if someone really was out to the destroy the Panama Canal. Later, as conditions worsened an attack on the Canal became a very real threat and caused me to spend many sleepless nights trying to anticipate what the local variety of lunatics were going to do next.

HANG ON UNTIL HELP ARRIVES

Then came the biggest surprise of all. I had been briefed at Fort Benning that at my first unit, I would spend a great deal of time slowly learning all phases of my job. However, someone forgot to tell Major General William R. Richardson, the 193 Brigade Commander, that I was to undergo a slow

---

PanCanal Employees. Their prices were even lower that at the Post Exchange or the Commissary. Balboa was the PanCanal main town on the Pacific side of the Isthmus and was like stepping back to the 1950s.

[31] Also called the S-3.

indoctrination. As an example of his outlook on how things should be run in the Army, he quietly arrived in the Panama Canal Zone with no fanfare several days before he was due to assume command. He went to the Brigade Headquarters around noon on a hot Wednesday and found a corporal in charge of the entire Brigade Headquarters. There were no officers or Non-commission Officers (NCO) to be found anywhere around the sparsely manned Brigade Headquarters. The Corporal suggested that the General might like to try the Golf Course.

I am told that General Richardson descended on the golf course like an avenging fury. I still run into retired military personnel who remember how the furious General, accompanied by several Military Police, went from hole to hole on the golf course, demanding to see the identification of everyone he met. If the individual was in the military and could not prove he was on a properly approved leave, General Richardson relieved every officer and NCO he found who was playing hooky. It seriously reduced the number of officers on duty in the Canal Zone, which was one reason that several officers from my IOBC[32] class were sent to the Canal Zone as replacements. Until the arrival of General "Wild Bill" Richardson, an assignment to the Panama Canal Zone was considered good preparation for retirement.

Once the Panama Canal Zone rejoined the army, so to speak, General Richardson established a training program that used up almost 2 years of fuel supplies for the Mechanized Battalion in the first six months of training. He demanded, and received, a cutting edge military force.

The 4th Battalion (M) 20th Infantry was the ready reaction force for the 193rd Infantry Brigade in case of war with Panama or invasion of the Canal Zone by enemy forces. The Panamanian Army was small, but incredibly mobile and periodically tried to goad us into fighting with them. On more than one instance during my tenure there, we went very close to an all out shooting match with the Panamanian military, though it was never reported in the US papers. Some of the actions taken by the Panamanians to goad us bordered on the demeaning. On one occasion, a Company Commander's wife went into Panama City to shop at the Farmer's Market. She was a very attractive lady, and a member of the Deny, Panama's version of the CIA decided to be frisky and pinched her rear end. She reacted by slapping him so hard it knocked him off of his feet. His response was to place her under arrest and haul her off to the local jail.

When her husband was notified that his wife had been arrested, he called out his unit, armed them with live ammo and got ready to invade Panama City. Luckily for all concerned, cooler heads prevailed. The General had the Captain arrested and relieved of command and the Ambassador was asked to try and get the wife released. The diplomatic negotiations were successful and she was returned to her husband, after, we heard through the rumor mill, being raped repeatedly while in Panamanian custody. In short order the husband and his wife

---

[32] Infantry Officer Basic Course

were sent back to the states. I frankly do not blame him for his reaction and I would have done the same thing myself.

As a result of the somewhat less than friendly relations between our two countries, there were contingency plans prepared for every possible event, to include the rescue of the United States Ambassador to Panama, who lived in a compound deep within Panama City.

Even as relatively inexperienced as I was, I quickly recognized that a determined enemy utilizing the narrow winding streets of Panama City could bottle our troops up for sometime if we tried to rescue the Ambassador by sending troops to the Ambassador's compound. So a very creative plan was developed to insure that the Ambassador at least had a chance of being rescued and this rescue job fell to the 4th Battalion (Mechanized) 20th Infantry, since we were the primary military force on the Pacific side and we were also the only mechanized unit in the Zone.

I must say that the rescue plan looked good on paper, but if it had come to putting the plan into operation, I am not so sure that I would have been so convinced of its chances of success if I had been called upon to actually put it into operation for real. What looks good in theory can many times be a nightmare for those that have to execute the plan. However, for daring, I would give the plan a solid A+.

Simply put, the plan called for the ready reaction platoon (usually mine[33]) to load onto four UH-1 (Huey[34]) helicopters, which would then be intentionally crash-landed inside the Embassy Compound. Unfortunately, there was not enough room even for a single helicopter to land normally inside the fenced enclosure, but it was decided that if we did not mind scratching the paint on the helicopters that we could get four of them inside the compound. According to the plan, we would then fan out from the compound and, hopefully, defend the Embassy and the compound until the rest of the Battalion could fight its way to the Embassy to rescue all of us.

Perhaps it would have worked, or perhaps, the Panamanians would have delayed the arrival of the rest of the Battalion long enough to have overrun our meager defenses. We will never know how this situation would have played out. However, the intense training that we underwent in how to occupy and defend the Embassy Compound was really an education for all of us. This was small unit

[33] The Brigade Commander's favorite Battalion was the 4th Battalion (M) 20th Infantry. It seems that all of the Battalion's senior officers had served together in Vietnam and Major General William R. Richardson thought that Lieutenant Colonel Lyman G. White, Battalion Commander of the 4th Battalion (M), 20th Infantry, hung the moon. LTC White's favorite Company Commander was the A Company Commander, Captain Randy Gallatin, my company commander and I was the junior Lieutenant in the Company. So it was somehow destined that I received most of these exciting opportunities for advancement.
[34] The workhorse helicopter of the Vietnam era.

tactics as they were meant to be carried out by daring soldiers. More than likely, we would have gotten our collective asses shot off, but at 22 years old, you feel immortal.

SEMI-PREPARED AT BEST

America was embroiled in the Cold War and the beginnings of the Korean Conflict in April of 1951 when the Commanding General of the U.S. Army, (Caribbean) was given the mission "to keep the art of jungle warfare alive in the Army." Recent worldwide events had demonstrated a need for proficiency in jungle operations. The French were struggling in the jungles of Indo-China against the Vietminh in hopes of reclaiming part of their pre-Second World War Empire. The British were successfully fighting a counterinsurgency war in the jungles of Malaysia, and the U.S. had recently fought numerous bloody campaigns in the tropics of the Burma-China-India Theater, and the South Pacific during World War Two (WWII). Given America's interests and responsibilities as an emerging superpower, and our global focus, it was felt likely the United States would again be called on to wage war in a jungle environment.

However, in the rush to gear up for the upcoming war with the Soviet Union that all of the "experts" were so eagerly anticipating most of our focus was directed toward conventional tactics. As those who had served in the jungle theaters of war left the service either because they wanted to return to civilian life or as a result of pending retirement from the service, the specialized knowledge of jungle and counter insurgency training was being lost. As has always been typical of this country, after a war, there was a rush by the Democratic Party to reduce the size of the armed forces so that more money can be poured into social programs to help the poor downtrodden of the nation. After World War II, it was felt that Russia would b e the next enemy, but times were good and there was more money in civilian life than in the military.

In this instance the rush was actually supported by the Doctrine Generals as a smaller force left more money for their fancy weapons systems to better get ready to fight those evil Russians. There was a great deal of talk at the time about the smaller, leaner professional military. The mere fact that this lessening of our defenses exposes all of us to danger has always been overlooked. Tens of thousands of experienced officers and men were sent home and not replaced. I will discuss this in more detail later in this story.

JUNGLE OPERATIONS AND TRAINING IN PANAMA

Until the Second World War, many military experts believed that jungles were impenetrable and unsuitable for modern military operations. The successful Japanese attack on the British in Singapore by way of the Malaysian jungles in 1942 changed conventional thinking. Until the first Japanese bullet was fired, the powers that be had turned a deaf ear to all of the warnings regarding the capabilities of the Japanese Army. The average individual's stereotypical view of the Japanese soldier was of a nearsighted midget, wearing coke bottle glasses, bumbling along in an inefficient manner. As is usually the case, the worst handicap facing the Allied soldiers was their unconscious reliance on the stereotypical view of the Japanese. The midget with the coke bottle glasses conquered a good portion of Asia before he was stopped.

However, American experiences in conducting training and maneuvers in the jungle began in 1916 with a cross Panama Isthmus trek by a U.S. Army infantry detachment. The defense of the Panama Canal required U.S. forces to operate and train in the jungle; thus elements of the U.S. Army serving in Panama had fairly extensive experience in jungle survival and movement prior to U.S. participation in WWII. The Japanese decisive defeat of British forces stationed in the China-Burma-India Theater of war during the early years of WWII caused an Army-wide examination of its ability to conduct operations in the jungle.

The Panama Mobile Force (PMF) was the primary Army element with experience in jungle operations. The PMF aggressively promoted their abilities to the War Department in order to secure a role in America's war effort. The PMF's higher headquarters, the Caribbean Defense Command (CDC) expanded training in jungle operations after being tasked by the War Department to train 1,500 replacements for the Pacific Theater; training camps were established at Pacora and Rio Hato, Panama. The first sixty-day training cycle was completed on 15 March 1943.

While these sites provided valuable training, the terrain was not as rugged nor the vegetation as thick as that of most jungle in the Pacific. Another jungle training site was then established at Camp Pina, just south of Fort Sherman; the terrain at this site was as challenging as anything in the Pacific Theater. This site was used until the end of the war.

Coincidentally, the most suitable area to conduct jungle warfare training under U.S. control at that time was Camp Pina and Fort Sherman; the site of coastal artillery and anti-aircraft artillery batteries located on the Atlantic side of the Panama Canal. The Fort Sherman Military Reservation covered in excess of fifty square miles of jungle and had an extensive infrastructure that included logistical and transportation systems. The combination of usable maneuver area and preexisting base facilities made Fort Sherman an ideal location for a jungle warfare school.

The famed 158th Infantry Regiment, also known as the Original Bushmasters, was the Army unit that started jungle training in Panama. This unit of the 45th Division was, after Pearl Harbor made a separate Regiment and in 1942 sent to the Panama Canal Zone for jungle training before being sent to the South Pacific. The Bushmaster, one of the most deadly snakes in the world became the mascot and the shoulder patch of the fighting 158th Regimental Combat Team. The Bushmasters became the Japanese worst nightmare.

FORT SHERMAN AREA

The areas used throughout the various incarnations of the U.S. Army Jungle Warfare School include Fort Sherman and the Pina Range Complex. Fort Sherman Military Reservation is bordered to the North and Northwest by the Caribbean Sea, on the South and Southwest by the Chagres River, and East by Limon Bay and Lake Gatun. It consists of 23,000 acres of single and double canopy jungle, which is cross compartmentalized with steep rolling hills, numerous tributaries, mangrove swamps and coastline. The cantonment area includes barracks and mess facilities, cadre headquarters and offices, a boathouse with docks, classroom and instruction sites, and recreation facilities.

Training areas on the Fort Sherman Military Reservation include the maneuver area with several fortified or semi-permanent objectives, a jungle land navigation course, and jungle combat maneuver lanes, helicopter landing zones, a drop zone, and two coastal artillery batteries that have been converted into small arms ranges and special warfare training sites.

The Pina Range Complex is immediately South of Fort Sherman, across the Chagres River. This complex includes several small arms live fire ranges and maneuver lanes, a mortar maneuver course, a live fire village, and a demolitions range. White Drop Zone and other areas of Gatun Lake are used for airborne insertions and small boat operations. The Chagres River is also used for small boat and tactical riverine operations and as part of the Sapper (light combat engineer) live demolitions maneuver course.

The coastal artillery batteries and anti-aircraft gun emplacements on Fort Sherman were obsolete by the mid-1940s; most of the large caliber guns had not been fired in years. Attack from the air was the major threat, and mobile anti-aircraft guns and missiles, and motorized ground forces had replaced most of the static defenses of the Canal. This left Fort Sherman with a caretaker garrison and the primary mission to billet troops stationed on the Atlantic side of the Panama Canal. The change in mission was another factor that made Fort Sherman a desirable location for jungle warfare training.

ORIGINS OF A FORMAL JUNGLE SCHOOL

The U.S. Army, Caribbean (USARCARIB) was still conducting limited jungle warfare and survival training for its forces, when the Commanding General received the formal mission from the Department of the Army of "keeping the art of jungle warfare alive in the Army" in April of 1951. In compliance with this directive, USARCARIB issued Training Memorandum

Number 9, which established a Jungle Warfare Training Board (JWTB). The JWTB was a study group "responsible for continued research and study, analysis, and reporting of final findings and recommendations on changes or additions to established U.S. Army doctrine and techniques of jungle warfare and equipment designed for jungle operations." Standards of individual and unit jungle training were established.

One major result of the JWTB's study was the establishment of a provisional headquarters to plan, organize, and evaluate a 2,000 man, field-training exercise. BRUSH BAY was conducted on Fort Sherman from 4 May to 4 June 1953. Elements of the 33rd Infantry, the 370th Engineer Amphibious Support Regiment, and the 45th Reconnaissance Battalion stationed in Panama were joined by nearly 1,000 paratroopers from the 82nd Airborne Division, organized in a Battalion sized Combat Team. The provisional HQ was later replaced by the 7437th Army Unit, Jungle Warfare Training Center (JWTC) on 15 June 1953 that later became the Jungle Operations Training Center (JOTC).

In November of 1953 the JWTC was attached to the 33rd Infantry; its focus was to train Panama based soldiers in jungle warfare and survival. Improvements were made to Fort Sherman facilities, and formal training of the 33rd Infantry was begun in the spring of 1954; the objective was to make the entire regiment proficient in jungle operations. In May of 1956 the 33rd Infantry was inactivated, and was replaced by the 20th Infantry Regiment, which inherited the JWTC and the mission of the 33rd Infantry.

The majority of soldiers trained by the JWTC were from the Panama area, though CONUS[35] based units were also being trained. An example of this was Exercise JUNGLE JIM, where a 1,200 man reinforced battalion combat team (2/188 AIR, 11th Airborne Division) received a month long (9 May to 7 June 1955) program of instruction (POI) and maneuvers very similar in scope of the POI used by the JOTC in the 1990s. In December of 1957, the JWTC began regular cyclic training of units from outside of the Panama area as part of the recently reorganized 1st Battle Group, 20th Infantry; this established the Jungle Operations Course.

The JWTC normally ran ten, three week long, cycles annually. Specialized cycles (some were taught completely in Spanish for instance) and support of training exercises also occurred in addition to the ten regular cycles. A normal cycle conducted training on three levels, individual soldier skills, small unit, and company. The bulk of the instruction was conducted for the infantry rifle company, but specialized training for a heavy weapons company, a heavy mortar company, a headquarters company, a combat engineer (Sapper) platoon, and a medical platoon was also available. Individual training included jungle survival, camouflage, navigation, mines and booby traps, and jungle plants and

---

[35] Continental United States

living. Upon completion of the "core" classes, the training focus shifted to small unit patrolling, attack, and ambush tactics and techniques.

Once the small unit was proficient in jungle operations, training moved to company and occasionally battalion level offensive field training exercises. By 1960 the JWTC had trained eleven infantry battalions, one artillery battalion, nine infantry companies, one mortar battery, three provisional non-commissioned officer groups, and three provisional officer groups from the Continental United States (CONUS). Concurrent with these cycles, numerous soldiers from the USARCARIB, La Guardia National (Panamanian Police), numerous soldiers from Latin American countries, and American Special Warfare Units received jungle-specific training.

On 1 July 1963 the mission and functions of the JWTC were assumed by the Jungle Operations Committee (JOC) of the School of the Americas, based at Fort Gulick, Canal Zone, Panama (the JOC continued to operate at Fort Sherman). Fort Gulick was located approximately ten kilometers east of Fort Sherman, adjacent to the city of Colon. The JOC extended the course to five weeks in duration, with the emphasis in jungle survival skills, and less focus on tactics. The reduction in tactical operations was mainly due to a shortage of resources and trained cadre available from the School of the Americas. Fortunately, an influx of Special Forces qualified instructors and increased supervision from the 8th Special Forces Group, in late 1965, brought fundamental changes to the program of instruction. The course was shortened to two weeks in length, most of which was spent in the jungle, and the training focus returned to combat tactics, techniques, and procedures.

VIETNAM AND JUNGLE WARFARE TRAINING

Although highly beneficial to the survival and combat effectiveness of U.S. troops in Southeast Asia, the Jungle Operations Committee remained fairly low profile throughout the early 1960s. However as American involvement in Southeast Asia increased, so did the importance and utilization of the JOC. An example of this increase is number of students who graduated from the course. In FY 1961, about 1700 students graduated from the course; 9145 students graduated in FY 1967.

One of the major reasons for this increase was the participation of 60 officers and non-commissioned officers from the 1st Cavalry Division (Airmobile) in July of 1966. Extensive positive feedback about the value of instruction was quickly brought to the attention of LTG Creighton Abrams, the U.S. Army Vice Chief of Staff. Soon the Department of the Army (DA) increased the quota of trainees for the JOC, and agreed to increase instructors and funds late in 1967. A rapid increase in class size and number of two week cycles occurred before additional funds and manpower was provided by DA; one of the

JOCs higher headquarters, U.S. Army South (USARSO) was tasked to provide additional resources in the interim.

The Jungle Operations Committee continually took measures to improve the quality of instruction. In addition to conducting course after action reviews, the JOC sent questionnaires to officers and NCOs that deployed to Vietnam about 90 days after they had been in country; this questionnaire asked for a reappraisal of course curriculum based on their experiences (see Appendix C). The commentary received was very positive overall, but valuable suggestions were made that led to modifications in the course. In October 1965 a team from the USARSO G3 visited a jungle operations course being taught in Hawaii. The POI was similar to the Panama jungle operations course, but the Hawaii course included a cordon and search of a mock Vietnamese village; this was added to the Panamanian course. This program of cadre/instructor self-critique and rotational unit after-action reviews (with the goal of constantly refining the Jungle Operations Course) continued until the school was closed in 1999.

JUNGLE OPERATIONS TRAINING CENTER DEVELOPMENT

The Jungle Operations Committee, of the School of the Americas was separated by the Department of the Army on 1 July 1968, and became the Jungle Operations Training Center (JOTC). The JOTC was placed under operational control of the 8th Special Forces Group on 1 July 1970. In July of 1975 the JOTC became an independent major subordinate command within the 193rd Infantry Brigade. These were primarily administrative moves, with little impact on the content of the Jungle Operations Course. The school did receive other responsibilities in addition to running the JOC; a USARSO RECONDO course was established in March of 1969, and operation of the USARSO NCO Academy was given to the JOTC in October 1971.

The Jungle Operations Course was three weeks long throughout the early 1970's with minor alterations in the POI; most of these were caused by technological improvements in night vision optics and heliborne mobility. Slots to the JOTC were given primarily to CONUS based light and airborne battalions. Slots were still allocated to individual soldiers in a manner similar to Airborne School. Organic units such as a squad from 1-504 Parachute Infantry Regiment did not attend the course. Soldiers from throughout the Army came to JOTC and were assigned to a provisional squad / platoon for the duration of the course. The jungle warfare skills learned and the opportunity for NCOs to test their leadership was undoubtedly very valuable, but a major change initiated in the mid-1970s vastly improved the benefits gained from attendance.

The Jungle Operations Training Center was reorganized in Fiscal Year 1976 to train battalion-sized units. The basic POI[36] was still taught, but soldiers

---

[36] Program of Instruction

now attended all training with members of their organic teams, squads, and platoons. This did much to improve unit teambuilding and to enhance leadership skills of junior NCOs and officers. After core week training, platoons went through situational training exercises (STX) where squad and platoon leaders were placed in difficult tactical situations. These exercises, in addition to live fire ambushes and react to contact maneuver courses, honed the war fighting skills and esprit of the small unit. The third week added company and battalion level operations during a battalion led field-training exercise (FTX). The FTX exercised the battalion command group, the battalion staff, and company leadership.

Units experienced the challenges of command, control and logistics in the jungle. The overall benefits of a rotation to the JOTC were now battalion wide and covered almost all of the Battle Operating Systems. Rotations were sought after throughout the Army light infantry community and the Marine Corps. Additionally, many Special Operations units received training from JOTC instructors or used JOTC facilities while conducting internal training events.

OPERATION JUST CAUSE

The unit that operated the Jungle Operations Training Center was re-designated the Jungle Operations Training Battalion (JOTB) during the invasion of Panama in December 1989. The battalion was notified of possible contingency operations as tensions between the American and Panamanian governments increased, and prepared and trained accordingly. The JOTB was augmented with additional combat and combat support assets and as JUST CAUSE began, was designated Task Force Sherman. The task force served with the 3rd Brigade, 7th Infantry Division (Light) as part of Task Force Atlantic.

Task Force Sherman successfully maintained the security and defense of Fort Sherman and the Gatun Locks[37] complex, including numerous key communications and transportation facilities, the Gatun Locks, dam, spillway bridge, and hydroelectric plant. The Task Force also cleared and 27 towns and villages, and 140 kilometers of coastline. They conducted 19 air assaults and Civilian Military Operations in four villages. Patrols from Task Force Sherman eliminated all Hunter Platoons south of the Rio Chagres, captured numerous prisoners of war, weapons, and large amounts of ammunition and equipment. They cleared the town of Portobello, Isla Grande and other villages located north of Colon during a joint operation with Navy SEALs and Special Operations Aviation.

Patrols continued until 12 January 1990, when Task Force Sherman became the reserve for Task Force Atlantic. The Jungle Operations Training Battalion was awarded a battle streamer for its actions during Operation JUST

---

[37] Located on the Atlantic Side of the Isthmus

CAUSE, making it the only TDA unit in the U.S. Army to receive this distinction.

THE JOTB IN THE 1990's

The JOTB returned to its primary mission of training light infantry units in the art of jungle warfare after Operation JUST CAUSE. By 1992, twelve light infantry jungle warfare courses, four engineer jungle warfare courses, and four aircrew survival courses were taught annually. In addition to these standard rotations, the JOTB provided support to numerous Special Operations units, U.S. Government, and law enforcement agencies.

The JOTB fulfilled a critical role in the U.S. Southern Command (SOUTHCOM) and USARSO military-to-military exchange programs (which included small unit exchanges, and guest instructor programs) that enhanced relations and aided our efforts to influence the further democratization of the Americas. Countries that participated in these programs included Argentina, Brazil, Chile, Columbia, the Dominican Republic, Ecuador, Guatemala, Guyana, Honduras, Paraguay, Peru, Uruguay, and Venezuela.

The Jungle Warfare Course

(JWC) was three weeks in duration and trained light infantry battalion task forces in jungle operations. The first week (core week) of training consisted of individual soldier skills and squad collective tasks that would be performed in a jungle environment. These tasks included: jungle plants and living, land navigation, mines and booby traps, jungle combat techniques, waterborne operations, and squad react to contact live fire lanes. Scout, mortar, and combat engineer (Sapper) platoons received additional specialized training during core week. The second week consisted of situational training exercises (STX) that included platoon deliberate attacks, raids, ambushes, a company cordon and search, and Sapper, riverine demolition missions. A battalion field training exercise (FTX) was conducted during the third and final week of the JWC. This FTX was normally a four-day long, free-play exercise that pitted the training battalion against a company-sized opposition force (OPFOR). JOTB observer/controllers provided both the training battalion and the OPFOR company with continuous feedback through comprehensive after action reviews.

The Engineer Jungle Warfare Course (EJWC) was similar in nature to the JWC, with additional focus on demolitions and mobility operations. The core week instruction was the same as the JWC, with the second week consisting of a four day FTX that required Sapper platoons to conduct numerous combat patrols, engineer reconnaissance missions, and route clearance missions on the Chagres River and jungle trails using live demolitions to reduce obstacles. The Sapper company would perform construction missions during the third and fourth weeks. These missions included basic masonry, carpentry, and pioneer tasks. The repair or replacement of footbridges in the jungle, repair of boat docks, and construction of training sites are examples of some EJWC projects.

The Air Crew Survival Course (ACS) was approximately two weeks in duration, and trained Army and Air Force aircrew personnel, U.S. Government, and law enforcement agencies in basic survival, escape and evasion techniques. Subjects included crossing water obstacles, improvised tools, weapons, traps, and snares, food procurement and preparation, and jungle navigation. The course culminated in a four-day survival, escape, and evasion exercise designed to test the student's ability to survive alone or in small groups, while in hostile territory.

Due to the Army drawing down after Operation DESERT STORM[38], there were only two light infantry divisions, one air assault division, and one airborne division left on active duty. Numerous low-intensity conflicts and sustainment and stability operations in Somalia, Haiti and the Balkans showed the need for skilled light fighters. Many of the battalions that participated in these operations had gone through a JOTC rotation. The environmental experience from the conduct of jungle operations was not the only benefit gained from training at the JOTC. Teambuilding, the focus on small unit combat operations and numerous live fire exercises, honed the critical combat skills of many battalions that participated in these operations.

The value of a JOTC rotation was recognized by all echelons of the "light fighter" community, from division commanders to team leaders. Infantry and Combat Engineer units from all CONUS based active Army, light, airborne, and air assault divisions, the 75th Ranger Regiment, and the United States Marine Corps continued to compete for course rotations to the JOTB until its inactivation in 1999.

Once again, the Military High Command had failed to learn from history and those who fail to learn from the lessons of history are fated to repeat the mistakes of the past. In spite of the fact that the Soviet Union was a thing of the past, the Doctrine Generals were still gearing up for a conventional conflict, ignoring the advances in weapons and technology. Once and for all they were determined to stamp out any of that evil Special Operations training that might be hiding around the Army[39].

---

[38] The fabled Peace Dividend after the collapse of the Soviet Union

[39] The following are a number of references that deal with the history of the Jungle Warfare School:

JOTB Historian. FY 97 Annual Historical Summary. USARSO Printing, 1998.

JOTB Historian. JOTB's Untold Story. JOTB Printing, 1990.

JOTB Historian. History of Fort Sherman and the U.S. Army Jungle Operations Training Center. JOTB Printing, date unknown.

JOTB Historian. History and Mission of Jungle Warfare Training. JOTB Printing, date unknown.

JOTB Historian. JOTB Historical Questionnaires. JOTB Printing, 1998.

Although this training proved highly beneficial to the survival and combat effectiveness of US troops in Southeast Asia, the Jungle Operations Committee remained fairly low profile throughout the early 1960 and in fact, never really received the support and accolades that it should. To the leaders of our military, all steeped in the need to doctrine, anything that smacked of the unorthodox, and jungle training was certainly one of those areas, was a frill that was not needed. For this school to have been closed at the end of 1999 was a crime and a serious blow to our military's readiness. But, the money was needed for more social programs. Political correctness was at its height of insidious power and even the President, a man who had avoided serving his country in the military, was alleged to be asking who needed a large standing army? Enlistments were down, budgets were being cut, and things did not look good for the future. At a time we should have been maintaining the size of our standing army, we were rushing to enjoy the "peace dividend." We were soon to find out that we all needed a strong military very badly.

WHY THE HISTORY LESSON?

I have gone into much detail, perhaps too much, in this chapter in order to make a point that certainly applies today. In spite of the very clear effectiveness of specialized training such as Jungle Warfare, whenever given the opportunity, the Army is always quick to determine that such training contrary to doctrine, is clearly unnecessary and the schools are closed. The funding that would have gone to the schools is directed toward new, more advanced weapons systems to be used by conventional forces and other "hard costs" of doctrine support. Except for a few visionary officers, the training for unorthodox warfare was, and has always, been a bastard stepchild.

Most of our leaders have taken the position that with the most powerful military in the history of the world, the very idea that the civilian population could be in danger from a potential enemy was laughable. Based on the concept that our doctrine assured victory for our forces, even civil defense training was terminated when the Soviet Union collapsed. The powers that be considered it an expensive frill when the money was needed to support the traditional forces.

It is a matter of history that each war this country has been involved in has found us ill prepared at its inception. The War on Terror has been no

---

Mc Garr, Lionel C. Training Circular: EXERCISE JUNGLE JIM. U.S. Army, Caribbean Printing, 1955.

USARSO Historian. Jungle Training Rooted in World War II Panama. USARSO Printing, date unknown.

USARSO Historian. Jungle Warfare Training in the Canal Zone. USARSO Printing, 1968.

exception. Unfortunately, for the survival of the American people, as I will show as we progress through the overview that the government has hidden just how ill prepared we are to deal with the problem presented by terrorist forces.

CHAPTER FOUR

FUN IN THE JUNGLE

The 82nd Airborne Division is the ready reaction force of the United States Army. The troopers that make up this Division are looked at as the most professional soldiers in any Army and the view of our military leaders is that there is not a problem that these professionals cannot handle. Unfortunately, the reality is not in keeping with the reputation. Like every other unit in the US Army, the 82nd has become a victim of the Doctrine Generals.

As a member of the 193rd Infantry Brigade, it was not felt necessary to send our units to the Jungle Warfare School at Fort Sherman, since we were operating in the jungle six days a week as it was. If we did not know how to operate in the jungles of Panama, then no one could. However, we were called upon quite often to act as aggressors against those stateside units that were sent to the Jungle School.

Under General Richardson's training program, we went to the jungle early Monday morning each week and we might be back early Friday morning. During the ensuing days we would establish base camps deep within the jungle and conduct training each as individual platoons or as part of company size units. Occasionally there would be Battalion and Brigade field exercises and we would operate as part of our parent unit, aggressing against whatever Battalion was chosen to be the bad guys. So I can safely say that we knew the jungle as well as someone knows the streets of his hometown.

It was during these exercises where my platoon was acting alone as an aggressor against a stateside unit that I began to get a truly practical idea of what a trained, determined force could do to a much larger, better equipment military unit that was not prepared for unconventional tactics. As I sit here almost three decades away from those days, I still remember the thrill it was to totally demoralize a large unit just using the terrain that was second nature to us, but was like being on a different planet to some of the Stateside units that attended the Jungle School.

I specifically remember one exercise where the unit attending the school was one of the top rated battalions of the 82nd Airborne Division and one of the units that was to come to our rescue if the Zone were ever to be invaded by an enemy force. The Battalion Commander was going to hand command over to one of his senior company commanders upon the unit returning to the states. I expected this unit[40] to make short work of my 35-man platoon.

We were dropped into Area of Operation Mosquito, a isolated training site so far back in the jungle that there were no roads and the only way in was by helicopter. As soon as we arrived I sent out some scouts and found out that the briefing that I had received had been wrong, there was actually one place along the coast, which was some five miles from my LZ[41], where troops could be landed by small boat. One of my NCOs was a close friend with one of the Jungle School evaluators stationed in the training area to grade the exercise. The evaluator happened to let slip that a portion of the 82nd was going to arrive by landing craft and conduct a by the book sweep using conventional tactics and close air support that would drop other elements f the Battalion behind us and then coordinate the movement of the two forces to flush us out and then capture us. I suspected that they could probably do it with very little trouble, but I had no intention in making it easy for them to succeed.

With the help of a helicopter pilot that owed me a favor[42], I had managed to obtain a substantial supply of pyrotechnics, including parachute flares, CS grenades, and a huge supply of artillery simulators and smoke grenades. My platoon sergeant was a Vietnam veteran who had a lot of experience sitting up booby traps. With this thought in mind, as a unit, we adjourned to the only beach where small craft could be landed and began to set up several little presents for the 82nd along the edge of the beach.

Looking at the map[43], it was clear that the only place that was open enough for the 82nd to land troops from helicopters was a large clearing near a

---

[40] As I recall, I was briefed that over 80 percent of this Battalion were men that had combat time in Vietnam.

[41] Landing Zone

[42] Quite often the aggressor force was not furnished with much in the way of pyrotechnic in order to assure that the unit going through the school would win the exercise. It was a great morale builder.

[43] There is a favorite saying in the Army that the most dangerous thing in the world is a 2nd Lieutenant with a map and a compass. I had both and I was using them freely.

deserted village some distance from the beach. Leaving a fire team[44] to wait for our visitors, I took the rest of the platoon to the village and we began to place some surprises there for our soon to be arriving guests. Once we had completed this enterprise, I left a fire team from my weapons squad with an M-60 Machine Gun and the rest of us adjourned to a nearby hilltop and made camp. It promised to be an interesting morning.

EASIER SAID THAN DONE

I will have to say that from my vantage point high in the big tree on that high hillside overlooking the village and its adjoining clearing, I had a ringside seat for the 82nd's air insertion. There was no doubt that this company of the 82nd was a well-trained outfit as the insertion proceeded like clockwork. That is until they touched the ground.

The 82nd was arriving in UH-1 helicopters, which normally could carry some 8 soldiers and their equipment. Figuring one squad per helicopters, this company sized insertion called for at least sixteen helicopters to off load 8 men each. Since it was desirous to get a complete unit on the ground at one time, there were four Hueys set to land during each insertion. Thus, in theory, one platoon would be on the ground at a time.

As called for in conventional doctrine when entering an uncontrolled LZ, the soldiers dove off the choppers while they were still several feet off the ground. Now this looks great in the movies and impresses the hell out of kids at Armed Forces day events, but in the jungle it is not wise. If you will recall, I mentioned the Elephant Grass that grows some six feet high around the Mira Flores Locks, well, this clearing contained Elephant Grass. When these gung ho soldiers dove out of the first four helicopters some two or three feet above the grass[45], they were actually diving out of the helicopters some eight feet above the ground. Some of them even landed on the trip wires that we had strung along the ground to our booby traps. In other words, all hell broke loose in more ways than one.

The first things we heard were the screams of the men who hit the ground after unexpected falls of some 8 or 9 feet. Then there were the booms of artillery simulators going off as our booby traps were sprung by the dazed soldiers, as they thrashed around in the tall grass. Then thick streams of smoke began to billow up into the clear morning air from other hidden booby traps we had secreted in the tall grass. My fire team, hidden in the village and not realizing

---

[44] At this time a rifle platoon consisted of three rifle squads and a weapons squad. Each squad consisted of two fire teams.

[45] From the air, Elephant Grass covered areas can be very deceptive and look just like a grassy meadow.

that there could be possible injuries, began to fire their weapons, adding to the confusion. Only a few of the 82nd soldiers were able to return fire.

After emptying their weapons into the confused airborne soldiers, my fire team made a dash across the clearing through the Elephant Grass, throwing canisters of CS gas into the midst of the totally disoriented soldiers. According to the plan that I had laid out, I was supposed to then rush the LZ with the remainder of the Platoon and capture the troops being inserted, but we were laughing too hard at their antics to have really been effective.

We later discovered that two or three of the 82nd soldiers had fallen onto Jungle Ant Beds and the little buggers had taken offense, swarming out of their burrows to literally cover the soldiers that had disturbed them. The unfortunate soldiers were now running through the Elephant Grass screaming insanely and stripping off their clothes as fast as they could in an effort to get rid of the ants. Those jungle ants, when they swarmed, could strip a carcass as fast or faster than Piranha and their bits were extremely painful. Of course, from our vantage point we had no idea what was happening and couldn't figure out why three or four men were throwing their clothes up in the air. My one regret was that I did not have a video camera. The situation became even more confused with the booby traps started several fires inside that Elephant Grass covered clearing. By morning, the grass was destroyed by the fire, as was most of the abandoned village.

Naturally, since the initial insertion had not gone as planed, the rest of that particular 82nd Company flew off, leaving their men on the ground basically stranded, and landed at their back up LZ, some six miles away as the crow flies. However, in Panama, six miles as the crow flies can become ten or twelve miles on the ground, as a lot of the Panamanian topography is either straight up or straight down. This left the stranded platoon at my mercy which no hope of support until the rest of their company could walk in from the back up LZ. Now the fun really began.

A NICE DAY AT THE BEACH

Meanwhile, at the landing site on the coast, it was later reported to me that several fully loaded LCT landing craft had rounded the headland and slid expertly onto the small beach. The front ramps dropped and the pride of the 82nd Airborne Division poured off the boats and onto that little beach looking suitably ferocious. After making sure that they had all of their gear, these highly trained, combat experienced troops started into the jungle and immediately set off our booby traps. Once my fire team added their weapons fire to the situation, the situation on that little beach became a total zoo. Those closest to the water tried to get back on board the boats, but as per their standing operating procedure, once they had unloaded their troops, the commanders of the LSTs had raised their ramps and began to pull back away from the beach.

Yelling men and equipment fell into the surf while Platoon Leaders and Company Commanders stormed around that little beach and tried to restore order. These efforts were of course helped along as my men tossed a few CS canisters into the crowd of soldiers now milling around the beach in some confusion, just to liven things up. Finally, in almost a mad dash, a mob that had shortly before been a well trained cohesive fighting force dashed into the jungle willy nilly, just looking for a way to get away from the gun fire, CS gas and booby traps. So just four men, with their superior knowledge of the terrain, and some well-placed booby traps, had totally demoralized and routed a Company sized element of the 82nd Airborne Division. So much for conventional tactics!

For the next four days, my platoon raised merry hell with the 82nd and never moved more than a mile from our hillside vantage point. For their part, the 82nd did their best to conduct their sweeps according to approved doctrine, but just as in the cities, the jungle undergrowth tended to channel their movements making them ripe targets for ambushes, booby traps and CS gas attacks when they least expected it[46].

The point of the story is that the 82nd Airborne was and is, one of our Army's best fighting units. However, they were going up against a smaller, highly mobile force that knew the terrain much better than they did and possessed some very devious minds unhampered by the requirement to follow standard doctrine. We used the terrain as an ally and to impede their best efforts to follow conventional doctrine. I truly believe that had we been using live ammo and not blanks, that we would have killed every one of them before the exercise was over at the loss of only a few of my men.

Of course, at the end of the exercise, it was decided that for the sake of the units' morale, the 82nd was allowed to receive a passing grade from the Jungle Warfare School. In a very formal ceremony the 82nd Airborne Battalion Commander, who was on the list for Brigadier General, was congratulated on the outstanding performance of his unit, by the Commander of 193rd Infantry Brigade. No mention was made of the debacle in the jungle as it would have showed some flaws in standard doctrine and this was not permissible. My unit that had routed the 82nd units in every engagement was told we had done a good job by a Captain and bundled onto the train that ran across the isthmus back to our base at Fort Clayton.

However, in spite of the continually demonstrated superior performance of the units of the 193rd at adapting doctrine to unusual situations, in its infinite wisdom, the United States Army has returned to standard Doctrine. We have developed the most sophisticated, well-armed military force in the history of the

---

[46] I might also point out that sweating and then being exposed to CS Gas just makes the effects of the gas that much worse. I can assure you that those airborne soldiers were sweating buckets under that thick jungle canopy as they searched high and low for us. I also have to admire their determination, not one of them gave up and quit.

world but we can't catch Osama Bin Laden and his merry band of misfits and we are being forced to withdraw from certain Iraqi cities due to our apparent inability to overcome insurgent activity inside those cities.

What is wrong with this picture, why does our Army appear so unable to deal with the insurgent menace? To get that answer you have to bear with me a little longer and then it will become clear to you, the Reader, what the powers that be are not able to see.

In retrospect, the 82nd had such problems not because I was a better field commander than the two company commanders that I faced, but because I knew the terrain much better than they did as this was my home, so to speak; I had time to prepare my surprises and most importantly, mine was a small highly mobile force compared to the 82nd's necessity for high profile transportation and clear lines of logistical support.

Rather than being required to receive addition training in Jungle Operations, the commanders of the two 82nd companies, through the "Power of the Ring[47]" were rated as qualified. Unfortunately, in real life situations where doctrine goes out the window, there are no raters to give West Point graduates passing grades. In real life, the pass or fail comes from the barrel of a gun and in urban warfare situations we are not the best that we can be.

---

[47] Just as Luke Skywalker had the power of the force, West Point graduates have the power of the ring to save them from most disasters. I am not anti-West Point by any means, they are a necessary evil, but I think that service academy graduation it is given too much importance in military circles. One of the finest General Officers that I have known is MG Stanley Green, a Mustang, or former enlisted man who has made it to General Officer.

CHAPTER FIVE

THE UNITED STATES ARMY INFANTRY SCHOOL

All things must end and so it was with my first assignment. My Battalion, the 4th Battalion (Mechanized) 20th Infantry had been turned over to a new battalion commander who only wanted West Point Officers under his command since they were so much better than ROTC Officers in his opinion[48]. After the events at the Jungle School, I was transferred to the position of Assistant Adjutant and assigned to develop the first experimental Battalion sized Personnel Administration Center (PAC) The idea behind this move was to consolidate all administrative functions normally handled at the Company level at the Battalion level and relieve the Companies of the necessity to have clerk typists and other administrative personnel assigned.

Shortly before Lieutenant Colonel Johnson[49] assumed command of my battalion, I had been transferred to lead the 2nd Platoon of Charlie Company. In the ensuing shuffle brought about by LTC Johnson assuming command, the Brigade Commander's aide (and fair haired boy), Lieutenant Jeffrey K. Beatty was sent to the battalion to be the new Company Commander of Charlie Company. He and I had never gotten along as I thought he was a jerk and still do. General Richardson specifically directed that Beatty was to have only West Point Officers leading platoons in his company, as they were so much better than non-West Point officers, so I had to go.

---

[48] Unfortunately, the new commander was fully supported by MG Richardson in this misguided belief.

[49] A six foot six inch descendant of General Albert Sydney Johnson of Civil War fame.

On the direct orders of the Brigade Commander[50], I was transferred to be the Executive Officer (XO) of the Headquarters Company at Fort Davis on the Atlantic Side. During the time that I served as XO, I was appointed as the Chemical, Biological, and Radiological Officer (CBR) for the Company. Normally, such as appointment was in name only as there was generally an NCO directly handing the troop training and the equipment, but for some bizarre reason, I was ordered to attend the CBR School being held at Fort Clayton. So for some two weeks, I studied everything the Army knew or suspected regarding chemical weapons, their use and their potential.

I received high marks as Company XO and when my Company Commander was slated for rotation, it was decreed by the new Brigade Commander[51], who felt ROTC officers could be useful, that I would become the new commander of Headquarters Company. This appointment would have made me the youngest Company Commander in the Brigade. However, by this time I had had my fill of the "if you are not West Point you are useless" philosophy of the 193rd and the Army's continual failure to properly diagnose the injury to my knees that was still troubling me and prior to this appointment, I had requested a transfer to another command. The Department of the Army in its infinite wisdom sent me to Fort Benning, Georgia and assigned me to the United States Army Infantry School (USAIS).

My first assignment at the Infantry School was to be the Chief of Academic Records for the Infantry school. This might seem like a backwater assignment, but it was actually a high profile position that brought me in contact with every officer and NCO in attendance as well as Generals and most members of Congress who had constituents attending the school. On more than one occasion, I had people like Senator Ted Kennedy and others of his peers call and ask for me by name. This was certainly heady atmosphere for a young First Lieutenant.

Then I was appointed to be the School's Representative at USAIS Military Boards. A military board was held whenever a student was unable to

---

[50] General Richardson did everything but adopt Beatty and as a result, an individual who would normally have been looked at as a complete and total ass kisser became a hero to the other officers in the Brigade. General Richardson even arranged for Beatty's wife, a beautiful young woman, to receive a direct commission as an Army Officer as well. But then Beatty was a West Point attendee, much better than a mere ROTC officer. I protested being reassigned to Fort Davis and asked to see the Brigade Commander. I was finally allowed to see the great man, but General Richardson told me that he didn't have time for Lieutenant problems; he was late for a Boy Scout luncheon. So much for an officer who looks after the welfare of his men; my career was less important to him than a Boy Scout Luncheon.

[51] Major General Richardson had gone on to his reward of being TRADOC Commander. Lieutenant Beatty was left on his own and had to perform without MG Richardson running interference for him which resulted in at least one dead soldier that I know about.

pass a course or if some regulation was violated by the student's behavior. My position was one that required me to determine the makeup of the Board and then act in a manner similar to a prosecutor and present the case against the Boarded soldier. In my two years in this position, I handled over three hundred boards of one type of another, many times with members of the JAG[52] Corp opposing me. I only lost two cases.

After a year as the Chief of Academic Records, I was assigned to be the Registrar of the School, a senior Major's position even though I was only a senior First Lieutenant. In fact, I was the youngest person to ever hold this particular position. I was now answerable directly to the School Secretary, an O-6[53] position and the Deputy Commandant of the Infantry School, an O-7[54]. My duties even took me to meetings with the TRADOC Forces Commander, a Lieutenant General. I had just made Captain.

My next involvement with Army Doctrine took place one morning when Colonel Bobby J. Harris, the Deputy Assistant Commandant of the Infantry School walked into my office and asked if it was true that I furnished the information to the civilian that was responsible for briefing the School Commandant and senior post staff (the senior briefer was a GS-14 position, technically far above a mere "Captain) regarding training and readiness. This information was then furnished to the Department of the Army and had a great impact on many areas of doctrinal development.

I confirmed that I was the one that furnished the raw data that was prepared and then presented during the briefings and to my horror Colonel Harris smiled. I might mention that his smile always raised my hackles. To get an idea of the smile from this particular, picture a smiling shark and this is close to the effect. His response was "Good, the briefer had a heart attack and died last night. You are to give the briefing to the Commanding General in an hour."

He left before I could think of a graceful way to say no to a man who did not have that word in his vocabulary when used by a subordinate. So an hour later, I was standing on a platform[55] briefing a room full of Generals and senior colonels. I really do not remember what I said, but apparently they liked it as I continued to give this briefing to the Commanding General until I was reassigned to the Instructional Department and even then I would be called back to give periodic briefings to visiting dignitaries.

However, during this entire time that I was in an administrative position, I continued to study advancements being made in chemical warfare and in small unit tactics. I even wrote some articles for the Infantry Magazine that were rarely

---

[52] Judge Advocate General

[53] Full Colonel

[54] A Brigadier General

[55] At the Infantry School when you are instructing or giving a briefing, you are said to be on the platform.

published, since they criticized conventional tactics in favor of special operations. Almost every article published in any of the service magazines was about the Soviet menace and our efforts to neutralize their superior numbers.

Then one day, I was called into the Office of the School Secretary, an O-6 named Hall who informed me that I was being transferred to the Defensive Tactics Department. He congratulated me on the job I had done as Registrar and then said that as an Infantry Captain, I needed to be with the troops, not behind a desk. He then criticized me for not being a poster soldier, since I had now developed a noticeable limp from my untreated Airborne School injury. He also cautioned me not to make too much mention of the fact that I favored special operations over standard doctrine. He said that some people might not understand.

As I look back now, it is clear to me that someone did not understand and that someone was the Chief of Staff of the Army. That is why we find ourselves at this time in history being unable to even protect our own borders, much less our civilian population centers. In the next chapters, I will show how our own procedures for waging urban warfare have been turned against us, why we did not have the capability to anticipate 9/11 and why it is only going to get worse.

CHAPTER SIX

INTELLIGENCE FAILURES

Before discussing urban warfare and the part played by the Infantry School and my own classroom instruction in the events of September of 2001, I want to take a moment and review some other actions taking place at about this same time in Washington DC that would have a long lasting effect on our ability to gather intelligence of the nature that would have warned us of such events as 9/11.

Seldom is the name of one particular individual historically associated with major governmental changes. Oh, people may know who was responsible at the time it occurs, but normally, this distinction fades with time. However, to many, the name of Frank Church will long have negative connotations whenever they think of him. Part of the blame for the success of the terrorist attacks against this country can be laid at the doorstep of this man from Boise, Idaho.

But who was Frank Church? Human memory is frail and things that are important today are forgotten tomorrow. Frank Church was born on July 25, 1924 in Boise, Idaho. This somewhat precocious young man went on to win the 1941 American Legion National Oratorical Contest with a speech titled "The American Way Of Life." In 1942 he entered Stanford University, but joined the US Army in 1943, becoming an Intelligence Officer in Burma during World War II. After the war, he returned to Stanford University and after graduating in 1950, he became a lawyer in Boise. He joined the Democratic Party, and in 1956, at the age of 32, he was elected as the fifth youngest member ever to sit in the United States Senate. With such a promising start, it is uniquely sad that he also inflicted one of the worst defeats to United States Intelligence gathering that it has ever suffered.

In 1959, Senate Majority Leader Lyndon Baines Johnson appointed Senator Church to the Foreign Relations Committee. Frank Church had many independent political views and in 1965 he began to criticize the War in Vietnam. In 1969, Frank Church joined with Senator John Sherman Cooper to sponsor an amendment prohibiting the use of ground troops in Laos and Thailand. This prohibition allowed the Viet Cong and their supporters to use Laos and Thailand as safety zones in which to lick their wounds and gather their strength. These same two senators joined forces in 1970 to limit the powers of the President to wage war.

His perceived lack of support for our military apparently went unnoticed by his constituency and Frank Church was returned to the Senate a number of times. He served on a large number of Senate Committees such as the Special Committee on Aging, Special Committee on Termination of the National Emergency and the Select Committee on Governmental Intelligence Activities. In 1975, Senator Frank Church became the chairman of the Select Committee to Study Governmental Operations with Respect to Intelligence Activities. The specific focus of this committee was the investigation of alleged abuses of power by the Central Intelligence Agency (CIA) and the Federal Bureau of Investigation (FBI).

The committee chaired by Senator Church looked at the case of Fred Hampton and discovered that William O'Neal, Hampton's bodyguard, was a FBI agent-provocateur who, days before the raid, had delivered an apartment floor-plan to the Bureau with an "X" marking Hampton's bed. Ballistic evidence showed that most bullets during the raid were aimed at Hampton's bedroom.

Church's committee also discovered that the Central Intelligence Agency and Federal Bureau of Investigation had sent anonymous letters attacking the political beliefs of targets in order to induce their employers to fire them. Similar letters were sent to spouses in an effort to destroy marriages. The committee also documented criminal break-ins, the theft of membership lists and misinformation campaigns aimed at provoking violent attacks against targeted individuals. One of those people targeted was Martin Luther King. The FBI mailed King a tape recording made from microphones hidden in hotel rooms. The tape was accompanied by a note suggesting that the recording would be released to the public unless King committed suicide.

In its final report, issued in April 1976, the Select Committee to Study Governmental Operations with Respect to Intelligence Activities concluded: "*Domestic intelligence activity has threatened and undermined the Constitutional rights of Americans to free speech, association and privacy. It has done so primarily because the Constitutional system for checking abuse of power has not been applied.*"

The committee also reported that the Central Intelligence Agency had withheld from the Warren Commission, during its investigation of the assassination of John F. Kennedy, information about plots by the Government of the United States against Fidel Castro of Cuba; and that the Federal Bureau of Investigation had conducted a counter-intelligence program (COINTELPRO) against Martin Luther King and the Southern Christian Leadership Conference.

As a result of Church's report Congress established the House Select Committee on Assassinations in September 1976. The resolution authorized a 12-member select committee to conduct an investigation of the circumstances surrounding the deaths of John F. Kennedy and Martin Luther King.

Additionally, a number of limitations were placed on the ability of the FBI and the CIA by Congress to conduct what is called Human Intelligence gathering. The Central Intelligence Agency, like the rest of our government, operates under a series of checks and balances to ensure each branch runs properly. The CIA works together with members of both the Legislative and Executive branches to ensure that the Agency is providing its customers with the information they need when they need it.

The policy makers may be the people who task the CIA to solve the puzzles and answer tough questions, but the business of intelligence is a team effort. As in any task, it is important that both sides work together and understand each other so the job is done well. On the Legislative side, the CIA works with the House Permanent Select Committee on Intelligence (HPSCI) and the Senate Select Committee on Intelligence (SSCI). These two committees, along with the Foreign Relations, Foreign Affairs, and the Armed Services Committees, are responsible for authorizing the programs of the CIA and other intelligence agencies and overseeing their activities. If the Oversight Committees do not authorize an intelligence gathering operation, it cannot happen. The CIA also works with the Appropriations Committees, which are authorized by the Constitution to appropriate funds for all US Government activities. Without the Oversight Committees' approval there can be no funding for an operation.

As a result of the Congressional desire to be involved in everything, there were no CIA Human Intelligence assets on the ground in Afghanistan where Osama Bin Laden was operating. Thus we had no advanced warning of the Al Qaeda plans for the attacks against our largest city. However, as I will cover in a later chapter, such assets may not have been so important after all.

THE NEED FOR INFORMATION

If the reader will recall from the first chapter, I discussed that in a normal campaign, the second stage of a normal military campaign is an extended intelligence-gathering phase, at least several weeks long. This intelligence gathering attempts to identify enemy command and control nexus, the enemy's assets and order of battle, significant enemy personnel, their habits, radio traffic, telephone systems, cable traffic, decryption, and any other information thought to be beneficial to US forces. A clear understanding the enemy and his military capabilities is a major advantage on the modern battlefield.

The U.S. uses significant space and human intelligence gathering assets in this phase of the operation. There are satellites orbiting the planet that are designed for multi-spectral imaging, and the collection and decryption of radio signals. The U.S. also has high-resolution radar mounted in aircraft, to detect land warfare assets and aircraft. These are crucial to the military commanders for maintaining battlefield situational awareness.

In the 1970's this doctrine was being formalized and there was a great deal of emphasis being placed on intelligence gathering about the prospective enemy. We relied on early versions of spy satellites, but most importantly, we had radio intercepts and human intelligence. As an aside it is important to note that as we have become much more sophisticated in the use of high tech intelligence gathering apparatus, we have turned away from developing human sources of intelligence. This lack of overseas human intelligence is one of the things that led to us being surprised on September 11, 2001[56].

As I studied the principles of conducting military operations in urban areas, it very quickly became clear to me that inside the confines of an urban area, military units that were victorious in the open could become helpless targets for hostile forces once inside cities. The primary problem in planning a campaign inside of an urban area was that in many cases, we had no specific up to date data regarding the military installations or permanently stations combat units inside large cities, especially no intelligence regarding underground installations. For this reason, in this time of let's have a war but not hurt the enemy's civilian population, indiscriminate large scale bombing of specific neighborhoods to take out specific installations was, and is, not feasible. A perfect example of this was in 1991 when we executed a bombing attack against the Iraqi Intelligence Headquarters, the Chinese complained that we had actually bombed their embassy instead. I guess "Smart Bombs" can't read.

Military decisions, and many times, political decisions are made based upon the intelligence gathered by all of this nation's intelligence agencies. The following are the types of "Intelligence Gathering Disciplines[57]" used by this country in the 21st century:

- **HUMINT** – This acronym refers to Human Intelligence – In the conduct of HUMINT, the information is gathered from another person on the ground. This information might be gained through interviews with indigenous personnel or following a suspect or through the use of various means of forcing involuntary revelations of information. It is the job of the Central

---

[56] This reference is from the audio portion of "All Things Considered" that aired on October 30, 2001, on National Public Radio. This reference can be found on the Internet at NPR.org.

[57] From *Intelligence Gathering Disciplines* in the Wikipedia Free Encyclopedia, which can be found at Wikipedia.org.

Intelligence Agency to gather Human Intelligence for the United States Government.

- **IMINT** – This acronym refers to Imagery Intelligence, that is intelligence gathered from satellite and aerial photography. This type of intelligence is collected via satellites and aerial photography.

Satellite Intelligence

There have been hundreds - perhaps thousands - of spy satellites launched by dozens of nations since the Soviet Union launched the first successful satellite, named Sputnik. While the vast majority of reconnaissance satellites and any information concerning them are strictly classified, some information (such as that concerning the US Corona program) has been declassified with the end of the Cold War.

The primary purpose of most spy satellites is to monitor visible ground activity. While resolution and clarity of images has improved greatly over the years, this role has remained essentially the same. Some other uses of satellite imaging have been to produce detailed 3D maps for use in operations and missile guidance systems, and to monitor normally invisible information such as the growth levels of a country's crops or the heat given off by certain facilities.

To counter the threat posed by these 'eyes in the sky' several nations have developed systems for destroying enemy spy satellites. This destruction is carried out with either with the use of another 'killer satellite', or with some sort of earth or air launched missile.

The spy satellite game has taken a strange new twist with the recent availability of high resolution, color images from commercial satellite imaging companies - allowing any country or any individual for that matter to get in on the action.

Aerial Intelligence

Aerial intelligence goes back hundreds of years. Long in the past hot air balloons were used to observe enemy formations long in the distance. The use of fixed balloons survived into World War I, when it was accompanied by observation from airships (zeppelins) and the newly invented airplane.

Low- and high-flying planes have been used all through the last century to gather intelligence about the enemy. At the start of the Cold War, foreseeing the need to observe the enemy in peacetime as well as war, the US started developing extremely fast, highflying spy planes. The first such plane, the Lockheed U-2, is still in service; its successor, the newer and faster SR-71 Blackbird, was retired in 1998. These planes have the advantage over satellites that they can usually produce more detailed photographs and can be maneuvered over the target more quickly and cheaply, but have the obvious disadvantage that they can be shot down.

- **MASINT** – This acronym refers to Measurement and Signature Intelligence, which is a general category that includes intelligence that does not fit within the definitions of Signals Intelligence (SIGINT), Imagery Intelligence (IMINT or Human Intelligence (HUMINT). This section includes the following sub categories:

> ACOUSTINT - Acoustic Intelligence - gathered from acoustical sources

> CBINT - Chemical and Biological Intelligence - gathered from chemical and biological weapons and hazards

> DEWINT - Directed Energy Weapon Intelligence - gathered from weapon related radio frequency, microwave, electromagnetic pulse, laser, and particle beams

> Effluent/Debris Collection - gathered from atmospheric effluents and debris

> EOINT - Electro-Optical Intelligence - gathered from optical monitoring of the electromagnetic spectrum

>> IRINT - Infrared Intelligence - gathered from the infrared spectrum

>> LASINT - Laser Intelligence - gathered from laser systems

> MATINT - Materials Intelligence

> NUCINT - Nuclear Intelligence - gathered from the analysis of radiation

> RADINT - Radar Intelligence - gathered from radar sources

> RF/EMPINT - Radio Frequency/Electromagnetic Pulse Intelligence - gathered from radio frequency and electromagnetic pulse emissions

> Spectroscopic Intelligence

URINT - Unintentional Radiation Intelligence - gathered from unintentionally emanated electromagnetic energy excluding nuclear sources

- **OSINT** - Open Source Intelligence - gathered from open sources Open source intelligence or "OSINT" refers to an intelligence gathering discipline based on information collected from open sources, i.e. information available to the general public. This includes newspapers, the Internet, books, phone books, scientific journals, radio broadcasts, television, and others. The term is unrelated to open source in the computer software community, which refers to programs whose source code is publicly available. Collection of information in OSINT is a very different problem from collection in other intelligence disciplines because, by definition, the information sources are publicly available. In other intelligence disciplines, a major difficultly is extracting information from non-cooperative targets. In OSINT, the chief difficulty is identifying relevant, reliable sources from the vast abundance of publicly available information. Obtaining the needed information once a source is identified is a comparatively minor problem. Sometimes overt HUMINT is considered part of open source intelligence. This is the use of non-clandestine human information sources; examples include interrogation of refugees, debriefing of legal travelers, and reports from overt agents such as attachés and ambassadors. A number of nations, notably Australia, Norway, South Africa, and Sweden, have created specialist units to focus on OSINT. Within the US government, the major provider of OSINT is the CIA's Foreign Broadcast Information Service, which also makes some of its information available to the public through the World News Connection.

- **SIGINT** - Signals Intelligence - gathered from interception of signals

SIGINT stands for Signals Intelligence, and refers to intelligence gathering by interception of signals, whether by radio interception or other means.

It became far more central to military (and to some extent diplomatic) intelligence generally with the mechanization of armies, development of blitzkrieg tactics, use of submarine and commerce raiders warfare, and the development of practicable wireless communications. For example, failure to properly protect its communications fatally compromised the Russian Army in its advance early in WWI and led to the disastrous defeat by the Germans under Ludendorff and Hindenburg at the Battle of Tannenberg. Similarly, the interception and decryption of the Zimmerman Telegram[58] was an important factor in the US decision to enter the War against the German Empire.

---

[58] Tuchman, Barbara W., The Zimmerman Telegram, Viking Press, New York, New York. 1958.

On the negative side, the inability of British commanders to take seriously traffic information from intercepts was instrumental in the failure to achieve more than they did at the Battle of Jutland, thus losing what might have been a major opportunity. Likewise, Admiralty dismissal of SIGINT information contributed to the loss of HMS Glorious in 1940.

The use of SIGINT had important implications during WWII as well. The Allied ability to intercept and decrypt the German Enigma code and the Japanese Purple code proved to be a great military advantage. Most notably, Japanese Naval intercepts yielded information, which gave Admiral Nimitz the upper hand in the ambush that resulted in the Japanese Navy's defeat at the Battle of Midway.

As sensitive information is often encrypted, SIGINT often involves the use of cryptanalysis. However, traffic analysis can produce information, often-valuable information, even when the messages themselves cannot be decrypted.

- **ELINT**- Electronic Intelligence - gathered from electronic sensors. However, even with this broad-spectrum gathering of intelligence information, intelligence failures can still happen. The problem seems to be the mindset of those who interpret the intelligence information gathered by all of the agencies. We had built the most powerful military machine in the history of the world with the focus being on the defeat of the Soviet Military machine. With the fall of the Soviet Empire, many of our senior military leaders expressed the opinions that as the last remaining super power, no other country would dare to challenge us in an all out war. Not even the military power of Communist China was sufficient to allow them to engage us in battle with a hope of success. And those who took this position were absolutely correct in their assessment; no other country could challenge us. It took a rag tag collection of former freedom fighters from the Afghanistan war against Soviet occupation to hand us the worst defeat this country has suffered since Pearl Harbor Day. How could such a thing happen? Easy, the terrorists (we will use this label to avoid confusion) knew their enemy, as we had trained most of them.

CHAPTER SEVEN

I MOUNT THE PLATFORM
AND
THE INSTRUCTION CONTINUES

As I mentioned earlier, in military parlance when you are giving instruction you are said to be on the platform. At the Infantry School, the classrooms inside Building 4, also called Infantry Hall, were set up similar to college classrooms with the instructor on a raised stage at the front of the room. At the rear of the rooms there were observation rooms overlooking the instructional area so that the senior officers could sit in secluded splendor behind one way mirrored glass and observe the conduct of the classes.

I was assigned to the Defense Committee of the Tactics Department. My boss, Major Robert K. Gifford was a robust gung ho officer who truly led by example. After some discussion of my areas of expertise, he finally assigned me to become the School's resident specialist in Military Operations on Urban Terrain (MOUT), otherwise known as urban warfare. It was now my job to develop the basic doctrine and training programs for the Infantry officer Advanced Course dealing with how best to conduct urban warfare operations. Though naturally, all training was to be geared toward a foreseeable US/Soviet conflict, I worked to make sure that my instruction was as broad as possible. At the same time, I feared small brushfire wars more than I did an all out nuclear war.

As I prepared my classes around the concept of defending an urban area against standard Soviet Doctrine, I began to also see that no matter how powerful the country, any major city could be a death trap for either a military invader, or the civilian population that inhabited the city and it would not take that much in the way of munitions to inflict tremendous death and devastation. It was becoming much more evident to me that there were serious flaws in our doctrine when it came to urban warfare, but unfortunately, no one would listen to a mere Captain in matters such as this. The Conventional Warfare Generals had spoken, and like the pronouncements from Mount Olympus, as it was said, so it shall be.

ONE SCENARIO

The Infantry officer Advanced Course classes that we taught were comprised of not only U.S. Army officers, but officers from many other countries as well. I recall that in one of my first classes, there were several Iraqi officers. One of these Iraqis was a Major who said very little, but who was clearly a man soaking up all of the information that he could. I had occasion to talk with him and found that he had also attended the British Military School before coming to Fort Benning. His grasp of tactics was as good as the best tacticians that I have ever met. It is my understanding that over the years, he and some of his fellow US/British trained officers became part of the Republican Guard and then joined the terrorists after the fall of Iraq. If so, this one man is worth several battalions to an enemy force.

Part of the Program of Instruction (POI) called for the classes to be taken to downtown Columbus, Georgia, the city closest to Fort Benning, for an afternoon of practical instruction on how this city could be defended against a Soviet attack. This required that the students have detailed information on all aspects of this old southern city. We walked the streets, examining railroad bridges and underpasses, power plants, as well as commercial enterprises that could be used to delay an advancing enemy. This particular class always elicited hundreds of questions from the more thoughtful officers.

As an assist in understanding some of the more esoteric aspects of urban warfare, I prepared a period of instruction using New York City as the background for a discussion on how to attack a major metropolitan area. We discussed blowing the tunnels and bridges in order to isolate the city, cutting off the water and the power to panic the civilian population and the use of civilian aircraft as "field expedient" missiles to further terrorize the population by attacking major buildings. In other words, this class was a prelude to 9/11.

Naturally, my every waking moment was not dedicated to teaching Urban Warfare, I also taught a large number of subjects such as the proper method establish, moving and dispersing convoys; the proper use of Indirect Fire and a number of other topics. If nothing else, the United States Army Infantry School was a firm believer in teaching soldiers how to do things by the book.

Of course, there were no classes on how to handle political meddling in military operations. This was the same time period when the Ayatollah Khomeni deposed the Shah of Iran; supposed Iranian students took hostage the staff of the US Embassy in Iran and a disastrous military rescue was staged to free the hostages. According to the story released by the White House, President Carter personally directed the rescue attempt that failed and resulted in the death of some of those in the rescue party.

FAST FORWARD TO THE 21ST CENTURY

Having established my credentials in the areas of counter terrorism operations and urban warfare, let me now update for the reader the instruction that I gave those many years ago. I have made an effort to stay current in my fields of interest and surprisingly, many of the doctrinal procedures that would be used today are the same as the 1970s. One of the weaknesses of doctrine is that it changes very slowly.

The 1970s was an era when many changes in our country took place, some of which were reflected in the makeup of the military force as well. With Vietnam behind us, the military became an all volunteer force, which resulted in a large percentage of those that enlisted being from the inner cities. The educational level of our soldiers suffered to the point that some training manuals were actually written as comic books to make it easier for the soldiers to read and comprehend. Some of the soldiers that I trained actually could not read at all, they looked at the pictures.

This was also the era when many of our weapons began to reflect the major advances in weapons technology that were coming from private industry. The TOW and the Stinger anti-tank weapons were just two of the examples of this technology being applied to weapons systems. The fire control systems of our newest tanks were incorporating computers, making this harder to use.

Our military force, as I have said several times, is currently the most powerful military force that the world has ever seen and no country, or group of countries could hope to hold their own against us in an all out war. However, this was not always the case. In fact, until only a few years ago, the Soviet Military was considered more than a match for our military and many of our strategic planners felt that in a head to head confrontation, there would be no clear winner.

The powerful Soviet war machine had its own doctrine by which it conducted operations and over the years since the end of World War II, it had shown itself to be a formidable fighting force. In fact, during the Nazi invasion of Russia in the last world war, the Russian war machine had at first been overrun, then held it's own and finally defeated the best that the German Military could throw against it. There can be little argument that, whatever may have been the economic problems of the Soviet society as a whole, the Soviet Army was a first class fighting force. Then came Afghanistan and everything that I had been saying about an unconventional force having the advantage over a conventional force was proven to be correct against the very bloody backdrop of one of the most isolated countries in the world.

THE MOST OVERLOOKED FACTOR

I now believe that when we give military instruction to the officers who are to lead out troops into these unfamiliar countries, we are setting ourselves, and them, up for failure if we do not stress that importance that religion plays in the every day lives of the Islamic fundamentalists. By this I mean do not just be intellectually aware of the importance of Islam to its many millions of followers, but insure that they truly understand what this truly means to these people.

Most of us in the West take religion with a grain of salt, but in the countries ruled by Islamic Fundamentalist governments, religion is the staff of life. Many of these countries are made up of separate tribes, some of which have been traditional enemies; their only common factor is the Islamic religion. It provides a way of life and a moral code to these people. The Soviet military quickly discovered that the Afghan people, though segmented into a number of tribes who were normally at war with each other, came together under the banner of Islam to fight the invaders. This joining of forces against a common enemy is what is now happening to us in Iraq.

THE DEATH OF A THOUSAND CUTS

The Pakistanis have a name for the battle plan used by the Afghani tribesmen against the Soviet forces in Afghanistan – *The Death of A Thousand Cuts*[59]. In fact these same tactics, under a variety of different names, have been the time test methods preferred by guerrilla forces the world over when facing a larger conventional force. Of course, the Afghani Mujahideen[60] did have the advantage of being trained by the personnel from the Afghan Bureau of Pakistan's Inter-Service Intelligence (ISI). From 1983 until late 1987, the guerrilla style ambushes, assassinations, attacks on supply convoys, bridges, pipelines and airfields were planed and coordinated by the head of the Afghan Bureau of the ISI for the Mujahideen, Brigadier Mohammad Yousaf. His unorthodox planning eventually defeated the Russian Army in Afghanistan.

Of course, the Soviet defeat[61] was not the first time that a European power had been defeated in Afghanistan. The British Army invaded Afghanistan three times and each time was driven out. In fact, of the 4,500 British troops that withdrew from Kabul in 1842, only one remained arrive to reach the safety of India. The continual harassment of the British force by the Afghan tribesmen has destroyed the force.

To give some idea of the size of the Soviet military force that invaded Afghanistan, the Soviet order of battle contained one four star general, five three

---

[59] Yousaf, Mohammad & Mark Adkin, Afghanistan-The Bear Trap: The Death of A Superpower, Casement, Havertown PA. 2001.

[60] This word translates as "Soldiers of God", giving some indication of the Afghani mindset in these matters.

[61] The Soviet defeat and evacuation of Afghanistan was the first time that a Soviet Army had been driven out of a country since Czar Peter The Great had begun Russia's southward drive of conquest over three hundred years ago.

star generals, fifteen two star generals and at least twenty-five Afghani generals commanding the communist Afghani Army that supported the Soviet effort. This was a formidable size military force to be met by a rag tag, ill equipped, and ill trained guerrilla army. The Mujahideen won, not because it was Allah's will (though let us not forget the power of belief) but because the Soviet Doctrine proved unable to handle the unconventional tactics of the Mujahideen.

This inability to deal with the tactics employed by the Mujahideen seems to have stemmed in part from the fact that the Soviets had gotten more sophisticated over the years coming to rely on interception of the enemy's communications and the ability to use air power to bring combat troops to the location of action in short order. However, the Mujahideen had no electronic communications for the Soviets to intercept. The Soviets were trying to fight a 21st century war and the Mujahideen were fighting a 19th century war. This primitive approach to warfare was one of the major advantages possessed by the Mujahideen[62]. As an example of their primitive ways, while the Soviets were scanning the airwaves to intercept Mujahideen communications, the Mujahideen, who only had a few walkie-talkies, were sending messages by riders on mule back.

According to Kaplan[63], evolution had arguably made the Afghans the toughest people on the face of the earth, able to go for long periods with food or rest. He was able to attest from a first hand view that keeping up with them on treks over impassable mountain trails reduced most westerners to tears. Another aspect that Kaplan felt was one of the Mujahideen strengths was that in the beginning they really had no strategy other than shooting the Soviets. As a result KGB and KHAD infiltrators were totally baffled in their attempts to ferret out the plans of the Afghan forces, as there was really no pattern to the guerrilla attacks.

IT WAS A MIRACLE

Of course, in spite of all of the so called advantages possessed by the Mujahideen, it is a major miracle that the Mujahideen won, since there were seven recognized Afghani political parties in exile in Pakistan and they all tried to get their hands into the planning of the battles. BG Yousaf, while charged by his superiors with the planning of the field activities was not able to give orders to the Mujahideen; he had to convince the Afghani field commanders to carry out the attacks. Naturally, I am not here to write about the defeat of the Soviets, but where information from this conflict does come to bear on current events in the United States, I think it is worth repeating.

---

[62] Kaplan, Robert D., <u>Soldiers of God: With the Mujahidin in Afghanistan</u>, Houghton Mifflin Company, Boston. 1990.
[63] Ibid

According to BG Yousaf, between 1983 and 1987, he and his Afghan Bureau of the ISI trained over 80,000 Mujahideen and distributed hundreds of tons of arms and munitions to these Soldiers of God. However, once again politics became the most important aspect of the war when, after having defeated the Soviet Military, the Mujahideen failed to capture Kabul, the capital of Afghanistan. BG Yousaf felt that this was the result of the United States Government not wanting another fundamentalist Islamic Republic to come into creation. Whatever the reason, this set the stage for the arrival of the Taliban.

In 1988, BG Yousaf's immediate superior until 1987, General Akhtar Abdul Rahman Khan, now the Chairman of the Joint Chief of Staff Committee and the man being groomed to replace the President when he decided to step down; General Zia-ul-Haq, President of Pakistan; U.S. Ambassador Arnold Raphel, BG Herbert Wasson, US Defense Attache in Islamabad, eight other Pakistani generals and their staffs were all killed with the C130 on which they were flying mysteriously crashed on takeoff. This created a major power vacuum that allowed the rise to power of Benazir Bhutto, daughter of the man that Zia had deposed and murdered[64]. It also stopped the creation of and Islamic Fundamentalist ruled Afghanistan, which the United States believed was Zia's ultimate goal[65].

The Pakistani Chief of the Air Staff immediately convened a board of inquiry. After a thorough investigation, that included laboratory tests carried out by Lockheed, the builder of the plane, the Board found that after eliminating every possible cause, there remained only one – a criminal act of sabotage that had killed 31 people. In fact, it was the belief of the Board that the crew of the cockpit had been instantaneously and simultaneously incapacitated by the use of a chemical agent such as a fast acting nerve agent[66].

This is an example of the deadly effectiveness of the weapons that we shall talk about later on in this book. But for now it is sufficient to say that these highly trained military men fell victim to an assassination that was very easily carried out by assassins who were some distance away when the event took

---

[64] Less there be some belief that I am accusing the United States Government of carrying out this assassination, let me point out that it was well known that General Zia was high on the hit list for both the Soviet KGB and the KHAD, the Communist Afghanistan Government secret police agency, as well as the terrorist group (called Al-Zulfikar – The Sword) created by Mir Murtaza, one of the exiled sons of Zulfikar Ali Bhutto and the brother of soon to be Prime Minister Benazir Bhutto.

[65] Yousaf, Mohammad & Mark Adkin, Afghanistan-The Bear Trap: The Death of A Superpower, Casement, Havertown PA. 2001

[66] As we will discuss later, the Board found that "the presence of an odorless and colorless gas would not have alarmed the crew so they would not put on their helmets and masks to make use of the plane's oxygen system. The Board commented that such a chemical agent could have been packed in a small innocuous container such as drink can, thermos flask or gift parcel, and smuggled onboard without arising suspicion."

place. While the death toll was only 31, the result was monumental for it almost assured that the Mujahideen were unable to complete their rise to power and the fanatical Taliban gained control of Afghanistan.

One of the points that I stressed in training is that the field commander needed to understand his enemy. As General Patton observed, if he could get inside his foe's head, he could beat him. BG Yousaf also made this same point in his book. Even though he worked with them and led them, after a fashion, it took him over four years to get to know the Afghani Warrior[67]. So the next chapter is dedicated to explaining, as thoroughly as possible, the Afghan Warrior. Many of the Mujahideen now following Osama Bin Laden and undertake terrorist activities around the world. So to understand the danger we face, we must understand our enemies.

The Death of A Thousand Cuts is even now being used against our forces in Iraq. During the initial invasion, we literally ran over the opposing forces, sometimes to the point that the support units could not keep up with the ground assault units. Casualties were very light. Now, however, the independent militia units of historical enemies, but bound together by the teachings of various radical clerics are rising up and inflicting more casualties on our forces than we ever dreamed possible. Iraq, the country to which we are trying to give democracy is on the edge of a major civil war and we are caught in the middle.

---

[67] Yousaf, Mohammad & Mark Adkin, Afghanistan-The Bear Trap: The Death of A Superpower, Casement, Havertown PA. 2001

CHAPTER EIGHT

UNDERSTANDING OUR ENEMY

THE MUJAHIDEEN

The individuals that made up the force that is called the Mujahideen are the nucleus of many of today's Islamic fundamentalist terrorist groups and many of those opposing our forces in Iraq were tempered in the fires of the Afghanistan conflict against the Soviet forces. Many of the original Mujahideen, or Soldiers of God, are from Afghanistan, though the infamous Al-Qaeda, the pre-eminent Mujahideen organization fermenting terrorism around the world, is actually an alliance of terrorists groups coming from many different countries. You must remember that the vast majority of those who were involved in the terrorist actions of September 11, 2001 were of Saudi Arabian extraction, a country that was, and is, supposed to be our friend. However, this being said, we will at this point focus our attention on those who were trained in the Afghani conflict.

However, before we look at the makeup of our enemy, let us stop for consideration of a few facts. The original Mujahideen were not always Islamic fundamentalist terrorists. Quite the contrary, the original Mujahideen movement was a movement without any political stand, revolutionary rhetoric, or supreme leader[68]. The original members of this group were not extremists, though they did believe in a fundamental interpretation of the Islamic religion. They had no politics as such other than a general common goal to kick the Soviet Union out of their country.

---

[68] Kaplan, Robert D., Soldiers of God: With the Mujahidin in Afghanistan, Houghton Mifflin Company, Boston. 1990.

Most of the original Mujahideen were actually Pathans, members of the largest ethnic group in Afghanistan[69] and the largest existent tribal society in the world. They live by a very harsh medieval code of honor called Pukhtunwali, and have been the source of all of Afghanistan's historical kings and political rulers. So in most cases when the Afghans are being discussed, the speaker is actually talking about the Pathans, some of the fiercest warriors in the world. The most outstanding attributes of these undefeated warriors found by Brigadier General Mohammad Yousaf and discussed in his outstanding study of the Afghanistan War[70] include:

- The Afghani Warrior/Mujahideen is brave

The Afghan Warrior has stood the test of time and he, or she, has never been conquered. Granted their country has been overrun on more than one occasion, but the warrior mentality of the Afghan people has never been truly defeated. In 1980, these defiant warriors banded together to take on the best military force that the Soviet Union could throw at them and by 1988, he had sent then packing. However, make no mistake, this is not a superman and his greatest failing is also his greatest strength, he is inflexible on he has embarked on his mission.

Much as the Apache Indian in the American Southwest, the Afghan culture was designed around the courage and heroism of its warriors. Just like the Apache's it was, and is, considered seemly for an Afghan is cry out, even if gravely injured. This stoicism is ingrained into the character of every child growing up in the isolated country that is Afghanistan. As an example, hit a five-year old Afghani child and like children the world over, he will cry. Hit a seven-year old Afghani child and his will hardly flinch and more than likely, he will try to take your head off of your shoulder for your troubles.

That is not the same as saying that the Mujahideen warrior knows no fear, for he does fear many things just like his US military cousins. However, the Afghani does not fear death – he fears failure and fear itself. At the top of the list of fears seems to be the fear of becoming disabled in an attack and then having to live as a cripple in a society where physical stamina and physical ability are revered to be point of becoming indispensable to survival.

- They Truly Believe in The Cause For Which They Fight

It is a remarkable thing in this jaded world that those of the Islamic faith see everything in terms of their religion. The Mujahideen are religion

---

[69] One of every two Afghans is a Pathan.

[70] Yousaf, Mohammad & Mark Adkin, <u>Afghanistan-The Bear Trap: The Death of A Superpower</u>, Casement, Havertown PA. 2001

fanatics when it comes to the spreading of their religion and their opposition to anything that smacks of the infidel. Where in the western world, it is normally the political leaders who call for war, in the Islamic world, it is the religious leaders who many times begin wars with the issuing of edicts calling for a Jihad or Holy War against a particular enemy of the faith.

Such is the case with the infamous Osama Bin Laden. He attended the very prestigious King Abdul Aziz University in Jeddah where he came in contact with the Muslim Brotherhood, an Islamist group dedicated to the spreading of the Islamic movement. Osama met and studied under two very prominent teachers in the Islamic world, Abdullah Azzam and Mohammad Qutb. Azzam went on to create a world wide Jihadist network and Mohammad Qutb was the brother of Sayyid Qutb, author of the work Signposts, the key text of the Jihadist movement[71].

These people that we call the terrorists actually believe that they are on a mission from God. They are dedicated and fanatical, truly believing that they will go to the Gardens of Allah and be served by 70 Virgins. They believe this as surely as a Christian believes in Christ, Heaven and Hell. Just as religious fervor lead the Crusaders to attempt to free the Holy Land, these modern day Crusaders believe that they are fighting the evil of the West.

We can get an idea of the depth of their belief by the reaction of the Islamic World to the Soviet invasion of Afghanistan. It did not matter to the men and women that joined the ranks of the Mujahideen that the government of Afghanistan was already communist, they saw instead, a sovereign Muslin Republic being invaded by non-believers. The Islamic warriors looked at this event in black and white terms, these were the godless Soviets. As it normally the case, the Islamic religious leaders called for a Jihad against the Soviet invasion, a crusade against the unbelievers. The fundamentalist Muslims follow the teachings of the Koran literally and a call for Jihad meant that it was every man's duty to go fight the Kafirs or unbelievers to save their faith, defend their honor, protect the independence f the country and protect their families. Unlike Western notions of patriotism, a call for a Jihad knows no limitations. Boys from 13 to old men in their seventies answered the call for Jihad against the Soviets and took to the battlefield[72].

Every Islamic fundamentalist that was able answered the clerics' call for a Jihad against the Soviets. These Soldiers of God were not young draftees, like many of the Soviet soldiers, but they were dedicated, believers in the Koran and in the teachings that they had received from a very early age from their clerics. They firmly believed that they were carrying out God's will.

---

[71] Bergen, Peter L., Holy War, Inc., Weidenfeld & Nicolson, London. 2001.

[72] Yousaf, Mohammad & Mark Adkin, Afghanistan-The Bear Trap: The Death of A Superpower, Casement, Havertown PA. 2001

Their belief, aided by the Pakistani Intelligence Service and CIA dollars brought down a superpower.

In addition to these two main tenets that BG Yousaf found in his study of the Mujahideen, there are a few other factors that must be considered when dealing with the members of the fundamentalist Islamic terrorist groups. For example:

- They are, first and foremost, Human Beings[73]
  One very basic premise that we must be sure not to overlook is that the terrorists are not the mindless, fanatical killing machines from the movies and our worst nightmares, but they are as human as are their victims. As human beings, they have emotions, feelings and concerns just like the rest of us. However, with the case of the Islamic fundamentalists, these basic human emotions have been channeled into lethal actions and they have been taught that any non-believer is an enemy. In many cases, these individuals truly believe that they are acting to protect their religion from being destroyed by the Western cultures.

- They are Revered Within Their Culture For Their Acts.
  In the western culture, we see acts such as the destruction of September 11, 2001 as inherently evil, but to those who carried out these actions, they were honorable acts. In the fundamentalist Islamic societies being a suicide bomber or a martyr bring great honor not only upon the one carrying out the acts, but upon his or her families as well.
  We have a tendency to judge everyone by our cultural standards and this is a terrible mistake. If we view some act as so totally abhorrent that it would be the worst act in the world for someone to commit, we can be blinding ourselves to the possibility that to the terrorist, it can be an act of atonement or an act that would bring them the highest honor in their culture.
  We must have professional respect for other cultures, no matter how foreign or bizarre we may think the beliefs of the culture may be. But if we treat each culture with respect and make a major effort to understand the philosophy or ideology that motivates the foreign culture, we may then be able to predict and stop their acts of destruction.

- Terrorists Are Generally Rational in Their Actions.
  The individual that we call a terrorist is rarely someone who is insane. These individuals are usually intelligent, clear thinking rational planners. Otherwise, they do not last very long in the terrorist business. By our western

---

[73] Nance, Malcolm W., The Terrorist Recognition Handbook, Lyons Press, Guilford Connecticut. 2003.

standards the fixated drive that these individual demonstrate when carrying out their mission may be viewed as insane, but it is generally the product of their upbringing and their religious fervor to do Allah's will as interpreted by their Clerics.

- They Are Almost Always Well Motivated

     Rather than outwardly instilled discipline learned over their training programs as in the West, the Islamic Fundamentalist warrior uses personal motivation to carry out acts necessary to show their determination.

- The Terrorist Has Mentally Justified His Or Her Actions

     The terrorist view the necessity for the mission as justifying any and all acts necessary to achieve success. For the modern day terrorist, steeped in radical religious ideas form a very impressionable age, the end nearly always justifies the means.

CLASSES OF TERRORISTS

As can be seen from the current crop of armchair experts that are making the rounds of the television talk shows, most of those who are employed in ranking and explaining the terrorists and their motivations are experts only from an intellectual point of view. Most would not know which end of the rifle the bullets comes from, much less the, sometimes, subtle distinctions between different levels of skill shown by various terrorist groups. However, there is a major difference between defending against a professional terrorist and one from the foreign equivalent of the "gang that couldn't shoot straight".

For the law enforcement member or the counter terrorist operative, this is a very important bit of information that would certainly have a dramatic impact on the tactics used to counter operations conducted by the various groups. This information also helps the intelligence analyst not only get an idea of who they are dealing with, but also how skillful and how deadly, if cornered they are apt to become.

Another reason this information is important is that the higher the level of training, the more professional, and actually more predictable, the terrorists are apt to be. For example, the Class One Terrorist is a true professional and they make every effort to blend into the local population, rarely calling attention to themselves until it is time for the execution of the mission. Then they will strike with deadly precision. An amateur, on the other hand, is apt to react to any obstacle with deadly force.

So who are these people that we call terrorists? The following is a ranking of the various classes of terrorists as outlined in The Terrorist Recognition Handbook[74]:

- Class I

A Class I terrorist is generally a government trained professional. This individual might have come from the ranks of the military, the state security or law enforcement ranks or even from the intelligence community. Of the various classes of terrorist, this is probably the most predictable of the classes. Their training is comparable to that given to every undercover operative worldwide and their mind set tends to run in predictable ways. A class one terrorist is also least likely to react to an obstacle with deadly force, preferring to use stealth and secrecy to achieve their goals.

A Class I terrorist may operate under an official cover such as a member of an embassy staff or purport to fill some other official position. If they are acting totally outside the intelligence channels of their country, they may also appear to be a legitimate businessman or woman, and some have even entered the United States as a student or through the immigration system. Make no mistake, while a Class I Terrorist is more predictable and less prone to panic than the other types of terrorists, they are every bit as deadly and just as dedicated to carrying out their mission.

A Class I Terrorist may be male or female, come from the middle to upper class and is generally between the ages of 22 and 50, though some have been younger and some certainly older. They generally have a university education and also receive much the same training as an intelligence agent. A Class I Terrorist is generally utilized in carrying out assassinations, bombing that call for skill and daring as well as the more important, high profile abductions.

Cuba, Chile, Libya, Iraq, Iran, China, the Soviet Union and North Korea have been known to use Class I Terrorists to achieve their goals. A classic example of a Class I Terrorist would be North Korean Intelligence Officer Kim Chun-Hyee whose actions resulted in the death of 115 people due to a bomb that she placed on a Korean Air airliner.

- Class II

The Professional Religious Extremist is considered to be a Class II Terrorist. These are individuals who are so immersed and dedicated to their religions that they have been induced to become an active part of a professional terrorist group in order to further the goals of their religion.

---

[74] Ibid

These are normally civilians who have made the decision to dedicate their lives to the cause, whatever the cause may be, and generally do not have any previous military experience. These are the individuals in a terrorist organization that maintains the systems necessary for the organization, as a whole, to function. They may work in logistics or fund raising or some other support feature. In rare circumstances, they may actually take part in live operations.

Generally, these individuals receive advanced training, including combat skills training; they are paid a wage, their families receive benefits and they receive advanced ideological training. With their family cared for, these individuals are free to concentrate on carrying out Allah's will as communicated to them by their religious leaders.

The individuals normally recruited for these positions are between the ages of 18 and 45, they may be male or female and they all generally have a university education. They come from devout families or, like Osama Bin Laden, have a religious conversion that returns them to their faith. These individuals are generally trained at local or overseas based schools that given them their training to be a terrorist. Class II Terrorists generally handle sophisticated bombing or suicide attacks, assassinations, raids, kidnappings, skyjackings, and attacks that attempt to make use of weapons of mass destruction. Many of the Al-Qaeda members fall in this category and were trained at training camps located in Afghanistan, Sudan, Lebanon, Iran, Iraq, Algeria, Yemen, and even in the United States.

It is also from the ranks of the Class II terrorists that the suicide bombers are drawn. The most devout are selected by the leadership and trained for this one mission in such groups as Al-Qaeda, Hamas, and Hezbollah.

Class II terrorists are used by such groups as Al-Qaeda, The Islamic Jihad, Hamas, Palestinian Islamic Jihad, The Al-Aqsa Martyrs Brigade; The Armed Islamic Group, the Egyptian Islamic Jihad, the Special Purpose Islamic Regiment, the Islamic Change Organization and a score of lesser known organizations.

Members of this Class of terrorist have been known to come from such countries as Algeria, Argentina, Bolivia, Bosnia-Herzegovina, Burma, Egypt, England, France, Germany, Indonesia, Italy, Kuwait, Libya, Malaysia, Morocco, Pakistan, Paraguay, the Philippines, Russia, Saudi Arabia, Somalia, Sudan, Tajikistan, the United Arab Republics, the United States and Uzbekistan. No longer is terrorism confined to a small radical group from some little known country, but it has become an international business. Even terrorist groups that have been traditionally lone wolves are starting to ally with other terrorist groups in order to gain logistical support, weapons and personnel.

- Class III

A Class III terrorist is normally considered to be a Radical Revolutionary or a Quasi-Religious Extremist. The Class III is the model upon which Hollywood designed its stereotypical radical. Those from this group are normally trained by the organization of to which they belong and then sent to external training camps for advanced training[75]. It might be said that Class III terrorists get their basic training through an OJT (on the job training) program. They learn as they spend their days and nights running to avoid the law enforcement organizations of the various countries through which they travel.

The terrorist organizations that rely primarily on the Class III Terrorist are:

- The Provisional Irish Republican Army and The IRA in Ireland;

- Euzkadi Ta Askatasuna in Europe;

- The Red Army Faction in Germany; and the

- The Abu Nidal Organization and the Popular Front for the Liberation of Palestine from the Middle East.

The typical Class III Terrorist may be male or female and from the age of 20 to 50. Educational levels range from none to some University education and they are generally drawn from average to upper middle class families. These are generally not the very poor with nothing to lose by rebelling against the system. Whether from some type of misplaced guilt related to their financial resources or a desire for some excitement in their lives, these children of the wealthy all seem to demonstrate a desire to destroy the very system that gave birth to them.

- Class IV

Classic guerrilla or mercenaries are considered to be Class IV terrorists. Just as with the Class I terrorist, a Class IV is predictable in that he or she tends to operate based upon their military training. They also tend to favor using standard military weapons in their operations such as the M-16 or the AK 47.

The distinction between a guerrilla and a mercenary is also one to keep in mind. A guerrilla is someone who fights the existing order within his or her country of origin for the purpose of overthrowing the existing order. A

---

[75] With the invasion of the Middle East by United States forces, these external training camps are becoming more difficult to find as they naturally are keeping an extremely low profile.

mercenary, on the other hand, is someone who goes to fight the existing order of another country, usually for money. Western mercenaries have been apprehended fighting in several countries since the 1960s, the most recent being the American who was caught fighting alongside the Taliban in Afghanistan against US forces.

Class IV terrorists are found in the ranks of UNITA and the Movement for Social Justice in Africa as well as Cuba's external force for the spread of communism in South America, the National Liberation Army.

A Class IV terrorist can be make or female and is generally between the ages of 10 and 50. IN many cases they have little or no education to speak of and come from urban or rural environments. In many cases, they are drawn form the ranks of minor criminals who have very little liking for the existing social order. They get most of their formal military training from within the organization itself.

- Class V

The Class V terrorist is the amateur, whether a civilian or a member of a militia/vigilante group. While the militia group may have a large number of members, most of them have only basic military or quasi-military training. Unless hired as foot soldiers by more sophisticated groups, the Class V terrorist normally takes part in small operations, such as raids or robberies. In the United States, militia groups will sometimes carry out follow up attacks after major external attacks within the US.

A Class V terrorist may be male or female and is generally between the ages of 10 and 65. Many times these terrorists have little if any education and come from an urban or rural area. Many times the families from which they come live in poverty conditions where, once again, they feel that they little if anything to lose by opposing a system that they see as oppressive.

These are the enemy that wants to bring war to the Untied States. For the first time, as we shall see in the next chapters, these individual terrorists groups have the ability to wage war on the same global scale once reserved for sovereign countries. We have entered a new era of warfare and none of us are safe.

PART II
THE SECURITY OF
OUR SOUTHERN BORDER

In spite of the horror of 9/11, most citizens in this country, whether they admit it or not, still believe that we are relatively safe at home. This could not be further from the truth. Our Borders are easy for illegal immigrants to cross; all the while, we are being told how safe the country is as a result of the formation of Home Land Security. In the next two parts of this book, I present verbatim testimony that was made to the Congress of the United States about drug smuggling, illegal immigrants and terrorist incursions across out borders for the reader's review.

If our efforts cannot stop the flow of drugs from Mexico and Canada into this country, how can we be sure of stopping the movements of terrorists and weapons of mass destruction?

CHAPTER NINE
ASYMMETRICAL WARFARE

When the Soviet Union collapsed, the free world celebrated. However, those in a position to know the real state of the world had a different view. According to Director of Central Intelligence James Woolsey, *"It is as if we were struggling with a large dragon for forty-five years, killed it, and then found ourselves in a jungle full of poisonous snakes – and the snakes are much harder to keep track of than the dragon ever was*[76]*."* We traded the possibility of a world war for a world full of small brushfire wars.

NO MORE CONVENTIONAL WARFARE

Against the Soviet Union, we were fully prepared to fight a conventional war and we proved out ability against the armies of Afghanistan and Iraq. However, now we are faced with hundreds of terrorist groups prepared to fight an "asymmetrical war" and this time, it is the American people who are the target, not our military in one sense of the word.

An asymmetrical war is where a numerically smaller, weaker group adopts those weapons and tactics that offer them the best advantage against a larger, stronger opponent[77]. As we shall see, some of those weapons make the Soviet arsenal of missiles and nuclear weapons look like fire crackers. The events of September 11, 2001 make it perfectly clear that asymmetrical warfare is a

---

[76] The U.S. Government Guide to Surviving Terrorism, Barnes & Noble Books, New York, 2003.
[77] Ibid

successful approach for the terrorists to use in carrying out their war against the United States. It is like the giant being bitten to death by gnats. One or two gnats have little or no effect, but hundreds and hundreds of gnats can drive the giant crazy with pain and frustration.

The plans to hijack planes, using something as simple as a box cutter, were so successful that in only one instance did their plan fail. The terrorists had correctly deduced that our security systems were not geared toward the simple weapons, but rather toward the more sophisticated guns and bombs of the classic terrorists. Why bring a bomb on board an airplane when the airplane itself is a larger bomb than the terrorist could hope to smuggle on board.

However, to be fair, in some locations apparently their plan failed. I was recently made aware that on September 11, 2001, there were attempts to hijack planes at four other airports, to include Chicago's O'Hare Airport that failed for one reason or another. There is also now evidence that the original plan called for hijacking ten planes, but that Osama Bin laden cancelled this larger effort in favor of the plan that took place.

Make no mistake we are in a war every bit as serious as any war that has ever involved this country, only this time the battlefield is in our front yards.

THERE ARE NO SAFE HAVENS

We here in the Untied States have, over the years, watched the world slowly chew itself up with wars, uprisings and terrorists attacks against the civilian populations of a large number of civilized countries and said to ourselves that it could not happen here. Well, those all of those who looked at our international cousins with sympathy and complacence, the events of September 11, 2001 were a serious wake up call. Osama Bin Laden had sent us a message that two oceans was not a barrier to him launching attacks in our largest cities.

IT WASN'T A FLUKE

The invading of our country by armed enemies is nothing new and happens much more often than our government wants to admit. As one example, reporter Phil Brennan of NewsMax.com wrote an article entitled Mexican Army Invades US[78]. I felt that the story was important enough to repeat in its entirety below:

"Mexican Army Invades U.S."
Phil Brennan, NewsMax.com
Wednesday, March 12, 2003

---

[78] Brennan, Phil, *Mexican Army Invades US*, NewsMax.com, March 12, 2003

It's the war nobody wants to talk about: well-armed Mexican soldiers storming across America's southern border, sometimes with guns blazing.

"We are in state of war," Edward Nelson, chairman of U.S. Border Control, told Soldier of Fortune magazine. "And we are fighting enemies who have brought the battle to our shores. If ever there was a time for the United States to put troops on the border, it is now."

A blockbuster exposé in the magazine's March issue notes that over the past five years, there have been 120 documented incidents of Mexican military/police incursions, sometimes resulting in the arrest of Mexican army personnel on U.S. soil by Border Patrol agents.

Thousands of Mexican soldiers, often ill-trained draftees, have been moved up to the border allegedly to fight narcotics smuggling. Many times these armed men cross the border chasing drug traffickers.

"Anytime you have the Mexican military running around with all these weapons and military gear it's quite frightening," said Raleigh Leonard, a Border Patrol public information officer.

The magazine cites incidents such as the one in March 2000 where soldiers in two Mexican Army Humvees fired on Border Patrol agents in El Paso, Texas, and another in October, when 10 Mexican soldiers fired at a Border Patrol helicopter in California.

Rep. Tom Tancredo, chairman of the Congressional Immigration Reform Caucus, said in a May 2002 press release that there were 23 incursions by Mexican authorities in 2001 alone.

In a letter to Soldier of Fortune magazine, a Border Patrol agent stated that, "The vast majority of the American people are totally oblivious that armed forces of a foreign nation routinely violate the sovereignty of the U.S."

Shockingly, the agent revealed, "Our government is aware of these incidents, but refuses to take any steps to stop these flagrant violations."

Soldier of Fortune cites a series of incidents that have taken place this year:

- Humvees full of troops pointing a rifle at Border Patrol agents.
- Incursions by "groups of six to eight armed men, possibly Mexican cops wearing black bulletproof vest and carrying machine guns.
- A Chevy Suburban hit five times by gunfire and containing 22 "undocumented migrants," more accurately called illegal aliens, eight of whom suffered gunshot wounds fired from a Mexican army vehicle, which then fled back across the border to Mexico.

Some of these "anti-drug-trafficking troops" are themselves trafficking in drugs.

"Many U.S. law-enforcement officials working along the border acknowledge the involvement of Mexican military troops and police in narcotics trafficking and migrant smuggling business," the magazine says.

"Many Mexican police agencies along the border are in the pay of the *narcotraficantes* and the corruption extends to high-ranking key Mexican military officers."

And "Drug cartels spend $500 million a year to pay off corrupt Mexican generals and police officials."

Said Congressman Tancredo: "There's no doubt Mexican military units along the border are being controlled by drug cartels, and not by Mexico City. The military units operate freely, with little or no direction, and several of them have made numerous incursions into the Unite States."

Tancredo warned that "unless we open our eyes and recognize that what's happening along the U.S.-Mexican border is real, one of our guys is going to get killed."

The feature story in the Stein Report[79], posted at 0:6:40 PM on December 2, 2002 was headlined as *"CITIZENS AT THE BORDER FACE RISKS DUE TO DRUG, HUMAN SMUGGLING"*

The alternative paper *Tucson Weekly* has a story about one border resident's experiences with the growing flow of drugs and illegal aliens across the Mexico-Arizona border. The Weekly includes previously unknown information about a shoot-out between Mexican drug smugglers and a Border Patrol Special Response Team. "One touchy topic for the Border Patrol may be the nature of the Special Response Team's mission in that area. Patrol sources told the *Weekly* that the team was operating close to the Mexican border along several miles of heavily traveled trails and newly blazed smuggler roads near Palominas. The purpose was not to arrest illegal entrants, but to turn them right back across the international line without having to process them through their countries' consulates, which would leave a trail of paperwork." The Border Patrol sector chief denied that agents were not processing illegal aliens to deliberately fudge the apprehension numbers.

A COMMON EVENT

Besides armed Mexican soldados, many others routinely violate our southern border with relative ease. One afternoon, I was privileged to watch a video recording taking by some of the Vietnam era sensors placed along the border to help apprehend drug smugglers crossing near El Paso, Texas. I watched in some amazement as a group of six or seven smugglers, each carrying one or two 40-pound duffle bags of drugs, moving through the grass working their way toward the closest road to their crossing point. The plan was for them to leave the

---

[79] The Stein Report is a weekday Internet news site about immigration featuring commentary, headlines and breaking news.

duffle bags beneath a particular tree and the next leg of the drug smuggling chain would then take charge of the drugs on their way north. A team of Border Patrol Agents who were monitoring the sensors caught this particular group of drug smugglers.

The guide that led the group across the Rio Grande into the waiting arms of the ever-vigilant Border Patrol was an older gentleman who sat quietly during the legal proceeding. During the initial meeting, as he was walking out the door, his defense attorney made the comment that he was glad it was the old man's first offense. With a slight smile, the old man responded that it was truly the first time he had been caught, but he had been leading drug smugglers across the border three times a week for the past two years or more.

I am sure that by this time the reader is wondering what drug smugglers have in common with terrorists. The point that I am wanting to make with these examples, is that if we are not able to stop the flow of drugs northward across the Mexican Border, what is to stop one of those 40 pound duffle bags from being full of chemical agent or the materials needed to make a dirty bomb? What if the next group that slips by the Border Patrol is not drug smugglers but dedicated terrorists from Al-Qaeda?

IF THEY CAN'T CROSS THE BORDER, THEY GO UNDER

It sounds like something from a Hollywood movie, the idea of terrorists using tunnels to enter the United States. However, it is a very real occurrence and happened more often than we would like to admit. The National Public Radio's Carrie Kahn Reports did the following story in these tunnels on April 19, 2004.

Tunnels Under the U.S.-Mexico Border
Big Increase in Discoveries of Smuggler's Routes

April 19, 2004 -- *Federal officials say they've uncovered something disturbing along the U.S.-Mexico border: more underground tunnels, used by drug traffickers and immigrant smugglers to evade tighter border enforcement.*

One tunnel a year used to be the average, but since a border crackdown after the attacks on Sept. 11, 2001, more than 10 passageways have been discovered. NPR's Carrie Kahn reports on two "hot spots" for tunnels -- the border at San Diego and Tijuana, and between the California border town of Calexico and Mexicali.

Armed with drills and ground-penetrating radar, U.S. border authorities are busy looking for tunnels running under the fences that separate the two countries. Officials say that if drugs and illegal aliens can come across, terrorists or even "dirty bomb" components could get smuggled across just as easily.

In an article in the San Diego Union-Tribune[80], there was a report of a cross border tunnel being discovered by accident in a San Ysidro parking lot. Luckily for all concerned, the only evidence of illicit activity was a van parked nearby packed with drugs. However, this could just as easily have been a tunnel for terrorists to move weapons of mass destruction into the United States. Even more disturbing, this particular tunnel was no amateur operation. This tunnel was professionally designed with electricity, ventilation and a pulley system for lifting whatever was being transported to the surface. It is estimated that this particular tunnel may have cost as much as a million dollars to build. How could such an undertaking not be spotted during the building stage?

What is even more disturbing is that this particular tunnel, actually discovered on April 4, 2003 was the fifth such sophisticated secret entrance from the south side of the boarder discovered in the prior fourteen months. Because of the possibility that terrorists may use such secret ways into this country, the war on drugs and the war against terrorism are converging.

The U.S. and Mexican law enforcement agencies are joining forces in the search for these elusive bolt holes that one U.S. official stated "may number at least a hundred if not several hundred." Imagine that, hundreds of hidden tunnels leading into the United States from Mexico.

HISTORICAL TUNNELS STILL EXIST

In addition to the modern tunnels being constructed by Drug Smugglers, very few people seem to know that there is a very sophisticated maze of much older tunnels that run beneath the city of El Paso, Texas. When I was doing the research for *Spirits of the Border: The History and Mystery of El Paso Del Norte*[81], I kept hearing stories about hidden tunnels running beneath the Rio Grande from Cuidad Juarez, Mexico into El Paso. I asked a local historian if he had ever heard about such tunnels and he laughed in a very dismissive manner. He assured me that there were no such tunnels and that it would be impossible to build a tunnel beneath the Rio Grande. Suitably chastened, I retreated to lick my figurative wounds. Then I sat out to find the tunnels. To my shock, I did.

My first clue to the existence of these elusive tunnels was found in a Masters

---

[80] Cearley, Anna, San Diego Tribune, May 7, 2003, *A Hole In Security?: Border Area Seems Even More Vulnerable in the Aftermath of 9/11.*

[81] Hudnall, Ken and Connie Wang, Spirits of the Border: The History and Mystery of El Paso Del Norte, Omega Press, El Paso, Texas. 2003

Thesis written by Nancy Ellen Farrar in 1970[82]. In her thesis, she talked about Chinese Smuggling Rings in El Paso, Texas in the years between 1882 and 1911. El Paso, Texas was the largest Chinese smuggling center on either border and as such, acted as the receiving point for most of the Chinese illegally entering the United States from Juarez, Mexico, the principal center of the Mexican Chinese smuggling trade[83].

As a result of Congress passing the Chinese Exclusion Act, Chinese could not immigrate into this country. Therefore, an underground railroad of sorts began taking Chinese from Ciudad Juarez, through El Paso to New York, Chicago, or San Francisco. Specially built houses were used, on both sides of the river that contained hidden underground rooms and concealed attics. Most of the Chinese buildings were constructed of boards or adobe and were linked by a honeycomb of underground passages in the area of South Oregon Street, the heart of El Paso's Chinese district.

In one case, part of a long underground tunnel believed to be a terminal for a tunnel that ran beneath the Rio Grande was found. There were several pictures of this particular tunnel taken that were recently found in the El Paso Public Library files. From the photos, this was not a slipshod operation, but a professionally made underground passage. This was no quick fix for the problem of getting the Chinese into the United States. This particular tunnel had walls two feet thick and ceilings made of railroad iron.

T.F. Schmucker, the officer in charge of the Immigration Office in El Paso, Texas stated that in certain alleys in Chinatown, houses were built so that the illegal Chinese could be hidden in chambers under the ground or in spaces between the roof and the ceilings. The smuggling of Chinese into El Paso was stopped primarily as a result of the Mexican Revolution, not because of US detection efforts. However, though the reason for the tunnels and hiding places has ceased, the tunnels and the secret rooms are still in existence.

Interestingly enough, according to another Thesis[84], when the adobe building that had stood at Mills and Oregon Streets in El Paso, Texas was razed to make way for the present customs house and federal court building, it was discovered that the Chinese had burrowed into the dirt floors of the building, making subteraneum (sic) passages from one cellar to another. In 1996, according to Alfonso Tellez, Historical Preservation Coordinator for the City of El Paso Planning, Research and Development Department, city crews routinely find

---

[82] Farrar, Nancy Ellen, *The History of the Chinese in El Paso, Texas: A Case Study of an Urban Immigrant Group in the American West*, A Thesis Presented to The Faculty of the Department of History of The University of El Paso at El Paso. 1970.

[83] Ibid

[84] Fahy, Anna Louise, Chinese Borderland Community Development: A Case Study Of El Paso, 1881-1909. Presented to the Faculty of the Graduate School of The University of Texas at El Paso. 2001

clandestine tunnels dug by Chinese through what is today's downtown area[85].

Finally, on another historical note, in 1937 Edna Hammond Dietrich of El Paso, Texas gave an interview to an El Paso Times reporter, saying "I think many persons will remember the underground settlement of Chinese near the railroad yards at Octavia and Main Streets[86]." This underground settlement was actually occupied until sometime in the late 1960s according to locals in El Paso, Texas.

I recently did a talk to a local group in El Paso about *Spirits of the Border: The History and Mystery of El Paso Del Norte*[87]. When I reached the part where I mentioned the tunnels, one gentleman raised his hand and told me that his father had been the manager of a local shoe store downtown in the 1950s. It had been this gentleman's job to clean up the store for his father after hours. One evening he had been cleaning the basement[88] of the store and discovered a sliding panel and a hidden staircase he had never seen before in dark corner of the basement.

When faced with a mystery, he did what any kid would do, he explored. He and a young friend had decided to see where the staircase led. To their surprise, they found a sub-basement that had long been forgotten. In the sub-basement, they found a doorway that led into a maze of old steam tunnels far beneath the city. To his knowledge these old tunnels have never been explored. In fact, there has been no modern investigation of these tunnels by any official organization, but only by authors such as myself.

Another gentleman[89] present at the talk chimed in at this point to confirm that a series of tunnels exists beneath El Paso High School. He stated that as a student at this old school, the track team had used the tunnels as a race course curing inclement weather. He also confirmed that the tunnels extended to the Rio Grande and were passable the entire distance.

PROHIBITION

This Fourth of July[90] my wife and I were invited to an out of town party. Sitting by a pool, I happened to strike up a conversation with an older gentleman who was a retired Customs Agent. His duty station had been the Mexican Border. He had heard about one of my books and the conversation turned to the topic of this book that you hold in your hands. He smiled and made mention of the many

---

[85] Alfonso Tellez, Historic Preservation Coordinator, Department of Planning, Research and Development, City of El Paso. Interviewed by Anna Louise Fahy in 1996.

[86] Ward, John, "*Mrs. Edna Dietrich Recalls Pond Where Depot Now Stands*", El Paso Times, 22 August 1937.

[87] Hudnall, Ken and Connie Wang, Spirits of the Border: The History and Mystery of El Paso Del Norte, Omega Press, El Paso, Texas. 2003

[88] Many of the older downtown buildings had full basements that were used for storage.

[89] While they gave me permission to use what they had said, neither man wanted his name mentioned in this book.

[90] 2004

years he had performed his job of Customs Agent. We talked a while longer and finally he began to tell me some of the stories of incidents he had been involved in prior to his retirement[91].

According to this retired Agent, El Paso had once been a primary smuggling route for bootleg liquor during Prohibition. He remarked that Joseph Kennedy had brought far more illegal alcohol through El Paso in those days than he ever did from ships waiting outside the 3-mile limit. There were a great many smuggling routes that bypassed the Customs checkpoints and in quite a number of instances, the smugglers had used the old tunnel system that runs from Juarez to El Paso.

He also went on to tell me that one of the very easy ways that terrorists could smuggle weapons of mass destruction into this country would be on one of the buses that run back and forth across the border. Under the North American Free Trade Agreement (NAFTA), it is prohibited for Customs to interfere with commercial traffic, such as buses. Agents are allowed to board buses and ask if the passengers are bringing in any contraband, but they cannot stop and search a bus. However, one morning, prior to his retirement, he had felt that a bus driver was acting suspicious so he ignored the rules and searched the bus, but found nothing. A drug sniffing dog was brought in, but found nothing. Then the agent happened to enter the lavatory of the bus and found that it was not working. Knowing that the bus would not be in service if the lavatory were out of order, he decided to check out the holding tank. When they opened the lavatory tank, it was crammed full of bags of marijuana. The lavatory chemicals had masked the odor of the drugs form the dogs. He was reprimanded for interfering with a commercial vehicle.

DRUG CARTELS AND TERRORISM

There is no doubt that there is a several drug problem in this country and a large portion of the drugs sold in this country come across our southern border with Mexico. However, consider, if you will, that any organization that can smuggle in sufficient drug supplies to meet the needs of a country the size of the United States could also just as easily bring in weapons of mass destruction. In fact it would be easier to bring in chemical weapons that it would be large supplies of cocaine. The War on Drugs and the War On Terror are actually one and the same, though many do not realize it.

Before we move on to address the problem along the southern border, let me present one more article that as a bearing on this situation.

Mexican Police Join And
Work With Drug Lords

---

[91] For obvious reasons, this retired Customs Agent did not want his name used.

By Jerry Seper
The Washington Times
9-28-2

SONOYA, Mexico - This isolated area of the U.S.-Mexico border, a 100-mile-wide stretch of wild desert between the Organ Pipe Cactus National Monument and Coronado National Forest, has become one of America's newest drug corridors.

Mexican drug lords, backed by corrupt Mexican military officers and police officials, will move tons of marijuana, cocaine and heroin this year over rugged desert trails to accomplices in Phoenix and Tucson for shipment to willing buyers throughout the United States.

Most of the smuggling routes pass through the Tohono O'odham Nation, a sprawling Indian reservation, where undermanned and outgunned tribal police will confiscate more than 100,000 pounds of illicit drugs this year, about 300 pounds a day.

"They keep us running like you can't believe," said Detective Sgt. David Cray, who heads the Tohono Police Department's anti-drug unit. "They have two-way radios, night-vision gear, body armor and carry automatic weapons."

"They've put people on the hills to act as lookouts and use portable solar panels to power their communications equipment," he said. "They have powerful four-wheel-drive vehicles and are under orders not to stop - to shoot their way through if they have to."

Heavily armed Mexican military troops and police, who have been paid handsomely to escort the drug traffickers and their illicit shipments across the border and into the United States, often protect the smugglers, according to U.S. law-enforcement authorities.

The drug lords are expected to spend more than $500 million this year in bribes and payoffs to a cadre of Mexican military generals and police officials to ensure that the illicit drugs reach their destination, the authorities said.

Mexican smugglers will account for 80 percent of the cocaine and nearly half the heroin that reaches the streets of America this year.

Law-enforcement authorities all along the U.S.-Mexico border are concerned about the involvement of Mexican military troops and police in the alien- and drug-smuggling business. Several officials said in interviews that many Mexican police agencies along the border have been "totally corrupted" by drug smugglers and that the corruption included a number of key Mexican generals and other commanders.

Violence along the border, fueled by the drug trade, has spiraled out of control, the officials said.

Corruption among Mexican police is so extensive, they said, that some U.S. law-enforcement agencies refuse to work with their Mexican counterparts. Mexican police officials have been tied not only to alien and drug smuggling, but *also to numerous incidents of extortion, bribery, robbery, assault and kidnapping along the border.*

Border Patrol agents in Douglas, Ariz., were pulled from their duty stations after police in Aqua Prieta, Mexico, tipped U.S. authorities of a pending drug shipment. Supervisors were fearful of putting their agents in the middle of a shootout between rival drug gangs, each supported by competing Aqua Prieta police.

About two dozen incursions by the Mexican military have been documented this year, some of which resulted in unprovoked shootings, including one recent incident involving a U.S. Border Patrol agent. Several law-enforcement authorities along the border questioned why the Bush administration has not made an issue of Mexican troops crossing into the United States.

"I'm not sure what other country allows foreign military troops such willy-nilly access," said one veteran Border Patrol agent, speaking on the condition of anonymity. "I've seen them come across the border, heavily armed and equipped, and I often wonder why we're not doing anything about it."

The Mexican military deployments have occurred all along the 1,940-mile U.S.-Mexico border, from Texas, where Border Patrol agents in El Paso were fired on in March 2000 by people in two Mexican army Humvees, to California, where 10 Mexican soldiers shot at a Border Patrol helicopter in October 2000.

Many of the incursions have occurred near this Mexican town, where drug trafficking by Mexican smugglers has reached new levels.

"There's no doubt Mexican military units along the border are being controlled by the drug cartels, and not by Mexico City," said Rep. Tom Tancredo, Colorado Republican, who recently returned from a tour of the Southwest border. "The military units operate freely, with little or no direction, and several of them have made numerous incursions into the United States."

"Mexican President Vicente Fox may be trying to take control of his military, but there is a major disconnect between him and them - particularly among the units along the U.S.-Mexico border," he said.

Mr. Tancredo, head of the 65-member Congressional Immigration Reform Caucus, said the amount of drug trafficking in the remote regions of the Southwest desert has become so intense that armed confrontations are a constant threat.

He said the trafficking has been tied to Mexican drug cartels, and the shipments often are protected - sometimes even delivered - by Mexican military units.

"There isn't a soul down there on that border, either the Tohono O'odham police or the Border Patrol, who do not believe that is exactly what the Mexican military is doing," he said. "U.S. law-enforcement personnel actually have watched the Mexican military unload drugs from their Humvees to awaiting vehicles for transport into the United States."

Military incursions into America

Over the past five years, U.S. authorities have documented 118 incursions by the Mexican military. It is not known how many times Mexican military units have crossed undetected into the United States.

"I am amazed our government is not up in arms about this, but I am not surprised," Mr. Tancredo said. "While we have the resources to actually take control of our borders, including a combination of the U.S. military and the Border Patrol, we lack the political will."

"Instead, we continue to send young men and women in harm's way, to be shot at and, perhaps, killed. We're asking them to fight a war against an invasion of illegal immigrants and drugs, but we fail to give them the support they need to win that war."

The most recent documented Mexican military incursion occurred on May 17, when a Border Patrol agent was fired on by three Mexican soldiers in a military Humvee near what is known as the San Miguel gate on the Tohono reservation, about 30 miles northwest of Nogales, Ariz. The gunfire, which erupted shortly after 8:30 p.m., shattered the rear window of the U.S. agent's four-wheel-drive vehicle.

The unnamed agent, after spotting the soldiers, had sought to avoid a confrontation and, according to U.S. authorities, had turned his clearly marked, green-and-white Border Patrol vehicle away from the Humvee when it was hit by gunfire. The Mexican soldiers were armed with assault rifles.

One bullet was deflected by the vehicle's prisoner partition, located directly behind the agent's seat. It then knocked out the right rear window. The agent involved has been on the job for about a year, authorities said.

Earlier that day and in the same area, Border Patrol agents had confiscated 2,200 pounds of drugs from a vehicle that had crossed into the United States, although a second vehicle had escaped back into Mexico.

Edward Tuffly, president of the National Border Patrol Council Local 2544, asked in a message posted online to union members why the U.S. government was slow to acknowledge the incident. "The politicians will run like hell to avoid 'offending' anyone," he wrote.

Local 2544 represents Border Patrol agents in the Tucson sector. The National Border Patrol Council represents more than 8,000 nonsupervisory Border Patrol agents.

The U.S. Immigration and Naturalization Service, which oversees the Border Patrol, is investigating the May incident. The INS has asked the Mexican government also to investigate the shooting.

In August, U.S. National Park Service ranger Chris Eggle, 28, was killed on the Organ Pipe Cactus National Monument while trying to apprehend two men fleeing Mexican law enforcement, who had crossed the border into the United

States. One of the men shot Mr. Eggle just below his bulletproof vest.

U.S. authorities have since identified the suspected assailant as Panfilo Murillo Aguila, a Mexican national known as "El Zarco," a known drug smuggler in the Sonoyta area. Arrest warrants also have been issued in the case for two former Mexican soldiers identified as Rogelio Velasquez Jocobi and Carlos Perez Sanchez.

Helping the drug trade

Questions concerning the Mexican military's involvement in the drug trade, however, are long-standing.

In 1998, the U.S. Drug Enforcement Administration reported an extensive connection between drug traffickers in Mexico and senior members of the Mexican army. The DEA said at the time that it avoided cooperating with Mexican army officers for fear that intelligence would be passed on to drug smugglers.

Former DEA Administrator Donnie Marshall told a House subcommittee in 1999 that drug traffickers "have long had the ability to corrupt public officials and institutions throughout the world," noting that the Mexican military was not exempt.

At the time, Mexican military officers assigned to an elite anti-drug smuggling group had been arrested in Mexico City on charges of drug trafficking and alien smuggling. Among those arrested were several captains and majors, all of whom had been assigned to the Mexican Attorney General's Office as anti-narcotics agents.

Since Mr. Fox's 2000 election there has been an increase in the number of arrests of Mexican government and military officials, along with the creation of a federal drug-enforcement unit that has seized tons of narcotics and made numerous arrests.

Mexican authorities also have been more willing to work with their U.S. counterparts, and a number of the leaders and top lieutenants from all four of Mexico's major drug cartels have been arrested.

The Mexican government has denied that any part of its military is working with the drug cartels, saying in a recent statement that military units along the border are working the same areas as the U.S. Border Patrol in fighting the illegal transport of drugs and people into this country.

The statement said that sometimes the troops "get lost in those areas," noting that there is "no clear marking for the border" in many regions. Mexican Defense Department officials have declined to say how many soldiers are patrolling the U.S.-Mexico border or to comment on the incursions.

Many U.S. law-enforcement authorities doubt the contention that the units were lost.

"Some of these 'lost' units are carrying drugs, and we've seen them before," said a second veteran Border Patrol agent, speaking on the condition of anonymity. *"Besides, if they are lost, why are they shooting at us instead of asking for directions?"*

The politics of immigration

The White House opposes the stationing of U.S. troops on the Mexican border for "cultural and historical reasons."

President Bush, former governor of Texas, has sought to appeal to Hispanic voters through such initiatives as promoting a Western Hemispheric free trade zone, giving amnesty to 4 million to 7 million illegal immigrants in the United States and allowing immigrants visas that would be renewable each year as long as they hold jobs.

"Some look south and see problems," Mr. Bush said in a speech last year to State Department employees. *"Not me. I look south and see opportunities."*

But Mr. Tancredo said he wants "an explanation of these 'cultural and historical' reasons why we can't protect our nation's borders." He said it was *"time"* for the U.S. government to order troops to the border to assist in controlling illegal immigration and drug smuggling, both of which he described as *"national security concerns."*

Earlier this year, some House Republicans called on Mr. Bush to station military forces along the Southwest border, citing a need to stop the persistent flow of illegal immigrants and to combat drug smugglers, who have taken over several areas of the lengthy border.

The lawmakers said the number of violent encounters along the border, including incursions involving the Mexican military, was increasing, "creating a need for immediate action on the part of our government."

"We are extremely concerned about the porousness of both our northern and southern borders," said Rep. Jim Ramstad, Minnesota Republican, who joined in the call for stationing troops. *"It is particularly disturbing that Canada and Mexico are still not adequately screening immigrant and cargo traffic in and out of their countries."*

The Bush administration has placed 1,100 National Guardsmen on the borders with Canada and Mexico after the September 11 terrorist attacks, but those deployments ended in summer.

Meanwhile, officials at the Border Patrol's Tucson sector office, which is responsible for 261 miles of international border, continue to negotiate with the Mexican military about the problems of drug trafficking, alien smuggling and incursions.

"We have attempted to maintain an active dialogue with a number of the generals in the Mexican army," said Carlos X. Carrillo, assistant sector chief. *"There is no question that when there is an incident, it is of grave concern to us."*

"The safety of our agents and the possible violation of U.S. law concerns us deeply."

Assistant Chief Carrillo also said Tucson sector supervisors have a "strong liaison" with Mexico and have been "very active" in reaching out to their Mexican law-enforcement counterparts. He said sector officials have "actively sought an open line of communication in an effort to reduce the potential of these kinds of incidents."

But despite the continuing dialogue, there has been no decrease in the amount of drugs coming out of Mexico into the United States. Additionally, the number of illegal aliens crossing annually though the Tucson sector has skyrocketed.

"Things have improved," said a top U.S. law-enforcement official. "But corruption is so deeply entrenched in Mexico, it will take years to identify and remove those who are still involved. Many Mexican military officers operate with total autonomy, particularly in faraway places like the border."

"The drug smugglers have a ton of money to persuade them to the dark side."

At the Tohono O'odham Nation, which shares 76 miles of international border with Mexico, the reservation's 75-member police department will spend more than $3 million this year on all border-related issues, including the towing of up to 40 cars a day abandoned by alien smugglers and drug smugglers.

"The problems of illegal aliens and drug smuggling impacts significantly on the level of service we can provide to our own community," said acting Assistant Police Chief Joseph Delgado. "The Border Patrol has pushed the illegal immigrants out of the cities and towns and to our reservation, where we do not have the manpower to deal with the crunch. The community is upset that we can't focus on them."

Chief Delgado noted that because of the flood of immigrants and drug smugglers, the reservation has become a violent place for the 13,000 people who call the Tohono O'odham nation home. He said alien smugglers and drug smugglers refuse to stop for police and often race their four-wheel-drive vehicles over the reservation's many dirt roads at speeds of up to 100 miles per hour.

"Our children are out in the community, and every day they have to face these ruthless people," he said. "It is very frustrating that we have had to divert our attention and our resources to focus not on our own community but to deal with this rising immigration and drug problem."

"We're literally the front line of defense for the United States, and we are doing the best we can," he said. "But I assure you, it's going to get worse before it gets better.[92]""

WHO CAN YOU TRUST?

The articles shown above make it perfectly clear that the drug problem is one that is growing and the authorities in Mexico seem to be helping. How difficult would it be to slip a few weapons of mass destruction into the flood of drugs coming across the border.

According to the retired Customs Agents that I met at the Fourth of July Party, there have already been some chemical strikes in this country. He told me that there had been a chemical strike that contaminated the area as far north as Las Cruces, New Mexico, some sixty or so miles north of the Mexican Border. The area had been decontaminated fairly quickly and very few people knew that it had happened.

CONFERENCE ON BORDER SECURITY

To show the attention that is being paid to the security of our southern border, in late May of 2004, Congressman Silvestre Reyes announced that a conference would be held regarding Border Security Issues. One of those involved asked me if I would like to attend as a speaker since I have experience in counter-terrorism and urban warfare. I agreed to attend and give my views. However, a day or so after being invited, I was uninvited as a result of Congressman Reyes' office not wanting me to attend. I seemed that the panel would be made up of "true experts" on terrorism: two professors from the University of Texas at El Paso (UTEP)[93] and a number f elected officials. It was felt by Congressman Reyes' Office that I would "confuse" the people. In other words, the views of someone experienced in evading patrols and slipping into areas was felt to be confusing.

Frankly, this is the typical government response to the concerns of the citizens – trust us, we've got it under control. Then a very carefully staged managed event such this conference on border security is held where so called experts give their very learned opinions, overwhelming any opposition with the many degrees that the speaker holds from institutions of higher learning. After the two UTEP professors spoke, I really feel safer, don't you?

A FINAL NOTE ON BORDER SECURITY

The insertion of terrorists and saboteurs into this country is nothing new. On June 13, 1942, during the early days of America's official involvement in World War II Kreigsmarine U-Boat Number 202 commanded by Kapitanleutuant Hans-

---

[93] One professor was from the Communications Department and one was from the Political Science Department, as near as I could determine, neither had any practical experience in urban warfare or counter terrorism, however, they were choice by Congressman Reyes' Office to speak on Border Security.

Heinz Lindner landed four German agents on the south fort of Long Island, New York[94]. These four were the first of a stream of agents that Adolph Hitler planned to insert into this country to carry out acts of sabotage and terror. It was only by a fluke that this plan was not wildly successful. Our open society will always make it easy for the enemy to infiltrate. Even with historic examples to point to of how easy it would be for enemies to cross the border, our government almost always sticks its head in the sand, not wanting to "upset" the public with the truth.

I want to add one other little tidbit of information that my retired Customs Agent friend told me during this Fourth of July party. He asked me if I remembered the ruckus that had been kicked up during the PAN[95] demonstrations in Juarez. Living only a few miles form the border as I do, I certainly was very much aware of various incidents in Juarez, Mexico.

He pointed out how easy it would be for terrorists to take advantage of the unrest to slip agents into this country. He went on to say that during the period of the demonstrations that the Customs Agents had been briefed on the plan to secure the border in case demonstrators decided to rush the Bridges connecting the United States with Mexico. According to the Border Security Plan, the first line of defense would be the Customs Agents, themselves, all suitably armed, but rigidly adhering to the Rules of Engagement. If the Agents could not handle the situation, then the El Paso Police Department would be called. If the El Paso Police Department could not handle the situation, then the US Military at Fort Bliss[96] would be summoned. If the US Military from Fort Bliss could not handle the situation, then the US Military forces at White Sands Missile Test Range[97] would be summoned. If all of these forces could not handle the situation then the next step called for the NUKING of the Border to create a five-mile wide strip of radiation, two and one half miles on each side of the Border. So much for El Paso!

---

[94] Abella, Alex & Scott Gordon, <u>Shadow Enemies</u>, Lyons Press, Guilford Connecticut. 2002

[95] PAN is a Mexican political party that held power for several decades, but recently lost control of the country.

[96] Fort Bliss, Texas is located on the outskirts of El Paso, Texas and is the home of the Air Defense Artillery.

[97] White Sands Missile Test Range is located in New Mexico, but is less than 60 miles from Fort Bliss.

122\ROBERT K. HUDNALL, JD

CHAPTER TEN
THE TRUE STATE OF BORDER SECURITY

Rather than listen to propaganda disseminated for public consumption, let's turn to the experts. The problem of drug smuggling and the true state of Border Security were considered by the 107th Congress, in 2001 and I think some of the testimony submitted to Congress certainly has a direct bearing on the potential for smuggling in weapons of mass destruction and terrorist operatives. A portion of the testimony is given below:

72–144 DTP
2001
DRUG TRAFFICKING ON THE SOUTHWEST BORDER
HEARING BEFORE THE SUBCOMMITTEE ON CRIME OF THE COMMITTEE ON THE JUDICIARY

HOUSE OF REPRESENTATIVES
ONE HUNDRED SEVENTH CONGRESS
FIRST SESSION
MARCH 29, 2001
Serial No. 3
Available via the World Wide Web: http://www.house.gov/judiciary

COMMITTEE ON THE JUDICIARY
Subcommittee on Crime

PREPARED STATEMENT OF DONNIE R. MARSHALL, ADMINISTRATOR, DRUG ENFORCEMENT ADMINISTRATION

Good Morning Chairman Smith, Ranking Member Scott, and other distinguished members of the Subcommittee. I am pleased to have this opportunity to appear before you today for the purpose of discussing our continuing efforts to address issues and concerns associated with Drug Trafficking on the Southwest Border. As always, I would first like to preface my remarks by thanking the Subcommittee for its unwavering support of the men and women of the Drug Enforcement Administration (DEA) and overall support of drug law enforcement.

The border that joins the United States to Mexico is currently an extremely porous part of the nation's periphery. In Fiscal Year (FY) 2000, 293 million people, 89 million cars, 4.5 million trucks, and 572,583 rail cars entered the United States from Mexico. Unfortunately, the growing volume of commercial and pedestrian traffic that plays an integral role in our nation's economy creates an infinite number of opportunities for drug trafficking organizations to introduce their illegal goods into the commerce of the United States. Illegal drugs are hidden in all modes of conveyances, including the compartments of cars and trucks, and the bodies and baggage of pedestrians. Some organizations may employ couriers who cross the desert in armed pack trains, or who act as human "mules" by strapping the drugs onto their bodies.

The means by which illegal drugs enter the United States range from, extremely sophisticated concealment methods, to simply tossing the drug laden package over border fences to be whisked away on foot or by vehicle. Drug trafficking organizations also utilize boats and ships to position their stash of drugs close to the border for eventual transfer to the United States.

Illicit drugs are smuggled in record levels into the United States via the *2,000-mile U.S./Mexico border*. Over the past few years, Mexican based trafficking organizations have succeeded in establishing themselves as the preeminent poly-drug traffickers of the world, using our shared border to smuggle illicit drugs into the United States. These organizations present an increasing threat to the national security of this country, with voluminous amount of drugs, violent crime, and the associated corruption of public officials in Mexico. Mexico is the largest transshipment point of South American cocaine destined for the United States, and 65% of this cocaine reaches American cities via the U.S./Mexico border. Mexico also remains a major source country for heroin and marijuana, and many of these Mexican based trafficking organizations are utilized by Colombian Cartels to transship drugs destined for the United States.

[AUTHOR'S NOTE: To give the reader an idea of how easy it would be to smuggle in Anthrax spores that could be used as a weapon of mass destruction, U.S. Army Commandos and CIA agents raided the home of

Sultan Bashiruddin Mahmood, Pakistan's former head of their nuclear bomb program and found diagrams of a helium balloon designed to release large quantities of anthrax spores into the atmosphere[98].

Before someone thinks that helium balloons in the Middle East are no danger to the United States as a whole, I would remind the reader that during World War II balloons released in Japan carrying bombs and other dangerous elements were released in Japan and landed in the Southwest United States.

As we shall see later in this text, weapons of this sort would be child's play for a man of Mahmood's demonstrated ability.]

ASSESSING THE THREAT: THE ROLE OF THE U.S./MEXICO BORDER IN THE DRUG TRADE

The drug threat presented by the U.S./Mexico Border is fairly consistent with the national drug threat, and to a certain extent, defines the overall drug threat against our nation. Clearly, the most distinguishable threat is the transformation and emergence of Mexican based trafficking organizations, whose activities now reach the highest echelons of the cocaine trade. Previously limited to marijuana and Mexican heroin smuggling, Mexican based groups have expanded and profited by maintaining a mutually beneficial relationship with Colombian based traffickers.

The U.S./Mexico Border continues to be the preferred corridor to smuggle cocaine, black tar heroin, methamphetamine, and marijuana into the United States. Overland smuggling constitutes a primary threat by secreting among the millions of pedestrians, cars, and trucks that the U.S. Customs Service (USCS) estimates cross the 39 legitimate crossing points from Mexico. There are 24 ports of entry (POEs) at the border as well as 15 additional crossing points. Some of these POEs include multiple crossing points. Preliminary El Paso[99] Intelligence Center (EPIC) statistics indicate that smuggling levels remained high: in CY-2000, authorities seized 17,660 kilograms of cocaine, 619 kilograms of heroin, 1,645 kilograms of methamphetamine, and 998,180 kilograms of marijuana along the U.S./Mexico Border.

These recent trends illustrate the vulnerability of the U.S./Mexico Border to Colombian and Mexican based trafficking organizations intent on introducing drugs into the United States market:

Cocaine is primarily transported from South America by vessel to the West Coast of Mexico and, to a lesser extent, the Yucatan peninsula, which is situated in the southeast portion of Mexico adjacent to the Gulf of Mexico. The use of vessels to transport bulk shipments of cocaine represents a departure from

---

[98] Carroll, Michael Christopher, Lab 257, William Morrow, 2004.
[99] El Paso, Texas.

the use of such modes of transportation as private aircraft and trucks utilized by drug transporters over the past two decades. From Mexico, bulk shipments of cocaine are then trucked to the United States, oftentimes secreted in produce and other perishable shipments.

Mexican black tar heroin is being smuggled into the United States in larger quantities than in the past; multi-kilogram seizures of heroin are becoming increasingly commonplace. South American heroin is transported by courier on commercial airlines or by private aircraft from South America to Mexico, and then by commercial airline or by private or commercial vehicle to the United States.

The DEA Tijuana Resident Office (TJRO) reported that 13 methamphetamine labs had been seized in Baja, California in fiscal year 2001 as compared with three (3) seizures in fiscal year 2000.

MDMA is being smuggled into Mexico for ultimate transshipment to the United States.

On February 26, 2001, U.S. Customs and DEA investigated the discovery of a 25-foot tunnel that took advantage of drainage lines that connect the U.S. and Mexico. A total of 375 kilograms of cocaine were recovered as a result of this effort.

COCAINE TRAFFICKING ACROSS THE U.S./MEXICO BORDER

Through the 1980s, most of the cocaine that entered the United States did so through the Caribbean and South Florida. Increased enforcement and interdiction efforts, however, forced traffickers to shift the majority of their smuggling operations to Mexico, a move that led DEA and other Federal agencies to mobilize along the U.S./Mexico Border. According to a recent interagency intelligence assessment, approximately 65 percent of the cocaine smuggled into the United States in 2000 crossed the U.S./Mexico Border.

Colombian based organizations rely on Mexican based groups in locations such as Guadalajara, Juarez, Matamoras, Sinaloa, and Tijuana to convey their cocaine into the United States. Mexican trafficking organizations have established themselves as transportation specialists for smuggling drugs across the U.S./Mexico Border. Frequently, these trafficking organizations are comprised of poly drug smugglers who transport marijuana, methamphetamine, and heroin in addition to cocaine.

Over the past decade, Colombian based drug lords and Mexican based trafficking organizations have entered into a symbiotic relationship that has resulted in the Mexican based traffickers playing an increasing role in the cocaine trade. Under this arrangement, Mexican based traffickers often receive shipments of cocaine directly from Colombian based organizations, and contract with the source to deliver a portion of the shipment to a contact of the Colombian based network operating in the United States. The Mexican based traffickers are allowed to keep the balance of the cocaine shipment as payment for their services, transporting the shipment to Mexican-controlled wholesale distribution networks that principally operate in the Western United States.

By the mid-1990s, Mexican based transportation groups were receiving up to half of each cocaine shipment they smuggled into the United States on behalf of the Colombian based traffickers. By relinquishing a portion of the cocaine destined for the U.S. market to Mexican based drug organizations, as opposed to attempting to unilaterally control every aspect of importation and distribution, Colombian based drug lords radically changed the role and sphere of influence of Mexican based trafficking organizations in the cocaine trade. In doing so, the Colombian based traffickers have minimized their risk of exposure to U.S. law enforcement authorities, and provided Mexican based traffickers with a valuable source of revenue and domestic customers.

As a consequence of this development, traffickers operating from Mexico now control a substantial proportion of wholesale cocaine distribution throughout the Western and Midwestern United States. Distribution of multi-ton quantities of cocaine once dominated by the Colombia-based drug traffickers is now controlled by trafficking groups from Mexico in cities such as Chicago, Dallas, Denver, Houston, Los Angeles, Phoenix, San Diego, San Francisco, and Seattle. In addition to cocaine transportation, some drug trafficking groups operating from Mexico appear to offer a range of services, including wholesale cocaine distribution and money laundering for Colombian clients, and direct delivery to wholesale-level customers on behalf of the major Colombian based cocaine groups.

[AUTHOR'S NOTE: This information is included in order to give the reader some idea of the magnitude of the smuggling that crosses the US/Mexican Border on a daily basis. Based on the amount of drug that is seized, it is not difficult to interpolate the amount that successfully makes the journey from the manufacturing end of the chain to the street user. If just one shipment is a hundred consists of the components for creating weapons of mass destruction, picture the ensuing death, destruction and chaos that would result!

To really understand the problem faced by this country, substitute the words chemical weapons every time a particular smuggled drug is mentioned in this testimony. The result is a real eye opener.]

Routes and General Methods

Over the past two decades, cocaine was primarily moved by air and land into Mexico from Colombia. During the late 1980s and early 1990s, traffickers used large commercial aircraft, such as 727's and 737's, to move cocaine from

South America to Mexico. Currently, maritime vessels are the most frequent method used to transport bulk shipments of cocaine to Mexico for ultimate distribution in the United States. Colombian based traffickers utilize fishing vessels to move cocaine usually to the West Coast of Mexico, and, to a lesser extent, the Yucatan peninsula. The cocaine is then off-loaded to "go-fast" watercraft for final delivery to shore. Once secured on land, the drug shipments are consolidated for overland movement to the U.S./Mexico Border.

Traffickers continue to use trucking routes through Central America and Mexico to the U.S./Mexico Border. Cocaine shipments transported through Mexico or Central America are generally moved overland to staging sites in or near northern Mexico, although intelligence suggests that small aircraft may play a role in moving some cocaine to the border area. At these staging sites, the cocaine is broken down into smaller loads for smuggling across the U.S./Mexico border.

Three of the four primary cocaine importation points within the United States are located along the U.S./Mexico Border in Arizona, Southern California, and Texas. Cross-border cocaine shipments generally are smuggled across the U.S./Mexico border in concealed compartments within cars, trucks, and recreation vehicles, or commingled with legitimate tractor-trailer cargo. Typically, the land vehicles are driven across the U.S./Mexico Border, and then either left in parking lots for subsequent pick-up, or driven directly to storage sites in the United States. Using this method, traffickers are able to shroud their illegal activities in the tremendous numbers of people and vehicles crossing the U.S./Mexico Border. These cocaine shipments typically consist of 20 to 50 kilogram loads secreted in concealed compartments that are primarily located under floorboards and/or in gas tanks of passenger cars, pickup trucks, and vans. Larger quantities, however, have also been seized. For example, in October, 2001,109 kilograms of cocaine were seized at a U.S. Immigration and Naturalization Service (INS) checkpoint in Falfurrias, Texas. The cocaine was found inside boxes onboard a tractor-trailer, commingled with a shipment of tee shirts.

Cocaine also is carried across the U.S.-Mexico border by couriers known as *mules*, who cross into the United States either legally through U.S./Mexico Border ports of entry, or illegally through undesignated points along the border. The couriers typically carry small, kilogram quantities of cocaine, thus minimizing the losses incurred by the courier's controller in the event of robbery, theft, or law enforcement intervention.

HEROIN TRAFFICKING ACROSS THE U.S./MEXICO BORDER

The U.S./Mexico Border is a significant transit point to the U.S. heroin market, not only for the Mexican black tar and brown heroin that dominate the markets west of the Mississippi River, but increasingly for South American heroin destined for the primary markets in the Northeast. Moreover, Nigerian and

Southeast Asia based traffickers have been known to move opiate/heroin products across the U.S./Mexico Border.

Mexican Heroin

Mexican Black tar and brown heroin has been a threat to the United States for decades. It is produced, smuggled, and distributed by poly-drug trafficking groups, many of which have been in operation for more than 20 years. Mexican based heroin distributors operating within the United States have historically been Mexican nationals with familial and/or geographical ties to the States of Durango, Michoacan, Nuevo Leon, and Sinaloa.

Mexican heroin primarily is smuggled overland and across the U.S./Mexico Border. Traffickers take advantage of easy border access and store bulk quantities of heroin in Mexico, where the perceived risk of discovery and seizure is low. When a transaction is arranged, the contracted amount, usually 1 to 2 kilograms, is smuggled into the United States, frequently by illegal aliens and migrant workers. By keeping quantities small, traffickers hope to minimize the risk of losing a significant quantity of heroin in a single seizure. Even large poly-drug Mexican organizations, which smuggle multi-ton quantities of cocaine and marijuana, generally limit smuggling of Mexican heroin into the United States to kilogram and smaller amounts. Nevertheless, trafficking organizations employing this "piecemeal" strategy are capable of regularly smuggling significant quantities of heroin into the United States.

Recent intelligence indicates that some heroin traffickers are smuggling 5 to 30 kilograms of Mexican heroin in tar and powder form from the interior of Mexico, representing a departure from the previous practice of Mexican based traffickers, who smuggled heroin into the United States in 1–2 kilogram amounts.

As recently as January 2, 2001, 92 pounds of black tar heroin was seized by the U.S. Customs Service in Del Rio, Texas. In December 2000, the U.S. Customs Service seized 59 pounds of black tar heroin at the Laredo port-of-entry. The U.S. Customs Service also reported several large seizures of black tar heroin at Arizona ports-of-entry. On October 3, 2000, for example, U.S. Customs Service Inspectors seized 101 pounds at the San Luis port-of-entry. This seizure ranks as one of the largest ever made along the U.S./Mexico Border.

Once heroin is smuggled into the United States, transportation is arranged to metropolitan areas in the western and southwestern states with sizeable Hispanic populations. Mexican heroin has also been transported to primary markets in Chicago, Denver, and St. Louis. Periodically, Mexican traffickers have attempted to find markets for black tar heroin in East Coast cities such as Boston and Atlanta. However, this effort at market expansion has, for the most part, met with failure. Although recent DEA cases have involved Mexican black tar heroin trafficking groups operating east of the Mississippi River, there has been no successful, long-term penetration of the East Coast heroin market by organizations selling Mexican-produced heroin.

South American Heroin

The availability of South American heroin, produced almost exclusively in Colombia, has increased dramatically in the Eastern United States since 1993. Despite having relatively limited production capacity and relying on unsophisticated smuggling techniques, traffickers of South American heroin have had a substantial impact on the U.S. market. The traffic of South American heroin has been characterized by the production of modest quantities of the drug in small laboratories in Colombia, the smuggling of heroin in quantities of 500 grams to 1 kilogram by numerous couriers aboard commercial airlines, and distribution of the drug through traditional retail outlets in northeastern cities, primarily New York City, Newark, Boston, and Philadelphia.

In response to increased drug law enforcement presence at eastern ports of entry, some South American based heroin traffickers have sought out alternative routes. Recent seizures in 2000 and 2001 reflect an increasing use of Mexico to smuggle South American heroin into the United States. In February 2001, for example, two separate seizures of South American heroin, totaling 4.9 kilograms, were made at the airport in Tijuana, Mexico.

METHAMPHETAMINE TRAFFICKING ACROSS THE U.S./MEXICO BORDER

Over the last decade, the methamphetamine trafficking and abuse situation in the United States changed dramatically. In the mid-1990s, methamphetamine trafficking and abuse increased in the United States, primarily in the West and Midwest. In 1997, this trend started to spread, to a lesser extent, to the Southeast. The entry of Mexico-based trafficking organizations into the methamphetamine trade contributed to this resurgence.

Historically, outlaw motorcycle gangs and many independent dealers dominated methamphetamine manufacturing and trafficking. Although independent trafficking groups continue to produce methamphetamine, in 1994, Mexican national drug trafficking organizations operating in California and Mexico began to take control of the production and distribution of methamphetamine in the United States. From their experience in the trafficking of cocaine, heroin, and marijuana, the Mexican organizations already had well established transportation routes.

The entree of Mexican traffickers into the methamphetamine production and distribution trade in the early 1990s resulted in a significant increase in high-purity supplies of the drug.

In 1994, Mexican national drug trafficking organizations operating out of

Mexico and California began to take control of the production and distribution of the methamphetamine in the United States. What was once controlled by independent, regionalized outlaw motorcycle gangs was taken over by major Mexican organizations and independent operators based in Mexico and California. Mexican national trafficking organizations now dominate wholesale methamphetamine trafficking, using large-scale laboratories based in Mexico and the western and southwestern United States. Outlaw motorcycle gangs are still active in methamphetamine production, but do not produce the large quantities that are distributed by Mexican groups.

In the early to mid-1990s, Mexican organizations had ready access to precursor chemicals on the international market[100]. These chemicals had fewer controls in Mexico and overseas than in the United States. The Mexican national organizations further developed existing international connections with chemical suppliers in Europe, Asia, and the Far East, and were able to obtain ton quantities of the necessary precursor chemicals, specifically bulk ephedrine and pseudoephedrine.

From their experience in the trafficking of cocaine, heroin and marijuana, the Mexican organizations already had well-established transportation routes. Initially offering inexpensive, high-purity methamphetamine, the Mexican organizations ultimately gained a foothold in the existing United States market and expanded their operations. Since they produced their own drug, they maintained greater control of the methamphetamine market and reaped greater profits than with the distribution of other drugs. It should be noted that high-purity methamphetamine produced by the Mexican groups, in combination with the marketing strategy of providing free samples, created new population of addicts.

Until 1999, the methamphetamine problem was increasing at an alarming rate. International chemical control efforts, particularly the international "letter of non-objection" program enacted in 1995, reduced the supply of those chemicals needed to produce high-quality methamphetamine. As a result, the national purity level for methamphetamine, as well as amphetamine, has gone down dramatically. The average purity of methamphetamine exhibits seized by DEA dropped from 71.9 percent in 1994 to 30.7 percent in 1999, rising slightly to 34.6 percent in 2000. Emergency room mentions and overdose deaths involving methamphetamine show an analogous decrease.

With the success of the international efforts to control the flow of bulk ephedrine and pseudoephedrine, such as bi-lateral meetings and the letter of non-objection program, Mexican traffickers turned to tableted forms of the precursors in the U.S. In 1997 and 1998, the vast majority of methamphetamine laboratories operated by Mexican organizations that were seized in California obtained their

---

[100] A lab capable of making these drugs is also capable of making simple chemical weapons.

precursor chemicals from sources in the United States. The Mexican organizations obtained their precursors from chemical wholesalers, rogue chemical companies, and back door/blackmarket sales of large quantities of ephedrine/pseudoephedrine tablets from unscrupulous retail and convenience store operators.

MARIJUANA TRAFFICKING ACROSS THE U.S./MEXICO BORDER

Drug trafficking organizations operating from Mexico have smuggled marijuana into the United States for over 20 years and are responsible for supplying most of the foreign marijuana available in the United States. Virtually all the marijuana smuggled into the United States, whether grown in Mexico or shipped through Mexico from lesser sources such as Central America, is smuggled across the U.S./Mexico Border.

Drug trafficking organizations employ a wide range of methods to transport the marijuana. The most common method is to smuggle marijuana in bulk quantities by truck and smaller quantities in vehicle tires, fuel tanks, seats, or false compartments. Traffickers use various vehicles to cross POEs: commercial vehicles, private automobiles, pickup trucks, vans, mobile homes, and horse trailers. Marijuana also is hidden inside agricultural products, and is smuggled across the border by horse, raft, and backpack. There are also sporadic reports of marijuana being smuggled via private aircraft; however, field offices do not consider border crossings by air to be a significant threat. They do report that private aircraft are used to smuggle marijuana up to the border on the Mexico side where large quantities of marijuana are stockpiled. The primary routes for marijuana, however, remain the overland routes.

MDMA TRAFFICKING ACROSS THE U.S./MEXICO BORDER

In the future, Mexico may increasingly be used as a transit zone for MDMA entering the United States. In the year 2000, several seizures of MDMA en route or in Mexico were reported. For example, in September 2000, Dutch authorities seized a 1.25 million-tablet shipment of MDMA destined for Mexico. On November 20, 2000, approximately 64,000 Ecstasy pills were seized at the Mexico City Airport.

CONFRONTING THE THREAT: A BALANCED RESPONSE

Given the expanse of the U.S./Mexico Border, it is clear that no single agency can "control" the border or completely filter illegal drugs from the massive quantities of legitimate commercial cargo that flow across our borders each day. Accordingly, DEA continues to implement a balanced approach to confronting the drug threat posed by the criminal organizations exploiting our

U.S./Mexico Border. The elements of this approach range from capitalizing on the latest advances in telecommunications technology, to our adhering to basic, time-honored principles of interagency cooperation.

As evidenced by the following program descriptions, DEA is continuously working to generate innovative enforcement initiatives that will serve to immobilize the most sophisticated international drug trafficking organizations operating today.

DEA's strategic approach to targeting major drug trafficking organizations is to initiate and pursue high impact, intelligence-driven, multi-agency, multi-jurisdiction/multi-nation investigations that employ a combination of intelligence, investigative technology support, and the coordinated efforts of DEA and its federal, state, local and foreign law enforcement counterparts. By strategically and comprehensively targeting international command and control centers of drug syndicates based overseas in conjunction with their domestic entry and transshipment routes and local distribution points, DEA has been able to dismantle drug organizations in virtually all arenas. This approach requires DEA's foreign and domestic enforcement, intelligence, and technology elements to work collectively to transform isolated investigations into large-scale, multi-agency, multi-jurisdiction/multi-nation investigations.

In 1991, DEA established the Special Operations Division (SOD), a program that utilizes sophisticated technology to coordinate the investigative and intelligence resources of the DEA, the Federal Bureau of Investigation (FBI), the U.S. Customs Service (USCS), and the Internal Revenue Service (IRS) to target the command, control, and communications of major drug trafficking organizations. These investigations are also coordinated with attorneys from the Department of Justice's Narcotics and Dangerous Drugs section. SOD performs the following mission-critical functions:

Provides significant up-to-date, real-time intelligence to field investigators;

Coordinates and supports complex investigations and prosecutions of multi-agency, multi-jurisdiction, and international targets;

Focuses sophisticated Title III technology and assets against specific targets;

Manages and oversees DEA's contract linguist program and prioritizes use of limited Title III resources; and Links and transforms isolated, local investigations conducted by single agencies into multi-agency, coordinated enforcement operations against multiple targets operating at regional, national, and international levels.

As the lead agency, DEA performs mission oversight responsibilities and provides the primary administrative services necessary to support the program's overall operations. DEA works closely with its partner agencies to set priorities and ensure a continued high degree of coordination and information sharing on supported investigations. SOD is currently staffed with a total of 228 personnel from DEA and other federal agencies. Of these personnel, 102 are DEA employees (48 Special Agents).

Southwest Border Initiative

One of DEA's primary functions is to coordinate the many drug investigations taking place along America's roughly 2,000-mile border with Mexico, an effort that involves literally thousands of federal, state and local law enforcement officers. As the threat from Mexican based poly-drug trafficking organizations continues to escalate, the workload steadily increases. Much of this increased workload is due to expansion by Mexican based traffickers into new geographic regions of the U.S., particularly the Midwest. Mexican based traffickers have become the world's preeminent drug traffickers, and their organizations are generally complex in nature and characterized by a high propensity for violence.

To counter this threat, federal drug law enforcement has aggressively pursued drug trafficking along the U.S./Mexico border. Through a cooperative and coordinated enforcement effort, DEA, the FBI, U.S. Border Patrol, U.S. Attorney's Office, U.S. Customs Service, and state and local law enforcement agencies have worked together to reduce the amount of illicit drugs entering the United States through the U.S./Mexico Border. The Southwest Border Initiative is intended to counter drug activity by identifying, penetrating, disrupting, and dismantling the major Mexican and Colombian based drug trafficking organizations using the border to smuggle illegal drugs into the United States. The strategy is to attack major Mexican based trafficking organizations on both sides of the border simultaneously, employing enhanced intelligence and enforcement initiatives, and cooperative efforts with the Government of Mexico.

As indicated by the case examples below, the Southwest Border Initiative has built a record of success in targeting, immobilizing, and dismantling major drug trafficking organizations.

Operation Green Air (Marijuana) was a multi-jurisdictional investigation targeting a Mexican/Jamaican marijuana smuggling and distribution organization with ties to Traditional Organized Crime. The organization smuggled multi-thousand pound quantities of marijuana by trucks and other conveyances from Mexico through U.S. Ports of Entry in Southern California to warehouses in the greater Los Angeles area. Several corrupt warehouse employees shipped the marijuana via Federal Express to distribution cells on the East Coast. Operation Green Air culminated in April 2000 with a nationwide takedown that resulted in the seizure of more than 15.25 tons of marijuana, $4,546,384 in U.S. currency, and the arrest of 106 individuals.

Operation Impunity II (Cocaine) was a multi-jurisdictional investigation targeting a Mexican drug trafficking organization responsible for the transportation and distribution of multi-hundred kilogram shipments of cocaine from Mexico to cities throughout the United States. This investigation targeted remnants of the Carrillo-Fuentes Organization and the Gulf Cartel Organization. Operation Impunity II culminated in December 2000 with a nationwide takedown that produced the seizure of 5,266 kilograms of cocaine, 9,325 pounds of marijuana, $9,663,265 in U.S. currency/assets, and the arrest of 141 individuals.

Operation Tar Pit (Heroin) was a multi-jurisdictional investigation targeting a Mexican heroin transportation and trafficking organization based in Tepic, Nayarit, Mexico. Primarily, this organization imported multi-kilogram quantities of black tar heroin from Mexico into the United States. The heroin was transported to the greater Los Angeles area and distributed to organization cell heads throughout the U.S., including San Diego, CA; Bakersfield, CA; Honolulu, HI; Portland, OR; Denver, CO; Cleveland, OH; Columbus, OH; Pittsburgh, PA; Phoenix, AZ; Yuma, AZ; Albuquerque, NM; and Charleston, WV. In June 2000, a multi-nation takedown was conducted against Operation Tar Pit targets that included the principal Mexican command and control members in Mexico; U.S. based cell heads, workers for each cell, and couriers. This investigation culminated in the seizure of 64 pounds of black tar heroin, 10 weapons, $304,450 in U.S. currency, and the arrest of 249 individuals.

Operation Mountain Express (Pseudoephedrine) was a DEA operation that targeted traffickers of the methamphetamine precursor, pseudoephedrine. Existing regulations allowed DEA registrants to obtain multi-ton quantities of tablet pseudoephedrine from gray-market importers. California-based Mexican production organizations took advantage of this fact by purchasing ton quantities of pseudoephedrine for use in methamphetamine production. Since January 2000, several multi-jurisdictional investigations targeting pseudoephedrine traffickers have been conducted. For the first time in U.S. drug law enforcement history, the illicit trafficking of pseudoephedrine was traced from bulk importers to rogue registrants and eventually to pseudoephedrine extraction laboratories. Operation Mountain Express resulted in the arrest of 189 individuals and the seizure of more than 12.5 tons of pseudoephedrine, 83 pounds of finished methamphetamine, $11,100,000 million in U.S. currency, and real property in excess of $1,000,000.

Operation Gas Mask (Precursor Chemicals) is a recently completed investigation targeting a California based supplier of HCL gas to Mexican national methamphetamine production organizations. This investigation resulted in the seizure of 10 operational methamphetamine Super Labs, 5 pseudoephedrine extraction labs, 497 gallons of methamphetamine in solution, 140 pound of finished methamphetamine, and assets totaling $1.5 million. Additionally, Operation Gas Mask resulted in the arrest of 48 individuals including Mexican National laboratory operators, chemical brokers, the California based supplier of HCL gas and two suppliers of solvents and reagents.

Eduviko Garcia Organization (Mexican Methamphetamine) Recently, DEA concluded an investigation, which targeted the Eduviko Garcia methamphetamine organization. Garcia received methamphetamine through a Nuevo Laredo, Mexico based facilitator who in turn received methamphetamine from a variety of Mexican based sources. Methamphetamine seized in the Garcia investigation has been tied to Francisco Zarragoza, a methamphetamine source based in Guadalajara, Mexico. The Garcia investigation resulted in enforcement actions in the states of Texas, Indiana, Washington, North Carolina, Oklahoma, Kansas and Kentucky and resulted in the seizure of 53 pounds of methamphetamine, 18 kilograms of cocaine, and the arrest of 50 individuals.

Other Enforcement Operations

Highway interdiction is central to drug enforcement, especially on the U.S./Mexico Border, since a vast number of seizures occur at checkpoint stops within 150 miles of the border in Arizona, California, New Mexico, and Texas. In addition to their drug and money seizures, state, local, and federal agencies generate valuable intelligence on trafficking patterns, concealment methods, and cell membership and structure. Presently, there are drug interdiction programs promoted and monitored by the El Paso Intelligence Center (EPIC), but carried out by state and local law enforcement officials. The operations are carried out along the highways and interstates most often used by trafficking organizations to move illegal drugs north and east, and illicit money south and west.

With DEA support, state and local highway officers are able to execute controlled deliveries of the drug shipments that they seize, thereby expanding the scope of their own investigations. These programs consist of three elements: training, real-time communication, and analytical support. With support from EPIC, training schools in support of these programs are designed and delivered to state and local highway officers across the nation. The training and implementation of these programs are conducted in accordance with the Attorney General's guidelines for Fairness in Law Enforcement, and prohibit the use of race, ethnicity or nationality as the sole basis for initiating law enforcement interdiction of suspected drug traffickers.

High Intensity Drug Trafficking Area (HIDTA) Task Forces

The mission of ONDCP's High Intensity Drug Trafficking Area (HIDTA) program is to reduce drug trafficking activities in the most critical areas of the country, thereby lessening the impact of these areas on other regions of the country. The HIDTA program strengthens America's drug control efforts by intensifying the impact of drug control agencies through the development of partnerships between federal, state, and local drug control agencies in designated regions and by creating effective systems for them to synchronize their efforts.

There are 28 established HIDTA's and 43 Investigative Support Centers (ISC's) with EPIC serving as the "national hub" for the HIDTA ISC's. EPIC has re-organized to implement this mission and has created a new HIDTA Coordination Unit that serves has the focal point for EPIC's relationship with the HIDTA ISC's. DEA recently approved the placement of 14 supervisory Intelligence Analyst positions in selected HIDTA ISC's and has proposed additional Intelligence Analyst positions in the FY 2002 budget to further enhance intelligence support to the HIDTA program.

Since the initiation of the program in 1990, the HIDTA program has expanded to 28 areas around the country, including one HIDTA that is comprised of five partnerships along the U.S./Mexico Border. These HIDTA Southwest Border Partnerships are located in San Diego, Tucson, Las Cruces, W. Texas, and San Antonio, and address important local issues such as methamphetamine trafficking, commercial interdiction, and intelligence collection.

With a strong infusion of DEA intelligence analytical resources, guidance, and expertise, the HIDTA intelligence program has become part of the nationwide effort to develop effective mechanisms for the collection and sharing of intelligence information that can be applied in the enforcement arena.

Intelligence Operations

The intelligence collection process is critical to the interdiction of drugs. Each time we dismantle an organization, DEA gains vital intelligence about the organization to use, both to further additional investigative efforts, and to increase the accuracy of intelligence information provided to the interdiction operations conducted by other law enforcement agencies. The domestic and international aspects of trafficking organizations are inextricably woven together. U.S. law enforcement must be able to successfully attack the command and control functions of these international drug trafficking syndicates on all fronts if ultimate success in diminishing the operational effectiveness of these organizations is to be achieved.

In addition to conducting numerous joint investigations with the United States Customs Service (USCS), DEA is working to optimize the operational efficiency and cost-effectiveness of U.S./Mexico Border operations conducted with other DOJ components, such as the Federal Bureau of Investigation (FBI) and Immigration and Naturalization Service (INS). Public Law 106–553, which was signed by the President on December 12, 2000, states, "DEA is also directed to better coordinate its operations with other Federal Agencies, including INS and FBI, along the U.S./Mexico Border, and to pursue co-location of offices whereas practical."

A Memorandum of Understanding (MOU) has been drafted and is currently pending endorsement by administrative program managers from DEA, FBI, and INS. By adhering to the provisions of this MOU, the enforcement components of the Justice Department will coordinate the review of their respective facility lease terms, and determine compatible opportunities for collocation.

CONCLUSION:

Drug trafficking organizations operating along the U.S./Mexico Border, which are controlled by Mexican based kingpins, continue to be one of the greatest threats to communities across this great nation. As a result of their alliances with Colombian organizations, Mexico based drug trafficking organizations increasingly have become organized, specialized and efficient, with individual components steadily consolidating power and control over well-defined areas of responsibility and geographic strongholds. The power and influence of these organizations is pervasive, and continues to expand to new markets across the United States.

The DEA is deeply committed to intensifying our efforts to identify, target, arrest and incapacitate the leadership of these criminal drug trafficking organizations. The combined investigations of DEA, FBI, the U.S. Customs Service and members of other federal, state, and local police departments continue to result in the seizure of hundreds of tons of drugs, hundreds of millions of dollars in drug proceeds, and the indictments of significant drug traffickers, and the dismantling of the command and control elements of their organizations.

Cooperative investigations will continue to serve to send a strong message to all drug traffickers that the U.S. law enforcement communities will not sit idle as these organizations threaten the welfare of our citizens and the security of our towns and cities.

The principal leaders of major drug trafficking organizations fear the threat of extradition to the United States more than any other law enforcement or judicial tool. Extradition of significant traffickers ensures that those responsible for the command and control of illicit activities, including drug smuggling and money laundering, will be held totally accountable for their actions and serve a prison sentence commensurate with their crimes.

In Mexico, the newly installed Fox Administration has given every indication of their intention to work as equal partners with American drug law enforcement, and we look forward to our future endeavors with optimism. Hopefully, these new endeavors will include the successful extradition of major Mexican based traffickers to the United States.

NOW FOR THE BAD NEWS

So there you have it, the DEA's position on their tremendous successes against the drug smugglers. However, unlike the fisherman, the DEA makes little mention of "the ones that got away." If the DEA is having such tremendous successes against drug smuggling rings and yet the flow of drugs has not shown any signs of lessening, just how much is being smuggled? Based on the reported statistics regarding the tremendous amount of drugs and cash seized, the total amount being smuggled must literally boggle the mind and yet more seems to be getting through than is being interdicted. *Even though this information is more than a year old, nothing has changed!* If our border defenses cannot stop drug smugglers, can we really expect them to stop terrorists from smuggling weapons of mass destruction across the border?

In the next chapter, we will hear from the Department of Immigration about their tremendous efforts to stop illegal aliens.

CHAPTER ELEVEN

A REVOLVING DOOR

The unfortunate fact is that it is practically impossible to ensure that terrorists do not smuggle weapons of mass destruction across the Border with Mexico. Part of the problem is that our Border Agents are trained to expect the expected. We look for those crossing the Rio Grande and trying to loose themselves in El Paso or some of the other border towns. Why? Because it is easy to watch the ways into the cities. The Border Patrol is stretched almost to the breaking point trying to guard a border than simply cannot be guarded.

As you read this information about how the problem is under control, remember that less than fifteen miles south of where I sit and write these words, I could hire a guide to bring me into this country for $200.00. Now this may not sound unnerving to the reader, but these guides make these illegal trips across the border three or four times a week and rarely are they caught. If they are caught, they are just deported.

WHAT DOES THE U.S. CUSTOMS SERVICE HAVE TO SAY?

On the same day that the DEA told Congress what a wonderful job it was doing stopping drug smuggling, the U.S. Customs Service came to blow its horn. Consider the following, if you will:

72–144 DTP
2001
DRUG TRAFFICKING ON THE SOUTHWEST BORDER
HEARING BEFORE THE SUBCOMMITTEE ON CRIME OF THE COMMITTEE ON THE JUDICIARY

HOUSE OF REPRESENTATIVES
ONE HUNDRED SEVENTH CONGRESS
FIRST SESSION
MARCH 29, 2001
Serial No. 3
Available via the World Wide Web: http://www.house.gov/judiciary

COMMITTEE ON THE JUDICIARY
Subcommittee on Crime

STATEMENT OF JOHN C. VARRONE, ASSISTANT COMMISSIONER, OFFICE OF INVESTIGATIONS, UNITED STATES CUSTOMS SERVICE

Mr. VARRONE. Thank you, Mr. Chairman and members of the subcommittee. I thank you for the opportunity to appear on this important issue and to discuss the efforts of the United States Customs Service in combating the drug threat along the Southwest border. Mr. Chairman, with your concurrence, I have a detailed statement that I would like to submit for the record.

Before presenting specifics on the Southwest border, I would like to first give the committee a sense of the overall challenges faced by U.S. Customs. Nationally, on a typical day, Customs personnel process an average of 1.3 million travelers and 410,000 conveyances. As a result, Customs averages 65 arrests, 118 narcotics seizures, 11 currency seizures and 128 other enforcement seizures, ranging from weapons to counterfeit merchandise to child pornography. This translates into the daily seizure of approximately 4,302 pounds of narcotics and $560,000 in U.S. currency.

Notwithstanding Customs' other enforcement responsibilities, drug interdiction and investigation is, without a doubt, our highest priority, and the Southwest border is the front line for this ongoing challenge. The windows of opportunity for would-be drug smugglers along the Southwest border are staggering. Specifically, a total of 293 million people, 89 million automobile and 4.5 million trucks crossed the Southwest border in fiscal year 2000.

To combat this enormous challenge, Customs dedicates approximately 4,000 inspectors, agents, analysts, pilots and marine enforcement officers.

Individual violators as well as complex criminal organizations operating on both sides of the border have been engaged in drug trafficking and drug-related money laundering for many years. Historically, Southwest border drug trafficking organizations principally smuggled marijuana and black tar heroin into the United States. Based upon successful law enforcement operations in the Caribbean and South Florida, Colombian-based cocaine traffickers expanded their drug smuggling operations to utilize the Southwest border.

The interagency cocaine assessment indicates that upwards of 50 percent, as Mr. Marshall said, up to approximately 65 percent of all the cocaine destined for the United States, we believe, enters via the Southwest border. Multi-agency investigative and seizure activity indicates that cocaine is being transferred from Colombian freighters and fishing vessels in the Eastern Pacific to go-fast boats destined for Mexico. This cocaine is ultimately smuggled into the United States via the Southwest border. Customs, along with DEA, FBI, Coast Guard and State and local law enforcement officers have been involved in the seizure of approximately 78 metric tons of cocaine in the Eastern Pacific during the last two fiscal years.

Sophisticated, well-financed and well-organized drug transportation groups are utilizing a wide variety of modes of conveyance and methods of concealment along the Southwest border. Customs records indicate that 79 percent of all Customs narcotics seizures in fiscal year 2000 occurred at the Southwest border. Marijuana seizures are up 12 percent, totaling 1.1 million pounds and accounted for 86 percent of the marijuana seized nationally by Customs. Thirty-five percent of the methamphetamine seized by Customs was identified as being produced in Mexico.

Our Southwest border enforcement efforts focus on the following areas: improved coordination of Federal interdiction efforts; utilization of advanced technology; effective intelligence gathering and multi-agency investigative operations. These collective enforcement operations have proven to be the most effective way to combat the threat.

To address the problem of drug smuggling, Customs has developed an investigative bridge strategy. The strategy involves greater integration of the Customs enforcement disciplines, which would be our investigative, intelligence, interdiction and air-marine operations; electronic surveillance operations; increased development of confidential sources of information; and the placement of additional U.S. Customs agents and intelligence personnel with the Drug Enforcement Administration in Mexico.

In addition, Customs participated in numerous multi-agency initiatives and task forces which complement the strategy, to include the Border Coordination Initiative; the high-intensity drug trafficking area; organized crime drug enforcement task forces; Special Operations Division and, most recently, the bulk cache HIFCA or high-risk money laundering and financial crimes area.

A very recent drug enforcement success which demonstrates both the threat of what our collective law enforcement efforts are challenged by occurred on February 26, 2001, when special agents from Customs and DEA executed a search warrant at a residence in Nogales, Arizona. The search warrant resulted in the discovery of a *tunnel leading to a local drainage system*. This drainage system was accessible from the international border. A search of the residence led to the seizure of approximately 840 pounds of cocaine. I believe we have a chart here, sir, in the room showing that photo right there to my right.

From an outbound currency threat perspective, Mexico remains one of the top 10 countries of concerns for the United States Customs Service. To combat the illicit movement of drug proceeds from Mexico, Customs routinely develops and employs currency interdiction initiatives. For example, last year, Customs developed and implemented two anti-money laundering operations called Power Play and Pressure Point. These initiatives resulted in the seizure of more than $16 million and 286 arrests, demonstrating our commitment to the interdiction of outbound drug proceeds.

To improve our drug interdiction efforts, Customs is aggressively pursuing a variety of technologies designed to complement one another and present a layered defense to smuggling attempts. These include mobile and fixed x-ray and gamma ray inspection systems for use in processing large trucks, cargo containers and rail cars. We currently have 36 of these systems deployed in the field.

Customs also continues to train canine teams at our national training academy to assist enforcement efforts in processing passengers, vehicles and cargo. We currently have 543 canine teams nationally, 366 of which are deployed along the Southwest border. Our aviation assets continue to support Mexican authorities as part of Operation Halcon. In this initiative, Customs air assets and aircrews assist Mexican law enforcement in airborne drug interdiction activities.

On behalf of the men and women of the United States Customs Service who are engaged on a daily basis in the counternarcotics activities along the Southwest border, I thank you and your committee for all your support, Mr. Chairman, and the opportunity to briefly describe our challenges, operations and successes. At the appropriate time, I would be glad to answer any questions, sir.

COLORING INSIDE THE LINES

So from the testimony made before Congress by those responsible for trying to halt the flow of drugs across our southern border, it is very clear that this problem is not solvable, at least for the foreseeable future. The most we seem to be able to do it try and limit the flow of drugs.

This being the case, there is no doubt that this would be relatively easy for a group to smuggle weapons of mass destruction across the border and into this country. These weapons could then be used to cause major destruction in our major cities and the deaths of potentially tens of thousand of innocent American lives.

As was pointed out in the testimony given above, several factors make Mexico an attractive location for drug trafficking: the 2,000-mile land-border with the United States that is comprised of difficult terrain, making it hard to regulate; the powerful criminal organizations that exploit weaknesses in Mexico's law enforcement and judicial systems; and, the rural and mountainous expanses throughout the country that are ideal for the cultivation, processing and manufacturing of illegal drugs or the smuggling of terrorists or weapons into this country.

The organizations that make use of the mules and other methods of transporting their illicit ware are sophisticated, well-financed and well-organized drug transportation groups. They are utilizing a wide variety of modes of conveyance and methods of concealment along the South Western Border. According to this same Congressional testimony, U.S. Customs enforcement records indicate that 79% of all Customs narcotics seizures in FY00 occurred at the southwest border. Marijuana seizures were up 12% to 1.1 million pounds, accounting for 86% of the marijuana seized nationally by Customs. Approximately 14 percent of the heroin seized in the United States comes from Mexico. An independent study indicates that Mexico is the source of 29 percent of the heroin used in the United States today. Thirty-five percent of the methamphetamine seized by Customs was identified as having been produced in Mexico. Mexico-based organizations have become the most significant distributors of methamphetamine in the U.S.

These facts taken as true, then it is equally clear that no matter how much is seized at the Border, it is still only a fraction of what is being shipped into this country. If we cannot keep out the drugs, then how can we keep out the terrorists who simply hike across country carrying their deadly cargo just as they did in the mountains of Afghanistan against the Soviet Military Machine?

Smuggling organizations operating along the southern border are abundant, innovative and resilient. Successful dismantling of these organizations requires a comprehensive strategy, one that interfaces the functions and expertise of all enforcement disciplines. Customs has developed the "Investigative Bridge Strategy" to address this problem. It involves:

The integration of the Customs enforcement disciplines, investigations, intelligence, interdiction and air/marine operations in an effort to exploit the interrelationship of drug transportation and distribution. By building an "Investigative Bridge" between border smuggling activity and criminal organizations located inland, further dismantling of these groups is possible.

The bridge is built when a drug seizure at a Port of Entry (POE) leads to the identification of an organization's inland command and control center and/or additional co-conspirators. Similarly, a bridge is also built when the investigation of an organization develops information leading to a drug interdiction at the border. Through this focus on integration and cohesion, the Investigative Bridge Strategy maximizes enforcement results.

Controlled deliveries and Title III wiretap investigations are an integral part of the strategy. These tools have proven to be extremely effective in identifying members of these organizations, locating narcotic consolidation locations, and uncovering persuasive evidence of criminal activity.

Controlled deliveries and cold convoys require close cooperation between inspectors, agents, and local law enforcement, at the interdiction site, along delivery routes, and at the ultimate destination. Timely notification and response by agents, coupled with a seamless hand-off are necessary elements to ensure success of the operation and a "building of the bridge".

Develop confidential sources of information and intelligence.

The placement of additional U.S. Customs resources in Mexico.

The following enforcement successes demonstrate both the threat and what is being done utilizing our investigative strategy:

On February 26, 2001, special agents from Customs and DEA executed a search warrant at a residence in Nogales, AZ, resulting in the discovery of a tunnel leading to the local drainage system[101]. This drainage system is accessible from the international border. A search of the residence led to the seizure of approximately 840 pounds of cocaine.

On March 5, 2001, Customs Special Agents from the Office of the Resident Agent in Charge, Charlotte, SC, arrested four members of a Mexican smuggling organization and seized approximately 8,125 pounds of marijuana discovered in an Allied Van Lines moving truck. In addition, special agents seized $1,411,568 in U.S currency.

On March 22, 2001, an investigation conducted by the Office of the Resident Agent in Charge, Brownsville, TX, resulted in the seizure of approximately 1,450 pounds of marijuana discovered on a train inbound from Mexico. Eight Mexican males were arrested in connection with this seizure.

Between March 15 and March 17, 2001, the Customs Service, Border Patrol and state/local law enforcement conducted a joint operation targeting smuggling activity at Falcon Lake located near Falcon Heights, TX. The operation culminated in the seizure of approximately 8,783 pounds of marijuana that had been smuggled by vessel from Mexico.

Numerous initiatives and task forces exist which embrace the concept of cooperative efforts to enhance our SWB interdiction and investigative efforts, and Customs actively participates whenever possible. Some specific examples of participation include:

---

[101] More and more of these tunnels are being found, but I have never read about the historical tunnels being found.

The Border Coordination Initiative (BCI) ensures comprehensive sharing of border intelligence and the coordination of enforcement operations between Customs and the Immigration and Naturalization Service (INS).

The High Intensity Drug Trafficking Area (HIDTA) program concentrates Federal, state, and local law enforcement efforts in 28 high-threat areas, such as the Southwest border.

The Organized Crime Drug Enforcement Task Force (OCDETF) focuses combined Federal, state, and local law enforcement efforts on significant, high-level drug trafficking and money laundering organizations.

The Special Operations Division, a multi agency initiative led by the Department of Justice, acts as a Headquarters based case coordination program. This unit, comprised of investigators and analysts from Customs, DEA, FBI, and IRS, has three sections, which concentrate on SWB narcotics and money laundering activities.

In the area of International Money Laundering, Customs has established the Money Laundering Coordination Center. This unit has been established to coordinate all Federal money laundering enforcement efforts, which have been mandated in the Treasury/Justice Money Laundering Strategy.

From an outbound currency threat perspective, Mexico remains one of the top ten countries of concern for the U.S. Customs Service. Intelligence indicates that large amounts of currency, in excess of tens of millions of dollars, continue to be smuggled out of the U.S. to Mexico.

Private vehicles have long been the dominant mode of choice for transporting illicit proceeds into Mexico. Outbound currency seizures (to include negotiable instruments) numbered over five hundred (500) for the years FY99 and FY00 at the southwest border ports of entry in which the majority were discovered within private vehicles. It is believed that Mexican transportation groups are also using other conveyances to move money to include possibly commercial trucks.

THE FUNNEL

Mexico acts as a "funnel" for illicit currency destined for the Colombian trafficking organizations. Intelligence indicates that staging areas have been set up in many SWB locations to facilitate the consolidation and movement of money between the two countries.

To combat the illicit movement of drug proceeds to Mexico, Customs routinely develops and employs currency interdiction initiatives targeting identified currency smuggling trends. For example:

In fiscal year 2000, Customs implemented Operation Powerplay, a six-week initiative that resulted in the seizure of $11,386,875 and 194 arrests. Of these funds, $3,074,456, or 27 percent, was destined for Mexico.

In FY 2001, Customs implemented Operation Pressure Point, a five-week initiative that took place in November and December. This initiative resulted in the seizure of $5,535,498 and 92 arrests. Of these funds, $1,217,810, or 22 percent, was destined for Mexico.

On March 28, 2000, the Departments of Treasury and Justice designated the Texas/Arizona borders with Mexico as a "bulk cash" High Intensity Money Laundering and Related Financial Crime Area (HIFCA). This HIFCA designation focuses not only on the geographic region, but also on the system through which large volumes of currency (mainly derived from drug trafficking) is smuggled or moved across the border between the United States and Mexico.

As part of the Bulk Cash HIFCA, Customs is concentrating its efforts not only on the transborder movement of currency involving Mexico, but also on Mexican money remitters and currency exchange houses, or casa de cambios, facilitating this activity.

On January 12, 2000, the governments of the United States and Mexico entered into a written agreement detailing the procedures to share information on reports of the cross border movement of currency. This agreement allows for the sharing of Reports of International Transportation of Currency and Monetary Instruments filed with the U.S. Customs Service, and Mexico's companion form, Article 9.

Mexico recently changed its reporting regulations to require the reporting of $10,000 U.S. equivalent into or out of Mexico to mirror the United States' currency reporting regulations. Originally, Mexico required only the reporting of $20,000 U.S. equivalent being imported into Mexico.

Customs seized the following quantities of unreported currency bound for Mexico via the SWB:

Fiscal	Year	1998	$14,466,186
Fiscal	Year	1999	$16,542,761

Fiscal   Year   2000 $17,089,183

Some specific examples of enforcement related seizures at the SWB are as follows:

On March 15, 2001, the U.S. Customs San Diego Financial Task Force conducted a joint southbound operation monitoring vehicle traffic exiting the United States at the San Ysidro, CA Port of Entry. During this operation, a vehicle exam resulted in the seizure of $449,905 in US currency.

On July 31, 2000, during U.S. Customs Operation Powerplay, a vehicle occupied by two Guatemalan citizens was detained while attempting to exit the United States into the Republic of Mexico. A search of the vehicle resulted in the identification of a false compartment found to contain $499,640.00 in United States currency. Both individuals were arrested.

Critical to all law enforcement operations is the routine sharing of tactical intelligence. Intelligence Collection and Analysis Teams (ICATs) have been created throughout the country to analyze smuggling trends and concealment methods, and to expeditiously disseminate intelligence to all border ports and Border Patrol checkpoints. The ICATs are comprised of Customs Special Agents, Customs Inspectors, INS agents, INS analysts, the US Border Patrol and the California National Guard.

Analysis by the ICATs and the intelligence community has been successful in identifying a multitude of smuggling and concealment trends. These include:

Current intelligence from all sources continues to point towards a highly diverse and constantly evolving smuggling environment that poses major threats all along the border. These threats continue to suggest strong pressure by major trafficking groups using all forms of transportation and all available means.

Drugs are being smuggling by a wide array of drug transportation groups that are using all major conveyances and concealment methods including cars, trucks, vans, oversize vehicles, rail cars, private aircraft and vessels, and pedestrians. A continuing problem that Customs faces is the use of sophisticated tunnels along the border.

One of the continuing trends is the proliferation of smaller, more tightly knit organizations that smuggle 100–150 kilos at a time in a rapid fashion. These groups are subsequently storing the drugs in warehouses and other locations, in preparation for the movement of large quantities to the interior of the United States for distribution.

Once a sufficient quantity of drugs is acquired, the groups then move the illegal drugs to major urban areas in the interior of the United States for distribution. These areas include Chicago, Los Angeles, Miami, and New York.

Like the criminal drug trafficking groups from the United States and

Colombia that preceded them, organized crime syndicates from Mexico are extremely violent and routinely employ intimidation and the corruption of public officials to achieve their objectives. Much of the drug-related violence that has become commonplace in Mexico has spilled over to communities within the United States.

Traffickers are attempting to design compartments that are impervious to detection. This includes identifying specific conveyances that are difficult for Customs to inspect and pose unique problems from an operational standpoint. Customs also has determined that traffickers along the border are using specific types of trailers called "low boy trailers", which due to their structure are difficult to examine, may pose problems for some x-ray machines, and are not easily searched by canine units. Recently, a meeting was held in El Paso with officials from railroad firms that conduct cross border trade. These firms indicated they are experiencing a large increase in false compartments discovered in railroad cars used in cross border trade.

The development of new and innovative technology has risen to the forefront of Customs' counter drug efforts. Customs is currently on the second year of a Five-Year Technology Acquisition Plan for the Southern Tier and continues to increase the smugglers risk of detection across the Southern Tier from Los Angeles, California, to San Juan, Puerto Rico. Without this across-the-frontier approach, our enforcement efforts in one area will be mitigated by the smugglers' ability to rapidly displace their criminal activity to an area where the threat of detection is lower.

Some of our efforts in the field of non-intrusive technology include:

Aggressively pursuing a variety of technologies designed to complement one another and present a layered defense to smuggling attempts. Such attempts are the direct result of increased funding that began in Fiscal Year 1999.

We are currently employing 36 pieces of Non-Intrusive Inspection (NII) equipment, including:

eight (8) mobile truck x-ray systems

nine (9) fixed-site truck systems

sixteen (16) relocatable Vehicle and Cargo Inspection Systems (VACIS)

two (2) mobile truck VACIS

one rail VACIS. This rail VACIS is the first system of its kind.

We are continuing the development of a higher energy x-ray system to examine sea containers as they arrive on our shores, as well as a system to exam large palletized cargo in the air, sea, and land environments.

Customs officers also have a wide range of hand-held tools at their disposal, including:

284 Portable Contraband Detectors (a.k.a. Busters)

135 Optical Fiber Scopes

67 Laser Range Finders

Without consistent funding to operate and maintain these technologies (large and small), benefits will be short-lived.

To assist our enforcement efforts, Customs continues to train Narcotics Detector Dogs at our national training academy. We currently have 543 K-9 teams operating in the field, 368 of which are assigned to the SWB.

In terms of making our land border operations more efficient at narcotics detection, while facilitating the flow of traffic, we have implemented several new programs. In conjunction with the Immigration and Naturalization Service, Customs has installed 236 license plate readers (LPR).

By automating the entry of the license plate data, the LPRs allow the inspecting officer to spend more time examining and questioning the vehicle and its occupants. LPRs have the capability to count the number of vehicles, identify stolen cars, and identify those that are positive IBIS and National Crime Information Center (NCIC) hits. LPRs will also allow Customs and INS to gather intelligence through data mining in order to enhance both inbound and outbound targeting.

The Customs Air and Marine Interdiction Division (AMID) plays a valuable role in interdiction efforts along the SWB. Customs continues to see short landings of drug-laden aircraft in Northern Mexico. To combat this threat, Customs has positioned Citation aircraft in Hermosillo and Monterrey, Mexico, to assist Mexican ground forces in the apprehension of these aircraft and their crews.

Some of the programs currently administered by AMID are:

The Air and Marine Interdiction Coordination Center (AMICC). AMICC, located in Riverside, California, provides command, control, communications and intelligence for counter-narcotics and designated homeland defense operations. It utilizes a wide variety of civilian and military radar sites, aerostats, airborne reconnaissance aircraft and other detection assets to provide 24-hour, seamless radar surveillance along the entire southern tier of the U.S., Puerto Rico and into the Caribbean.

Training to improve coordination between U.S. and Mexican assets on Interceptor Operations.

AMID currently has two advisors assigned to the U.S. Embassy in Mexico to enhance in-country coordination, communication and safety.

A Mexican liaison has been assigned to the AMICC to further enhance coordination, communication and safety.

The Customs Service relies on the Tethered Aerostat Radar System (TARS), which is currently operated by the Department of Defense, to identify suspect aircraft and vessels inbound to the U.S. The DOD has recently reduced the system by 21% and plans to make another 38% reduction in the system in FY 2002.

The answer to the narcotics smuggling challenge at the SWB border is effective coordination, joint planning and joint implementation. This is precisely what the Border Coordination Initiative (BCI) does and does effectively. The BCI is an approach to integrating the efforts of several of the U.S. Government's border law enforcement agencies. Customs and INS began BCI as a means of creating a seamless process of managing cargo and travelers at our nation's SWB. A process which incorporates the multitude of skills and expertise within each of our organizations, in order to more effectively interdict the flow of narcotics, illegal aliens and other contraband.

The structure of BCI is founded upon the officers at our frontlines. Their input and daily actions have always provided the basic building blocks for this initiative and continue to keep our efforts focused on those challenges presently facing us along the SWB. We have been able to build upon this information by establishing a solid foundation for the program through:

The establishment of an Office of Border Coordination, Co-Managed by a "Border Coordinator" from Customs and INS.

Setting eight (8) priority areas for the field to focus on: Port Management, Investigations, Aviation/Marine Support, Intelligence, Communications, Technology, Integrity and Performance Measurement.

Selecting national Co-Team Leaders from Customs and INS for each of these priority areas and requiring jointly prepared action plans from BCI field managers addressing these topics, Stressing Community involvement by providing and exchanging information with the trade and community groups relating to our enforcement effort.

Addressing the concerns of these groups regarding service and the movement of goods and people.

Eliminating conventional bureaucratic barriers between agencies in terms of equipment and technology sharing, joint enforcement efforts and procurement

Integrating local and state law enforcement entities into the national interdiction effort.

Establishing a scheduled, multi agency reporting system which tracks success, failures and support requests from all SWB areas.

Providing funding in support of the innovative and creative means to apprehend violators of our nation's laws along the SWB.

Providing overall coordination at and between ports of entry to address drug and alien smuggling.

On behalf of the men and women in Federal law enforcement who are engaged on a daily basis in counter-narcotics activities on the SWB, and specifically our U.S. Customs officers, I thank you and your committee for all your support, and the opportunity to present our enforcement activities and recent successes here today.

This concludes my remarks. I will be glad to answer any questions the Committee may have. Thank you.

GIVE US YOUR MONEY AND WE WILL SUCCEED

The upshot of this testimony by the US Customs Service is that "we are doing a great job, but give us more money and we will do a better job. While I agree that more money needs to be spent on security, I question whether this money should be spent on doing the same old things that we have always done. The question is not whether weapons of mass destruction will be smuggled across the border and used in this country, but when. As related earlier, there has been at least one instance where such weapons have already been used here.

But let's look at what the State of Texas has to say.

CHAPTER TWELVE

EVEN THE EYES OF TEXAS
DON'T ALWAYS SEE THE PROBLEMS

Since we are talking about the border with Mexico, I would believe that the views of the law enforcement agencies that police that border for the states would be appropriate. Certainly a large portion of that border with Mexico, over 1,500 miles, is policed by the law enforcement agencies of the State of Texas so it is only natural that the Department of Public Safety of Texas should be heard from[102].

72–144 DTP
2001
DRUG TRAFFICKING ON THE SOUTHWEST BORDER
HEARING BEFORE THE SUBCOMMITTEE ON CRIME OF THE COMMITTEE ON THE JUDICIARY

HOUSE OF REPRESENTATIVES
ONE HUNDRED SEVENTH CONGRESS
FIRST SESSION
MARCH 29, 2001
Serial No. 3
Available via the World Wide Web: http://www.house.gov/judiciary

COMMITTEE ON THE JUDICIARY
Subcommittee on Crime

---

[102] The World Famous Texas Rangers are part of the Department of Public Safety.

STATEMENT OF MICHAEL D. SCOTT, CHIEF, CRIMINAL LAW ENFORCEMENT DIVISION, TEXAS DEPARTMENT OF PUBLIC SAFETY

Mr. SCOTT. Thank you, Mr. Chairman and members. I appreciate very much you holding these hearings today to discuss the problems of drug trafficking along the Southwest border. I realize also that there is a degree of disenchantment spreading throughout this country with the progress or perceived lack thereof with our drug control efforts. However, the drug problems facing this country are problems of morality mixed with socioeconomic and health issues, and I believe we will be fighting those problems for many years to come, but I applaud the committee for holding these hearings and for bringing attention to this problem.

In 1993, a former DEA administrator testified before Congress that in the late seventies, the majority of all cocaine entering this country entered through South Florida. He also testified that there was a great infusion of Federal resources into South Florida to address that problem. The result was to cut off the flow of cocaine through South Florida, but by the mid-1980's, Colombian drug traffickers had countered by developing a Mexican connection, and the flow of cocaine and other illegal drugs into the United States shifted from Florida to Mexico.

Mexican traffickers that were once known only as mules for the powerful Colombian cocaine cartels today are drug lords in their own rights. We have heard a lot of estimates this morning about the flow of cocaine across the border. My estimates are between 50 and 70 percent of cocaine entering this country comes across the Southwest border. More importantly, approximately 55 percent of that cocaine, we believe, enters in South Texas alone.

Sixty-eight percent of the Border Patrol seizures along the Southwest border occur in Texas. It is an important thing, however, to note that the vast majority of the drugs crossing the Southwest border do not stay in the border region. These drugs are shipped across the country to places like Marietta, Georgia; Greensboro, North Carolina and Fort Smith, Arkansas, not to mention many other cities in this country. Suffice it to say that drugs smuggled into this country from Mexico ultimately flows into the streets and schools across the country.

Although many agencies at the Federal, State and local level have increased their resources along the border, I suggest that we have not seen an equivalent infusion of resources that were used to address the problem in South Florida in the seventies. The North American Free Trade Agreement, NAFTA, was passed in 1994 to facilitate open trade between the United States, Canada and Mexico. The approximately 365 million consumers in these North American countries are expected to benefit in many ways economically from NAFTA.

We in Texas share rich cultural, social and economic ties with our neighboring country of Mexico. Many citizens on each side of the border cross over to visit family members, to shop and to attend school. While I believe strongly that the economic benefits produced by the NAFTA concept are good for all three countries involved, it is clear that there have been some serious unintended or overlooked consequences of NAFTA.

The United States and Mexico share a 2,000-mile border. It is the busiest border in the world. In 1999, an estimated 295 million pedestrian, 88 million passenger vehicles and 4 million commercial trucks crossed our border from Mexico, and these numbers are only expected to increase. Texas has a 1,248-mile border with Mexico, and along that border, there are 10 ports of entry; 26 international bridges. In the year 2000, over 48 million passenger vehicles and 3.1 million commercial vehicles crossed our border. That is approximately 75 percent of all commercial traffic entering this country from Mexico crosses in Texas.

U.S. Customs officials estimate that only 5 or 10 percent of the commercial trucks entering this country are subjected to any type of search or inspection. This is a prescription for failure. Mexican drug trafficking organizations have exploited our inability to inspect vehicles and pedestrians entering this country. They have purchased trucking companies and maquiladoras in Mexico in an effort to promulgate their illegal drug industry. It is critically important that with continued implementation of NAFTA, we must not overlook the need to improve methods for our inspection. There must be a balance between free trade and the undesirable consequences of little or no inspection on the trucks.

In spite of these overwhelming numbers, our interdiction efforts continue to outpace our ability to conduct follow-up investigations and to prosecute the violators. Simply interdicting drugs along the border is not the answer. Each interdiction case made by the Customs Service or the Border Patrol must be investigated. Oftentimes, DEA, because of a lack of resources, are forced to simply process the mules apprehended by the Customs agents or Border Patrolmen. Furthermore, the volume of drugs along the Southwest border has had significant impact on our State prosecutors as well as Federal prosecutors and the courts.

Over the past year, State prosecutors along the border have complained that handling smaller drug cases generated by the Federal officers have cost local taxpayers millions of dollars. I am not suggesting that additional funding is the only solution to this problem. However, appropriate levels of funding across the board in the areas of interdiction, investigation, prosecution and the courts is critical for us in the criminal justice system to be able to maintain a holding action.

Drug-related violence along the border has increased significantly over the last several years. In August 1997, four suspected drug traffickers entered a popular restaurant in Ciudad Juarez, just across the border from El Paso. They opened fire, killing five and wounding four others. On their way out of the restaurant, they killed an off-duty Mexican police official who was approaching the restaurant. Although violence among rival drug gangs is commonplace in Mexico, rarely has it spilled over into public places. This gangland style killing at a restaurant in Ciudad Juarez may have ushered in a new era in drug-related crime along the border.

Saul Martinez Gutierrez was a newspaper editor in Matamoras, Mexico, just across from Brownsville. His newspaper often published articles attacking the drug traffickers. Last weekend, his body was found with four bullet holes to the head. His press credentials were thrown on his body. He may be the latest casualty in a drug war that turns the Texas-Mexico border into a violent intersection of supply and demand.

Mr. SCOTT. In closing, I recognize that law enforcement efforts alone cannot solve the problem. However, our collective efforts in supply reduction, combined with successful demand reduction and treatment efforts, can have a positive effect. Anyone who has seen the recent movie Traffic or has watched the Nightline news series last week could easily be discouraged. It is oftentimes that our successes along the border are overshadowed by the enormity of the problem. I can tell you that our officers along the border are totally committed to the problem, and I will close and be happy to answer questions at any time.

FURTHER SUPPORTING EVIDENCE FROM MR. SCOTT

The violence being demonstrated by the Mexican Drug rings make it clear that they have little if any respect for the law. They are totally motivated by money. So what happens if these drug rings are offered substantial sums of money to either poison the drugs they are carrying across the border or they transport weapons of mass destruction into the United States? Either way, they make money and large sums of people die.

Mexican drug trafficking organizations rely on violence and the threat of violence to carry out their trade. Since the summer of 2000, there has been a significant increase in drug-related violence in the contiguous border area with Mexico. Mexican law enforcement officials and the media in Mexico have reported numerous drug-related homicides of drug traffickers and police officials in northern Mexico. The Mexican media also reports that 60% of the drug-related homicides occurred in the region bordering South Texas.

Much of this drug-related violence is now being aimed at US law enforcement personnel. Violent assaults against federal agents along the southwest border have increased from 156 just five years ago to 500 in 1999. In January 2000, US officials learned that leaders of the Carrillo-Fuentes cartel offered a $200,000 bounty to anyone who murdered any US law enforcement official. Border Patrol agents find it increasingly difficult to patrol the US-

Mexico border, especially when we learn of these bounties being offered by the drug cartels. With our knowledge of the high levels of drug-related violence in Mexico, we must always take these threats seriously.

Drugs present the leading crime challenge in the border region but other crimes are also a problem. In 1996, there was an average of 60 violent crimes and 654 property crimes each and every day along the Texas border. In other words, a border resident in Texas became the victim of a violent crime every 24 minutes while a property crime occurred in the border region every 2.2 minutes.

CORRUPTION

Corruption of public officials has been a way of life in Mexico for many decades. Corruption in Mexico extends into almost all walks of life, from driving a taxi to operating a business. Mexican drug organizations, such as the Carrillo-Fuentes, Arellano-Felix, and Caro-Quintero cartels, have built their multi-billion dollar drug trafficking networks after making impressive strides buying up the government of Mexico through the exploitation of corruption. These and other drug organizations alike, have the resources and the motivation to take any measures necessary to facilitate their trade including bribery, corruption, violence, and intimidation. Corruption in Mexico is not always voluntary or motivated by cash payments. It is documented that if a local official refuses to take "mordida" or bribery money, he or his family members are terrorized or murdered by the drug organizations.

Corruption has not stopped at the border. Now, the drug traffickers are looking for US officials who might be for sale and, unfortunately, they are finding them. During 1999 and extending into 2000, an FBI-led public corruption task force in Arizona resulted in the arrest of ten federal officers, three local and county officers, and one local judge on drug-related corruption charges. The increase in public corruption, particularly as it relates to drugs, has and will continue to have a negative impact on the public trust and confidence our citizens have in elected officials—government in general and law enforcement in particular. Whether it is paying off a Customs inspector to pass a vehicle through without an inspection or paying a local sheriff's deputy to help get a load of drugs through the Border Patrol checkpoint, everyone agrees that the problem of corruption in this country is bad and only getting worse.

The FBI has made public corruption one of its top priorities. Just last week, the San Antonio office of the FBI announced the arrest of eight San Antonio police officers and one deputy sheriff all on charges of drug-related corruption. The four-year investigation revealed that the officers accepted cash payments from purported drug traffickers to provide protection for their drug shipments. Some of the officers were on duty, in uniform, when involved in the alleged corrupt conduct. After the arrests were made, San Antonio Police Chief Al Philippus was quoted as saying, "We are sickened and shocked by the inexcusable actions of these officers. They have betrayed the honor of every San Antonio police officer who wears the uniform, every law enforcement officer in this nation, but mostly the community who they swore to serve and protect."

LAW ENFORCEMENT INITIATIVES

In spite of the outcry in recent years that the drug war has been a failure, drug enforcement officers across the southwest border, and particularly along the Texas border, are more committed than ever. While it would be easy to get frustrated and discouraged, I continually observe a total commitment among the officers charged with enforcing the drug laws of this country. It is important to point out that our effort along the border is focused on the interdiction of drugs at the border and on the investigation of major drug smuggling organizations. We do not focus our efforts on the user or abuser of drugs.

The overall success of our national enforcement efforts to combat the availability of illegal drugs in this country depends heavily on the coordination and cooperation of the many law enforcement agencies involved. This coordination and cooperation is enhanced by the willingness to share intelligence and other drug-related information across jurisdictional lines. The High Intensity Drug Trafficking Area (HIDTA) program has helped create an atmosphere in the drug enforcement arena that promotes this coordination and cooperation among law enforcement agencies. It allows agencies at the federal, state, and local level to leverage their resources and maximize intelligence sharing capabilities for the common goal of reducing the flow of drugs into this country. The South Texas HIDTA is a partnership between law enforcement agencies and prosecutors from all levels that serves as a model for other HIDTAs across the country. The multi-agency, multi-jurisdictional initiatives sponsored by the South Texas HIDTA have proven to be extremely successful in our overall drug enforcement effort in South Texas. This success is exemplified by the drug seizure statistics referred to earlier in this report. I am appreciative of the support we continually receive from this committee and from the Congress as a whole for the HIDTA program.

I would also like to express my appreciation to the members of Congress for the continued support of the Southwest Border Anti-Drug Information System (SWBSADIS). With your support, we have built a secure, automated intelligence network across the southwest border that connects the criminal databases in the states of California, Arizona, New Mexico, and Texas, along with the Regional Information Sharing System. Additionally, we are working with the El Paso Intelligence Center (EPIC) to further expand the capabilities of this system. In Texas, access to this system is being made available to drug enforcement agents within DPS, drug task forces, and the HIDTAs.

CLOSING

I recognize that all the law enforcement efforts in the world cannot solve the drug problem in this country. However, our collective efforts across the spectrum of supply reduction combined with successful demand reduction and treatment efforts can have a positive impact on this problem. We may have declared a "war" on an unconventional enemy that we cannot completely defeat. However, we must not listen to the naysayers and the advocates for legalization. We must stay they course. We all recognize and accept the fact that to deal with the problem of drug abuse and the related drug trafficking, we must deal with it on all fronts simultaneously. We should further recognize that the solutions require initiatives from a variety of mutually exclusive sources, including public health and treatment providers, schools, churches, community organizations, the military, as well as law enforcement.

Anyone who has seen the recent movie *Traffic* or who watched the "Nightline" news series last week could be easily convinced that our drug enforcement efforts along the border are failing. It is clear that oftentimes, our success along the border is overshadowed by the enormity of the problem. There is no question that federal, state and local drug enforcement agents along the border often feel overwhelmed and frustrated by the challenges they face trying to reduce the flow of drugs into this country. However, I commit to you today that the officers along the border charged with the interdiction, investigation, and prosecution of drug traffickers have not admitted defeat and continue to risk their lives daily in an effort to reduce the availability of drugs in this country.

REGARDING MR. SCOTT'S STATEMENT

Mr. Scott was quite correct in that the border separating Mexico from the United States is over 2,000 in length. Only a few thousand-law enforcement officers patrol this vast area. How then, can we be sure that terrorists are not leading parades of their followers through the desert to inflict death and destruction the unsuspecting citizens of the United States? Before we answer this question, let us hear from the judiciary in the next chapter.

CHAPTER THIRTEEN

FROM THE BENCH

It is a fact of life that many lawyers hope to become District Attorneys and every district Attorney wants to become a Judge and every Judge has a secret yearn to become a Congressman or a Senator. So it is not surprising that into the testimony regarding the drug smuggling problem came the voice of a Judge.

72–144 DTP
2001
DRUG TRAFFICKING ON THE SOUTHWEST BORDER
HEARING BEFORE THE SUBCOMMITTEE ON CRIME OF THE COMMITTEE ON THE JUDICIARY

HOUSE OF REPRESENTATIVES
ONE HUNDRED SEVENTH CONGRESS
FIRST SESSION
MARCH 29, 2001
Serial No. 3
Available via the World Wide Web: http://www.house.gov/judiciary

COMMITTEE ON THE JUDICIARY
Subcommittee on Crime

STATEMENT OF HON. ROYAL FURGESON, UNITED STATES DISTRICT JUDGE, UNITED STATES DISTRICT COURT FOR THE WESTERN DISTRICT OF TEXAS

Judge FURGESON. Thank you very much, Mr. Chairman and members of the subcommittee. I appreciate so much this invitation to come before you and discuss the challenges facing Federal courts on the Southwest border. I have submitted a written statement and a fact sheet, and I would ask that they be included in the record of these proceedings.

Mr. SMITH. Judge Furgeson, without objection, both your complete statement and the complete statement of the other witnesses today will be made a part of the record.

Judge FURGESON. Thank you so much, Mr. Chairman, and I would be remiss if I didn't bring greetings from our chief judge, Jim Nowlan, to his good friend, Mr. Chairman.

Mr. SMITH. Thanks.

Judge FURGESON. May I begin by asking you to consider 10 facts? Fact number one: since 1993, marijuana seizures on the Southwest border have increased fivefold. Fact number two: since 1993, cocaine seizures on the Southwest border have increased 50 percent. Fact number three: since 1993, alien apprehensions on the Southwest border have increased 35 percent, to a record 1,644,000 illegal entries. Fact number four: since 1993, the number of criminal cases filed in Southwest border courts, the number has increased by 161 percent. Fact number five: since 1993, drug prosecutions in border courts have almost doubled. Fact number six: since 1993, immigration prosecutions in Southwest border courts have increased sevenfold.

Fact number seven: our Federal courts are divided into 94 districts. Of these 94, five are located on the Southwest border. These five now handle 27 percent of all Federal court criminal filings in the nation. The other 73 percent are divided among the remaining 89 districts. Fact number eight: our Southwest border courts are basically beyond capacity to handle our increasing criminal dockets.

As the fact sheet, which is attached to my testimony, illustrates, the average criminal caseload per district judge outside the border courts is just over 75 cases. However, the caseloads of our border courts by district are Southern Texas, 205 as compared to 75; Arizona, 282 as compared to 75; New Mexico, 343 as compared to 75; Western Texas, 442 as compared to 75; and Southern California, almost 500, 492, as compared to 75.

Fact number nine: lack of judgeships on the Southwest border is hampering the successful, really successful, law enforcement efforts of Federal and State agencies involved in the Southwest border initiative. We simply can't handle any more of their cases. Here are two examples of the problem: on the immigration side, in El Paso, while Federal law enforcement officers stopped almost 20,000 illegal aliens last year with false documents, only 664, or about 3.3

percent, were prosecuted, and all across the Southwest border, while 1,644,000 illegal aliens were apprehended, less than 1 percent were prosecuted.

Fact number 10: since 1993, when this explosion of filings began, only one of the five Southwest border districts, Arizona, has received more than one new judgeship. At the end of last year, three, New Mexico, Western Texas and Southern Texas, each received one new judgeship, and thus far, Southern California has received no new judgeships since 1993.

Now, will you please consider these three predictions? Prediction number one: Federal law enforcement efforts along the Southwest border will continue the same or increase. Prediction number two: narcotics seizures and alien apprehensions along the Southwest border, if they do not remain the same or increase, will not diminish significantly; and prediction number three, criminal filings in the Southwest border districts will remain the same or increase. The Congress has done some things to address our problems, and we are deeply appreciative. You have increased our budget; you have helped us with probation and pretrial services officers. We appreciate that very much.

The last piece of the puzzle, we believe, is to give us more judgeships so that we can expand our capacity and therefore be available to handle the larger number of prosecutions that we see mandated by the Federal law enforcement efforts here. There are two bills pending which we believe will do the job that is needed. One is Senate 147, and the other is H.R.272. Those bills, we believe, meet our needs, and we wholeheartedly support them.

We appreciate what Congress has done to support the courts over the years, and we will tell you that we are going to do our part to make sure that the quality of justice expected from our system remains high. We do hope that you are able to respond to this final piece of the puzzle for us. I am deeply grateful for the opportunity to speak to you, and I will be glad to answer your questions when appropriate.

[The prepared statement of Judge Furgeson follows:]

PREPARED STATEMENT OF THE HONORABLE ROYAL FURGESON, UNITED STATES DISTRICT JUDGE, UNITED STATES DISTRICT COURT FOR THE WESTERN DISTRICT OF TEXAS

Mr. Chairman, and Members of the Subcommittee, my name is Royal Furgeson. I am a United States District Judge for the Western District of Texas. I appreciate the opportunity to testify before you today about how drug trafficking on the U.S./Mexico border affects the criminal justice system in the federal judicial districts along the border.

To be frank with you, our criminal justice system along the Southwest Border is at a crossroads. Since 1995, the Southwest Border Initiative, the national strategy designed to crack down on illegal immigration and drug smuggling, has produced record numbers of federal prosecutions along the border. Operating under a congressional mandate and increased funding, the Department of Justice has significantly expanded its presence along the U.S./Mexico border, stationing thousands of additional Border Patrol, INS and DEA agents there since 1994.

As a result of the Southwest Border Initiative, the five district courts that span the border with Mexico, the Southern District of Texas, the Western District of Texas, the District of New Mexico, the District of Arizona, and the Southern District of California (the "Border Courts") have experienced unprecedented, massive increases in their criminal dockets. As the Crisis in the Border Courts Fact Sheet that I have provided to you shows, those five Border Courts now handle 27% of all federal court criminal filings in the United States. The other 73% of federal criminal filings are divided among 89 other district courts. The number of criminal cases filed in the Border Courts has increased by 161%. Drug prosecutions in the Border Courts more than doubled between 1994 and 2000, and immigration prosecutions increased more than seven-fold during that time.

Unfortunately, in contrast to the skyrocketing caseload and massive expansion of prosecutorial resources, judicial resources in the Border Courts have fallen far behind. The average criminal caseload per district judge in the Border Courts is more than quadruple the average for the rest of the nation. We have, in short, reached our limits to how many criminal cases can be prosecuted in the five Border Courts with the current number of authorized federal judgeships. We are desperately out manned and under funded. In fact, insufficient judicial resources already drastically restrict the numbers of cases that could most likely be prosecuted if we had more judges. For example, as I will discuss later in my testimony, last year Immigration and Border Patrol agents encountered 19,531 illegal aliens in the El Paso area. Of this number, 13,929 had some form of false or fraudulent document, and the remaining 5,602 made false claim to United States citizenship. However, only 664 of these illegal aliens were prosecuted. The remaining illegal aliens were returned to their country of origin. While 3.3% of the apprehensions were prosecuted, all could have been. In fact, almost all could have been prosecuted as felonies. Indeed, last year the Border Patrol alone made 1,644,000 apprehensions along the Southwest Border. Yet, less than 1% of those cases were prosecuted. One significant factor retarding our ability to prosecute more of these cases is that we simply do not have enough federal judges in those districts.

My message here today is simple: the Border Courts are beyond their capacity to handle their caseloads. Washington cannot increase the crackdown on illegal drugs and immigration along the Southwest Border without more judges to allow these cases to be prosecuted. I will discuss my specific situation in Texas as well as the general situation along the entire border. I will also discuss alien smuggling as well as narcotics trafficking because both go hand in hand to cause a logjam effect on the Border Courts. Finally, I will end with a recommendation about how to alleviate the problem.

THE SOUTHWEST BORDER INITIATIVE

The United States and Mexico share a 2,000-mile open border. To the concern of both nations, the Southwest Border has become such a crossroads for narcotics trafficking and alien smuggling that the very security of the region is threatened. The Congress and the President recognized the problem in the early Nineties and, in 1994 and 1995, set up the Southwest Border Initiative to deal with it. In 1993, before the Initiative began, 1,213,000 persons were apprehended for illegal entry into the United States, along the entire border from Brownsville, Texas to San Diego, California. During the same year, narcotics seizures on the Southwest Border totaled 512,000 pounds of marijuana and 34,000 pounds of cocaine. Much lesser amounts of heroin and methamphetamine were seized.

To implement the Southwest Border Initiative, the Congress and the President significantly increased federal law enforcement efforts along the border. Between 1994 and 2000, the number of Border Patrol agents almost doubled, the number of INS agents increased by 93%, the number of Customs agents increased by 28% and the number of DEA agents increased by 155%. In addition to these tremendous increases in law enforcement personnel, there have been significant increases in equipment of all kinds, including technology-enhanced equipment, and increases in infrastructure, such as fences, lights and access roads.

The Southwest Border Initiative has resulted in substantial drug seizures and illegal alien apprehensions. Indeed, the numbers are huge. As I have previously stated, in 2000, 1,644,000 persons involved in some violation of our immigration laws were arrested by the Border Patrol alone, a 35% increase over 1993. In 2000 as well, marijuana seizures amounted to 2,478,300 pounds, an increase of almost five times over 1993; cocaine seizures amounted to 49,900 pounds, an increase of almost 50% over 1993; and heroin and methamphetamine seizures also increased, to 520 pounds and 3,060 pounds, respectively.

QUANTIFYING THE RESULTS OF THE SOUTHWEST BORDER INITIATIVE

As impressive as these figures are, we know that the federal law enforcement effort has not shut down narcotics trafficking and illegal alien smuggling on the Southwest Border. There is, of course, no way to quantify how much or little success the effort has achieved. We do know, however, that in the areas where there has been a maximum federal law enforcement presence, local crime rates have dropped considerably. For example, phase one of the Southwest Border Initiative focused on the two areas that had the highest volume of illegal entries: San Diego and El Paso. From 1994 to 1998, local crime in San Diego dropped 60% and local crime in El Paso dropped 19%. The next phase of the Initiative centered in Brownsville and McAllen, which saw local crime decline more than 20%. Thus, while narcotics traffickers and alien smugglers continue to ply their trade on the border, it seems clear that the federal law enforcement effort is making the trade more and more of a risky business. Unfortunately, so long as the demand for drugs and cheap labor in our country remains so high, the risks will apparently be worth it.

It should also be observed that narcotics smugglers are not without their own strategies for minimizing risks. In the Pecos Division of the Western District of Texas, there is a Border Patrol checkpoint on Interstate 10 just west of Sierra Blanca, stopping all eastbound traffic. Every day, ten or more passenger buses come through the Sierra Blanca checkpoint. Routinely, the buses are diverted to a secondary location so that agents can check the citizenship of the passengers. While this is being done, drug-sniffing dogs circle the outside of the buses in an effort to detect drugs in the baggage stored in the luggage bays underneath the buses. The agents inside the bus are also alert for evidence of narcotics smuggling, as they perform their immigration checks.

Before 2000, Border Patrol agents at the Sierra Blanca checkpoint made it a practice of touching and manipulating the passenger carry-on bags in the overhead bins of the buses. After a court challenge to the practice, the United States Supreme Court determined it to be a violation of the Fourth Amendment's proscription against unreasonable searches. See *Bond* v. *United States*, 529 U.S. 334, 120 S.Ct. 1462 (2000). Of course, narcotics traffickers have access to our court decisions. Within months after the decision in *Bond*, the Border Patrol agents at the Sierra Blanca checkpoint noted a steep decline in drug dog alerts to the luggage bays under buses and a substantial increase in the volume of carry-on bags in the overhead bins. It appears that narcotics traffickers adjusted their strategies to reduce their risks of detection by placing their drugs on buses in the one place where law enforcement inspection had been restricted.

The *Bond* case is an example of the challenging Fourth Amendment jurisprudence that has developed on the border. More about this will come later in this testimony. As far as assessing or quantifying the results of the Southwest Border Initiative, however, it is clear that the effort is very much a work in progress. While the numbers indicate that the Initiative has had a major impact on illegal activity on the border, whether the ultimate objective of the entire strategy will be realized remains to be seen.

SEIZURES AND APPREHENSIONS VS. PROSECUTIONS

Every narcotics seizure and illegal alien apprehension on the border by a federal officer does not turn into a federal prosecution. For example, 1.6 million apprehensions of illegal aliens in 2000 does not equate to 1.6 million prosecutions thereafter. The vast majority of persons apprehended are photographed, fingerprinted and taken back across the border and dropped off in Mexico. The practices along the Southwest Border with respect to the decision to prosecute vary considerably. In some areas, if an alien is not a smuggler of aliens or drugs and does not have a criminal history, he is not prosecuted for entering the United States in violation of the immigration laws until he has entered illegally at least four times. In other places, it requires more than ten illegal entries before an alien is prosecuted. As I have stated earlier in my testimony, of the 1.6 million apprehensions along the border last year, less than 1% were prosecuted. There are multiple reasons why: (1) the Department of Justice does not have enough prosecutors to prosecute all who enter illegally, (2) the U. S. Courts do not have enough judges to handle the ensuing cases, and (3) the Bureau of Prisons does not have enough prison space to imprison those convicted. That latter point is not hard to understand when you compare the 1.6 million apprehensions in 2000 with the federal prison population for the entire United States in the preceding year of 130,000. If most of the people who were apprehended were charged, convicted and imprisoned, our federal prison population would increase more than tenfold in just one year.

The illegal entrants who are prosecuted in the federal courts are persons whose entries involve possession of drugs, alien smugglers or persons with criminal histories, many with lengthy and aggravated criminal histories. The illegal entrants who are actually prosecuted are not simply persons who entered looking for work; they are frequently very dangerous people.

The same prosecution disparity holds true with federal narcotics seizures as well. In the past, federal prosecutors on the Southwest Border have coordinated with local state prosecutors to divert low-level seizures (sometimes less than a pound of marijuana) to state courts, where they could be handled more efficiently and expeditiously. With the significant increase in caseload, however, these diverted cases began to overload the border counties that were cooperating in the diversion program. While they wanted to do their share, these counties (which are among the poorest in the nation) simply could not afford to deal with the rising crush of extra cases and the corresponding increases in costs for housing, investigation, prosecution and trial. So that the diversion program could continue, the Congress appropriated funds for these counties so that the cooperation could continue. It is hoped by all that these appropriations can continue. The costs are between $10 million and $15 million each year and, when considered in the context of the overall expenses to prosecute the smaller cases on the federal level, are well worth it.

THE GROWING DOCKET OF CRIMINAL CASES ON THE BORDER

While not all seizures and apprehensions on the Southwest Border have resulted in federal prosecutions, there have been enough to dramatically grow the criminal dockets of the Border Courts. As stated in the Introduction, the Border Courts cover five federal judicial districts: Southern California, Arizona, New Mexico, Western Texas and Southern Texas. Today, these five districts handle 27% of the criminal filings in all federal courts throughout the nation. That means that less than 6% of the federal judicial districts (5 our of 94) handle 27% of all criminal case filings.

This large percentage is attributable to the increase in filings since the beginning of the Southwest Border Initiative. From 1994 to 2000, criminal filings have increased in the Southern District of California by 112%; in the District of Arizona by 193%; in the District of New Mexico by 95%; in the Western District of Texas by 212%; and in the Southern District of Texas by 179%. Because of sheer numbers, the Western District of Texas, the Southern District of California and the Southern District of Texas rank first, second and third in the nation in criminal case filings in the United States.

It is the goal of the federal courts to process all criminal cases in a fair, just and expeditious manner, according to the Constitution and the rule of law. This goal is increasingly difficult to achieve on the Southwest Border, because of the sheer volume of filings. For example, while the national average of weighted filings in the United States per federal judgeship is 479 (including both criminal and civil cases), the weighted filings for Southern California are 978 (more than double the national average); for Arizona, 589 (23% above the national average); for New Mexico, 668 (39% above the national average); for Western Texas, 864 (80% above the national average); and for Southern Texas, 581 (21% above the national average).

Local examples are instructive, too. When I took over the docket of the Pecos Division in 1995, 45 criminal cases were filed. Last year, in 2000, 447 criminal cases were filed, a tenfold increase, without a corresponding increase in any judgeships. It is also revealing to examine the number of trials border judges try as compared with those tried elsewhere. For the fiscal year ending September 30, 2000, for example, the federal judges of the Southern District of California completed 55 trials per judge, compared with 11 trials per judge in the Central District of California, 15 in the Eastern District and 13 in the Northern District.

Numbers alone are not adequate to tell the tale. As the case of *Bond* v. *United States* illustrates, Fourth Amendment issues abound on the Southwest Border. Questions constantly arise about the limits of search and seizure law and answers are not self-evident. The matter is even more complicated because the statutes defining the authority of the Border Patrol do not reflect the growing responsibility of the Border Patrol for federal drug law enforcement. For instance, in *United States* v. *Martinez-Fuerte*, 428 U.S. 543 (1976), the Supreme Court upheld the constitutionality of the brief seizure of travelers at permanent immigration checkpoints by Border Patrol agents for the purpose of making brief immigration inquiries.

Though not a deciding issue in the case, the Court noted that the authority for the Border Patrol to establish such checkpoints and to make such inquiries of travelers was expressly authorized by Title 8 of the United States Code, section 1357(a). Subsection (a) states that:

"Any officer or employee of the [Border Patrol] Service authorized under regulation prescribed by the Attorney General shall have power without warrant—

(1) to interrogate any alien or person believed to be an alien as to his right to be or to remain in the United States;

(3) within a reasonable distance from any external boundary of the United States, to board and search for aliens . . . any railway, car, aircraft, conveyance, or vehicle . . . for the purpose of patrolling the border to prevent the illegal entry of aliens into the United States.

Most would assume that the Border Patrol is charged with the detection of narcotic smuggling in the same manner that it is charged with the interception of illegal aliens. Indeed, the smuggling of illegal aliens and illegal narcotics are the two problems inherent in law enforcement challenges on the Southwest Border. However, the authority for Border Patrol agents to take actions to enforce narcotics laws is derived largely from their cross-designation by the Attorney General, not by any express provision of the United States Code. This difference in the creation of authority raises legal questions as to whether Border Patrol agents enjoy the same scope of powers to enforce narcotics laws as to enforce immigration laws. Accordingly, what actions the Border Patrol may take within their authority to enforce federal drug laws is somewhat ambiguous. Because of the statutory void, the actions of the Border Patrol in connection with narcotics seizures raise recurring questions for Border Courts assessing Fourth Amendment issues. None of these difficult legal problems confront courts outside the border.

A NOTE OF THANKS

Before I share the recommendation of the federal judiciary about how we think this problem of escalating dockets can be addressed, I first wish to thank the Congress for what you have already done for the Border Courts. Last year, we came to you and expressed our concerns about the stress being experienced by our courts on the Southwest Border. We asked for an increase in the Judiciary's budget to fund the needs of the Border Courts for more probation officers, pretrial services officers and clerks. You responded with help. We asked for adequate compensation for court-appointed counsel on the border. You responded with help. We asked for more Deputy Marshals on the border. You responded with help. We asked for support for local border prosecutors to take the overflow of cases from federal prosecutors. You responded with help. We asked for the new construction of needed courthouses on the border. While this is a long-term item, you were responsive. Finally, we asked for new judgeships along the border. While you were unable to provide all the help we asked for, you did add one judgeship each to the District of Arizona, the District of New Mexico, the Western District of Texas and the Southern District of Texas.

THE MORALE OF THE STORY

At its best, Congressional testimony is dry and boring and I know that I have presented many pages of this testimony for the reader to absorb. However, I must submit that there is a very valid reason for submitting this material in this form. It makes it very clear that the drug problem is totally out of control in spite of all of the money and manpower thrown at the problem. It also makes it abundantly clear that the southern border of this country cannot effectively be policed and that smugglers cross it at will.

This being the case, I would suggest that this material be re-read and the words weapons of mass destruction be substituted every place that drug smuggling is mentioned for the problems are one and the same. If terrorists should decide to smuggler either warriors or weapons into this country, they could do it with a very good chance of succeeding it they brought them in through Mexico. There is no doubt that those living along the border are in danger of being the victims of terrorist attacks. Perhaps living along the Canadian Border would be a solution? Or would it?

PART III

THE NORTHER BORDER

It seems fairly clear that there are severe problems policing our 2,000-mile long border with Mexico. Every day drugs move into the United States and being the long journey to the streets of our cities. I would have to ask if we can't stop the drugs, how could we stop the terrorists.

Along our Northern Border, the problem is even worse. The population in the northern part of our country is greater than along the Southern Border. Therefore, it is easier for the illegal border-crossing terrorist to blend into the population. It is also easier to cross into the United States from Canada, so many would be illegal immigrants fly to Canada in order to get into the United States. This ease of crossing is an open door for any terrorist with an itch to kill Americans.

If the reader does not believe me, then read on for more Congressional testimony about problems along our Northern Border and don't say that I didn't warn you!

CHAPTER FOURTEEN

THE NORTHERN BORDER: THE CONGRESSIONAL VIEW

When agencies talk about drug smuggling and illegal immigrants, most readers assume that it is the border with Mexico being discussed. However, this is not always the case. The problems along the northern border are as bad if not worse than the southern border. Congress is also aware of the problems along out border with Canada so in the same series of hearings where the problems along the Mexican Border were discussed, the problems with the Canadian Border were also discussed. To fully understand the dangers facing us form the threats of terrorism, we need to fully understand the existing problems with border security.

63–123

2000
LAW ENFORCEMENT PROBLEMS AT THE BORDER BETWEEN THE UNITED STATES AND CANADA: DRUG SMUGGLING, ILLEGAL IMMIGRATION AND TERRORISM

HEARING BEFORE THE SUBCOMMITTEE ON IMMIGRATION AND CLAIMS OF THE COMMITTEE ON THE JUDICIARY

HOUSE OF REPRESENTATIVES
ONE HUNDRED SIXTH CONGRESS
FIRST SESSION
APRIL 14, 1999
Serial No. 17

Smith, Hon. Lamar, a Representative in Congress from the State of Texas, and chairman, Subcommittee on Immigration and Claims

WITNESSES

Brandland, Dale, Sheriff, Whatcom County, Washington State

Bromwich, Michael, Inspector General, U.S. Department of Justice

Davis, Eugene, Deputy Chief, United States Border Patrol, Blaine, WA

Hall, Mark, President, National Border Patrol Council Local 2599, Detroit, MI

Harris, David, President, Insignis Strategic Research, Ottawa, Ontario

Papademetriou, Demetrios G., Senior Associate, International Migration Policy Program, Carnegie Endowment for International Peace

Pearson, Michael A., Executive Associate Commissioner, Field Operations, INS Headquarters

Trotter, Robert, Assistant Commissioner, United States Customs Service

LAW ENFORCEMENT PROBLEMS AT THE BORDER BETWEEN THE UNITED STATES AND CANADA: DRUG SMUGGLING, ILLEGAL IMMIGRATION AND TERRORISM

OPENING STATEMENT OF CHAIRMAN SMITH

Mr. SMITH. The Subcommittee on Immigration and Claims will come to order.

I have an opening statement; I know the Ranking Member has an opening statement as well; and then we will proceed to our first panel as quickly as possible.

This subcommittee has never held a hearing specifically addressing the northern border. In recent years, there have been an increasing number of reports highlighting the lack of Federal resources on the northern border and the resulting threat to U.S. national security and community safety. Three threats need to be addressed: drug smuggling, illegal immigration and terrorism. All these threats are exacerbated by the lack of resources on the northern border. In fact, the Border Patrol currently has only 289 agents along the 3,500-mile northern border. It is obvious that if we do not know who comes into our country, we do not know what comes into our country, like illegal drugs. A porous border is an open invitation for illegal drug smugglers and for terrorists and their goal of mass destruction.

Drug smuggling at the northern border is a significant concern. Numerous articles have documented the alarming rise in the smuggling of a type of highly potent marijuana grown indoors in British Columbia. This marijuana is five times as potent as regular marijuana and is more likely to increase drug addiction.

A 1998 report from the National Drug Intelligence Center "warned that marijuana exports from Canada to the U.S. are becoming a significant problem." Also disturbing to Americans and Canadians alike is that U.S.-Canada drug enforcement officials have reported that drug smugglers in the U.S. are exchanging British Columbia marijuana pound for pound for cocaine, which "has begun fueling a fledgling crack-cocaine trade north of the border."

U.S. officials believe that the vast majority of drug smugglers make their way into the United States without detection. "If we are getting one to 2 percent at the border, we are being lucky," said Tom Kelly, who worked as resident agent in charge of the U.S. Drug Enforcement Agency of Blaine, Washington until earlier this month. Gene Kerven, Port Director for U.S. Customs, puts it at less than 5 percent.

There have been reports of drug smuggling at other points along the northern border as well. On June 8, 1998, for example, United Press International reported that a joint investigation between U.S. and Canadian law enforcement officials culminated in the arrest of 18 individuals, 14 Canadians and 4 Americans, in the seizure of $3.7 million worth of drugs.

What about illegal immigration? In fiscal year 1998, fewer than 300 agents apprehended 12,146 aliens attempting illegal entry. The question is, of course, how many did they miss? So few agents cannot monitor a border thousands of miles long, 24 hours every day. The Border Patrol knows that the drug and alien smugglers monitor the Border Patrol's shifts and simply wait until agents go off duty.

The crackdown on illegal drugs and immigration along our southern border has caused more illegal aliens to enter the U.S. from the north. A former Acting Associate Commissioner for Enforcement stated, "As southwest border enforcement continues to stiffen and the price charged for smuggling escalates, many choose the alternative of illegally entering the U.S. from Canada." Drug and illegal alien smugglers and terrorists are, of course, going to enter at the least secure point of entry.

It may surprise many people to learn that Mexican nationals can enter Canada without visas, so it is often cheaper for them to fly to Canada and walk across the northern border than to have smugglers bring them across the southern border.

The number of Asian nationals being smuggled into the U.S. also is increasing. Regarding third country nationals, Canadians themselves make up the fourth largest group of illegal aliens in the U.S.

One of the most dangerous threats to our national security is the risk of a terrorist crossing our northern border undetected. This happened in 1997 when Gazi Ibrahim Abu Mezer crossed the northern border and attempted to blow up the New York subway system. In this case, the terrorist was caught before the crime was carried out. Next time, we may not be so fortunate. Since 1995, there have been at least 13 other cases of terrorists crossing the border from Canada, two in Blaine, Washington alone.

In 1998, the Director of the Canadian Security Intelligence Service acknowledged the presence of 50 terrorist organizations in Canada and outlined their activities: fundraising in aid of terrorism, smuggling, providing logistical support for terrorist acts and providing transit to and from the United States, "one of the world's pre-eminent terrorist targets."

Drug smugglers, terrorists and illegal aliens travel both ways across the border. Canadians as well as Americans will benefit from better border security. The United States and Canada already have engaged in cooperative efforts to combat illegal alien smuggling and to share intelligence information regarding drug smugglers and terrorists.

Both countries have much to gain by supporting joint and individual efforts to reduce the threats to both Americans and Canadians.

[The prepared statement of Chairman Smith follows:]

PREPARED STATEMENT OF HON. LAMAR SMITH, A REPRESENTATIVE IN CONGRESS FROM THE STATE OF TEXAS, AND CHAIRMAN, SUBCOMMITTEE ON IMMIGRATION AND CLAIMS

This Subcommittee has never held a hearing specifically addressing the Northern Border. In recent years, there have been an increasing number of reports highlighting the lack of federal resources on the Northern Border and the resulting threat to U.S. national security and community safety.

Three threats need to be addressed—drug smuggling, illegal immigration, and terrorism. All these threats are exacerbated by the lack of resources on the Northern Border. The Border Patrol currently has only 289 agents along the 3,500-mile Northern Border.

It's obvious that if we don't know who comes into our country, we don't know what comes into our country, like illegal drugs. A porous border is open invitation for illegal drug smugglers and for terrorists and their goal of mass destruction.

Drug smuggling at the Northern Border is a significant concern. Numerous articles have documented the alarming rise in the smuggling of a type of highly potent marijuana, grown indoors in British Columbia. This marijuana is five times as potent as regular marijuana and is more likely to increase drug addiction.

A 1998 report from the National Drug Intelligence Center "warned that marijuana exports from Canada to the U.S. are becoming 'a significant problem.' " Also disturbing to Americans and Canadians is that U.S.-Canada drug enforcement officials have reported that drug smugglers in the U.S. are exchanging British Columbia marijuana pound-for-pound for cocaine, which "has begun fueling a fledgling crack cocaine trade north of the border."

U.S. officials believe that the vast majority of drug smugglers make their way into the United States without detection:
If we're getting 1 to 2 percent at the border, we're being lucky,' said Tom Kelly, who worked as resident agent in charge of the U.S. Drug Enforcement Agency at Blaine (Washington) until earlier this month. Gene Kerven, port director for U.S. Customs, puts it at less than 5 percent.

There have been reports of drug smuggling at other points along the Northern Border as well. On June 8, 1998, United Press International reported that a joint investigation between U.S. and Canadian law enforcement officials culminated in the arrest of 18 individuals (14 Canadians and 4 Americans) and the seizure of $ 3.7 million worth of drugs.

What about illegal immigration? In Fiscal Year 1998, less than 300 agents apprehended 12,146 aliens attempting illegal entry. The question is, how many did they miss?

So few agents cannot monitor a border thousands of miles long 24 hours every day. The Border Patrol knows that the drug and alien smugglers monitor their shifts and simply wait until they go off duty.

The crackdown on illegal drugs and immigration along our Southern Border has caused illegal aliens to enter from the North. A former Acting Associate Commissioner for Enforcement stated that "as Southwest border enforcement continues to stiffen and the price charged for smuggling escalates, many chose the alternative of illegally entering the U.S. from Canada." Drug and illegal alien smugglers and terrorists are going to enter at the least secure point of entry.

It may surprise many people to learn that Mexican nationals can enter Canada without visas. So it is cheaper for them to fly to Canada and walk across the Northern Border than to have smugglers bring them across the Southern Border.

The number of Asian nationals being smuggled into the U.S. also is increasing. Regarding third country nationals, Canadians themselves make up the fourth largest group of illegal aliens in the U.S.

One of the most dangerous threats to our national security is the risk of a terrorist crossing our Northern Border undetected. This happened in 1997 when

Gazi Ibrahim Abu Mezer crossed the Northern Border and attempted to blow up the New York subway system.

In this case, the terrorist was caught before the crime was carried out. Next time, we may not be so fortunate. Since 1995, there have been at least thirteen other cases of terrorists crossing the border from Canada, two in Blaine, Washington, alone.

In 1998, the Director of the Canadian Security Intelligence Service (CSIS) acknowledged the presence of 50 terrorist organizations in Canada and outlined their activities: fundraising in aid of terrorism; smuggling; providing logistical support for terrorist acts and providing transit to and from the United States, "one of the world's pre-eminent terrorist targets."

Drug smugglers, terrorists and illegal aliens travel both ways across the border. Canadians as well as Americans will benefit from better border security. The United States and Canada already have engaged in cooperative efforts to combat alien smuggling and to share intelligence information regarding drug smugglers and terrorists.

Both countries have much to gain by supporting joint and individual efforts to reduce the threats to both Americans and Canadians.

Mr. SMITH. The gentlewoman from Texas is recognized for her statement.

Ms. JACKSON LEE. Thank you very much, Mr. Chairman, and good morning.

I am delighted that you are holding this hearing this morning regarding issues along the northern border between the United States and Canada.

Beginning in 1994, the North American Free Trade Agreement opened the Mexican market to Canada and the United States. Two-way trade in goods, services and income between Canada and the United States totaled $390 billion in 1997, the largest bilateral exchange in the world. In my home State of Texas, because of NAFTA, there has been an increase in trade. Texas and Canada have a balanced and mutually beneficial exchange.

According to the Drug Enforcement Agency, however, in 1997, Canada continued to serve as a destination and a transshipment point for drugs, particularly marijuana, cocaine and heroin. The Canadian Government estimates the worth of Canada's illicit drug market at $10 billion as compared with the U.S. National Drug Intelligence Center's estimate of $57 billion in the U.S. market. However, only 300 U.S. Border Patrol agents are stationed on the northern border whereas 7,000 agents are stationed on the southwest border.

According to recent reports in the Associated Press in the Seattle Times, drug arrests along the U.S.-Canadian border has jumped 400 percent since October 1998, with more than 355 pounds of narcotics with a street value of $5.4 million. According to recent Border Patrol statistics, Border Patrol agents at the

Spokane, Washington sector confiscated 2,850 pounds of narcotics between September 1997 and September 1998.

There is a problem along the northern border, Mr. Chairman. However, I would like to suggest that there is a great desire on behalf of Canada and its officials to work with us to help stem this problem. I believe more cooperation and collaboration can see us be more successful. Canadians, as our southern border friends, are our friends and they too want to have strong law enforcement.

Let us review for a moment Section 110 as proposed in prior legislation. The question is, how do we deal with and solve this problem. Is the solution Section 110 of the Illegal Immigration and Immigrant Responsibility Act of 1996? Section 110 requires an automated entry and exit system at all airports, seaports and land border crossings to record departures and arrivals of every alien entering and exiting the United States. Under Section 110(a), this system must record every alien departing from the United States and match with the record of the alien arriving to the United States. If an admitted alien remains in the U.S. beyond the period authorized, the Attorney General will be able to identify the alien with an on-line computer procedure.

However, I have some concerns with this proposed procedure. One, the implementation of an exit-entry removal system at the border would not indicate where non-immigrant overstays are to be found and would therefore not lead to any apprehension or removals.

Second, it would provide or produce a databank of non-immigrant overstays of which no action can be taken with this information. The implementation of Section 110 would also possibly increase traffic, discourage tourism and trade and increase costs of the Border Patrol.

Third, by duplicating the process for returning traffic from Canada, the process would cause extreme delays and congestion. The massive congestion problems will discourage Canadians from coming to the U.S. border communities.

However, will the implementation of Section 110 deter or stop drug trafficking or even identify drug smugglers? There are many who say that it would not. I would hope we would want to collaborate on what might be most effective. Section 110 would be of no use for this purpose because the proposed entry controls would not add any screening value in terms of either enhancing the quality or quantity of the intelligence available or applying it through lookouts at visa offices and border crossings. The proposed exit controls would obviously be of no use in this respect either.

Section 110 would be especially difficult to enforce with respect to drugs, the vast majority of which are smuggled into the United States as part of commercial freight shipments, not by individual traders. I think the best resolution to this would be a strong and definitive feasibility study as to how this might work or assist us.

There is also the issue of terrorism. As a member of the Subcommittee on Crime, international terrorism is something that I have been working on for quite some time. We have had to deal with the bombings of the World Trade Center and let us not forget one of the most devastating and heinous acts of terrorism in American history, which was perpetrated by Americans, the bombing of the Federal building in Oklahoma City.

All Members of Congress and all Americans want to stamp out terrorism and the people who commit these heinous acts, whether it is domestic or international. However, will the implementation of a provision such as Section 110 stop or even identify these terrorists? Again, many have said not. Experts from the Americans for Better Borders, the American Immigration Lawyers Association say that it would be difficult.

Much publicity has been given to the case of Mr. Gazi Mezer who was arrested in Brooklyn in August 1997 after the police were informed that he and a friend were planning a bomb attack on the New York subway. Mr. Mezer had been apprehended three times while attempting to smuggle himself into the United States from Canada. He was never detained or prosecuted as a terrorist prior to his arrest because there was no intelligence in either country suggesting that he was one.

The most effective way to prevent the admission of terrorists is t develop the ability to identify them and deny them access ideally at the visa post and as a last resort, at the point of entry. Section 110 would be of little use for this purpose because the proposed entry controls would not add any screening value in terms of either enhancing the quality or quantity of intelligence available or applying it through lookout visa offices or Border Patrol points.

In order for terrorists to be identified at the border, the INS or U.S. Customs must have the intelligence about these people. The implementation of a procedure as a screening procedure is not enough. Section 110 is designed to track visa overstays; it will not do anything to prevent drug smugglers and terrorists from entering the United States.

If an entry and exit system is implemented, I do want to ensure fairness in the process. If, in fact, controls are put in place at the southwest border, then those same controls should be put in place at the northern border. While both Mexico and Canada are different and have different problems facing their borders, both countries have benefited from NAFTA and both have the same kinds of problems.

In conclusion, Mr. Chairman, let me suggest that a screening strategy that does not track or identify smugglers or terrorists is not enough. However, the best enforcement strategy should be a regional one that will ultimately focus key screening efforts of the two countries' external borders through the use of joint intelligence and homogenized or harmonized lookouts.

The Lookout Program is a State Department program that targets a suspected terrorist by computer. If each of the law enforcement agencies work together, the DEA, the U.S. Customs Service, the INS, the Department of Justice, and the Royal Canadian Mounted Police, this will be an effective way of increasing public safety as opposed to spending billions of dollars on what might be the cost of the infrastructure.

However, Mr. Chairman, I think this is an excellent hearing. I thank you so very much for having the hearing and I look forward to listening to the panelists on the issues and problems of the northern border.

CHAPTER FIFTEEN

THE NORTHERN BORDER: THE INS VIEW

STATEMENT OF MICHAEL A. PEARSON, EXECUTIVE ASSOCIATE COMMISSIONER, FIELD OPERATIONS, INS HEADQUARTERS

Mr. PEARSON. Thank you.

Mr. Chairman, Congresswoman Jackson Lee and members of the subcommittee, I am very pleased to have the opportunity to talk with you today about the Immigration and Naturalization Service's role in enforcing our Nation's immigration laws along the northern border. I am pleased to be joined this morning by my colleague, Deputy Chief Patrol Agent, Gene Davis, from Blaine, Washington.

I want to assure you that while our work and resources on the southern border tend to get more attention, INS is just as committed to strengthen control along our border with Canada.

Our border with Canada is the longest, non-militarized border in the world, nearly 4,000 miles excluding Alaska. This is a testament to the longstanding, friendly relationship between our countries, but it does not mean that this frontier is unmonitored or uncontrolled. INS maintains 114 Ports-Of-Entry, 8 Border Patrol sectors and 44 patrol stations along the border. This year, we are adding 22 new Border Patrol agents to the northern border, an increase of nearly 8 percent.

INS personnel on the northern border are responsible for approximately 27 percent of our inspections and 1 percent of our Border Patrol apprehensions. Nothing multiplies the effectiveness of personnel and equipment more than teamwork. Our longstanding tradition of cooperation and coordination which is critical to our success on the northern border with our Canadian counterparts is formalized in the United States-Canada Accord on our shared border. This 1995 joint agreement seeks to address common enforcement concerns, including the smuggling of people and contraband, the abuse of asylum processes, and the pooling of resources.

Technology at Ports-Of-Entry allows us to facilitate the flow of legal traffic, while strengthening our enforcement capabilities. Two examples are the dedicated commuter lanes where we expedite precleared, low-risk passengers and remote video inspection systems, which provide inspections around-the-clock in remote, low volume ports. We are further enhancing enforcement with the deployment of other technology to the Border Patrol including night vision goggles, infrared scopes and ground sensors. In addition, integrated surveillance intelligence systems, which use high-tech cameras, are currently planned for installation in Blaine and Buffalo.

Successful deployment of state-of-the-art technology is not the only thing we have achieved by working closely with our Canadian counterparts. The partnerships we have forged with Citizenship and Immigration Canada, the Royal Canadian Mounted Police and other agencies have produced impressive results in the investigation of alien smuggling operations, a prime example of which is Operation over the Rainbow II.

This yearlong, multi-agency investigation directed by our Buffalo District crippled a syndicate that had smuggled as many as 150 Chinese nationals monthly into the United States over the past 2 years, charging a fee of $47,000 per person. To deliver their human cargo to the United States, the organizers attempted to take advantage of the complex law enforcement situation on Native American territory that straddles the northern border. Both the Royal Canadian Mounted Police and the Toronto Police dedicated considerable resources to this investigation.

Illegal immigrants often exploit the fact that Canada, like the United States, has a long and cherished tradition of embracing immigrants, especially those fleeing conflict or political repression. Some enter Canada using fraudulent documents, claim to be refugees and are released by Canadian authorities pending a hearing freeing them to attempt entry to the United States.

A few of those who seek to exploit the relative openness of U.S. and Canadian societies are terrorists. Last fall, the director of the Canadian Intelligence Service told his senate that CAIS was investigating 50 terrorist organizations that had established infrastructures in his country.

Let me assure you that INS personnel nationwide are vigilant to the potential of terrorist entry into the United States. INS inspectors at Ports-Of-Entry and Border Patrol agents who monitor areas between ports have access to a variety of databases, including TIPOFF a repository of classified information on suspected terrorists collected by Federal intelligence and law enforcement agencies.

In urban areas along the border, such as Detroit, our special agents participate in FBI joint led terrorism task forces, which proactively investigate and detect aliens suspected of involvement with or support terrorist activities.

As you can see, the situation along the northern border presents unique challenges and because of our close relationships with Canada, unique advantages and opportunities. Through increasingly cooperative efforts, the United States and Canada are seizing these opportunities to strengthen control of our shared frontier, but clearly there is more to be done.

In closing, I would like to emphasize that inherent in our strategy is the flexibility to respond to emerging conditions and changing tactics. As we have demonstrated in the past, INS is prepared to shift the deployment of new and existing resources to meet any threat anywhere.

I look forward to working with the subcommittee to ensure that INS can continue to meet today's demands and tomorrow's challenges.

Thank you, Mr. Chairman. I would be happy to answer questions that you and the members of the subcommittee may have.

[The prepared statement of Mr. Pearson follows:]

PREPARED STATEMENT OF MICHAEL A. PEARSON, EXECUTIVE ASSOCIATE COMMISSIONER, FIELD OPERATIONS, INS HEADQUARTERS

Mr. Chairman, Congresswoman Jackson-Lee, and Members of the Subcommittee, I am pleased to have the opportunity to talk to you today about the Immigration and Naturalization Service's (INS) role in enforcement of our immigration laws at the Northern Border of the United States that we share with Canada. I am also pleased that my colleagues, Mr. Gene Davis, Deputy Chief Patrol Agent, Blaine, Washington, and Mr. Thomas Leupp, Chief Patrol Agent, Swanton, Vermont, are here with us today.

Our border with Canada is the longest non-militarized border in the world. This is a testament to the longstanding, friendly relationship that exists with our northern neighbor. This border, however, is not unmonitored or uncontrolled. The INS maintains 114 Ports-of-Entry (POEs), 8 Border Patrol Sectors and 44 Patrol stations along the 3,987 miles of border with Canada (excluding Alaska).

Before I cover our border enforcement strategy, I want to discuss four important, related issues. The first is the importance of our close cooperation with Canada. Second, is the means by which we utilize the latest improvements in technology to control illegal immigration on the Northern Border. The third subject is our anti-smuggling effort as it relates to both alien and drug smuggling. And lastly, I will discuss the serious topic of terrorism and the use of Canada as a staging area for terrorists seeking entry to the United States.

COOPERATION

The joint United States/Canada Accord on Our Shared Border, announced February 24, 1995, committed the United States and Canada to a number of commercial goals. The Accord also addressed common enforcement issues, including:

- Combating the misuse of asylum applications;

- Enhancing border protection with more effective inspection efforts which target drugs, smugglers and the illegal movement of people; and

- Continuing our commitment to pool our inspection and enforcement resources.

Since 1995, the two countries have worked as partners to implement a number of Accord initiatives. A steering committee, made up of representatives from the various government departments involved, is guiding this implementation. Together, the United States and Canada are sharing technology that will detect movement of illegal persons and contraband. Together, the United States and Canada are working toward the long-term goal of preserving and further developing the unique nature of this shared border, while jointly addressing concerns about illegal migration to North America.

The Royal Canadian Mounted Police (RCMP) actively assists in investigations of alien smuggling organizations. One unique indicator of the good working relationship between the United States and Canada is that in Canada it is a crime to conspire to break U.S. laws. This Canadian law gives the RCMP the legal leverage necessary to act against organizations planning to commit crimes in the United States. The RCMP has devoted considerable personnel and money to assist U.S. law enforcement efforts. As an example, for Operation Over the Rainbow II, the RCMP and the Toronto Police dedicated approximately 15 officers on a full-time basis for six months.

Operation Over the Rainbow II, coordinated out of the INS Buffalo District Office, involved alien smuggling activities through the St. Regis Mohawk Territory at Akwasasne, located near Massena, NY. Alien smugglers, using Native American guides, smuggled Chinese aliens. With the assistance of the RCMP, a total of 46 individuals were indicted. Currently, 36 defendants in the United States are in custody. Three of the defendants have accepted plea agreements. The remaining ten defendants were indicted in Canada. The case highlights how shared intelligence and close coordination between the two countries, in both undercover operations and in the execution of the various arrest warrants, is essential to the dismantling of an organization that straddles an international border.

TECHNOLOGY

The United States and Canada are able to detect and refuse admission to criminals through shared data contained in systems that are quickly accessed in coordination with border operations. This technology is a small part of the advanced systems being utilized on the Northern Border.

Other technology advances utilized along the Northern Border have assisted INS in expediting low-risk, high volume traffic through our Ports-of-Entry (POEs), while maintaining effective enforcement. These inspections enhancements allow the Service to concentrate our enforcement personnel on higher risk border crossers

Dedicated Commuter Lane/CANPASS—programs to expedite pre-cleared low-risk, frequent crossers at land ports, currently in Buffalo, NY; Blaine, WA and Detroit, MI.

INSPASS/CANPASS—programs to facilitate low-risk, frequent air travelers are in place in pre-clearance sites in Vancouver and Toronto.

Remote Video Inspection Service (RVIS)—This provides 24-hour access to inspections at low volume land ports of entry. It ensures inspection at remote locations. RVIS is currently deployed to 11 Northern Border locations, with plans for expansion to additional sites.

Outlying Area Reporting Station (OARS) Videophone inspections systems have allowed INS to expand the hours of operation at smaller POEs and provide a means to inspect persons from remote locations. Without videophones we were unable to offer the enhanced benefit of longer hours and the inherent enforcement benefit of conducting an inspection where none previously existed. The system allows private pleasure boats to report for inspection at remote stations where no previous inspection site existed. OARS is currently deployed to 35 Northern Border locations, with plans for further installation.

We continue to enhance Border Patrol technology for enforcement efforts as well. Northern Border Patrol Sectors have received 9 LORIS infrared scopes, 152 night vision goggles, 35 pocket scopes, 1,333 sensors, 110 ASTRO portable Encrypted Voice Radio Program (EVRP)-capable radios and 82 ASTRO Spectra EVRP-capable mobile radios.

In addition, two new technology camera systems are currently planned for installation on the Northern Border. These systems, known as Integrated

Surveillance Intelligence Systems (ISIS) consist of high-resolution day cameras and infrared night vision cameras. These cameras provide live video to the Border Patrol. This video is used to monitor the border, identify the source of ground sensor activations, detect illegal activities and dispatch agents as needed.

The Blaine Border Patrol Sector will get the first Northern Border ISIS installation, expected to be completed this year. A second camera project, now in the planning stages, will be located in Buffalo Sector near the Niagara River. We estimate that project will be completed early next year.

SMUGGLING

Along the Northern Border our efforts against alien smuggling continue to increase, especially in the area of criminal prosecutions. Like our other enforcement efforts, cooperation and coordination with the Canadians is key to our efforts. The Northern Border is a favored transit point for aliens from the Asia, particularly China. Canada's asylum law permits persons to enter Canada, claim asylum and be free while their cases are processed. Some of them attempt entry to their real destination—the United States. Chinese nationals typically board Canada bound airliners with fraudulent passports or other travel documents. Upon arrival, the aliens then claim to be refugees and are released by the Canadian authorities pending a hearing. Groups of Chinese then travel to large cities such as Vancouver, Toronto or Montreal, where they are staged for the smuggling attempt into the United States. Other nationalities typically follow this format, with variations, dependant on applicable Canadian law. For example, some nationalities need only a passport and no visa to enter Canada. The most active entry points are through Swanton Sector in Northern New York and Vermont, Blaine Sector in Washington State, and Buffalo Sector in Western New York.

With increased INS anti-smuggling activity, and with the support of U.S. Attorneys on the Northern Border, the number of smuggling case prosecutions for the Northern Border have increased from 184 in FY 1997, to 194 in FY 1998, to 137 in just the first six months of FY 1999.

The INS Inspections Division is involved in combating drug smuggling in cooperation with the U.S. Customs Service at POEs, while the Border Patrol as the primary agency responsible between the POEs.

The Inspections Division of INS participated in 303 drug seizures on the Northern Border in FY 1998, about 13% of the Inspections national total, i.e. less than 1% of the marijuana and cocaine by weight. Border Patrol Sectors along the Northern Border were responsible for 217 (4%) of the 6,665 national drug seizures made by the Border Patrol in FY 1998. By weight, the Northern Border was responsible for less than 1% of the marijuana and less than 1% of the cocaine seized by the Border Patrol.

The INS is not the primary agency responsible for drug investigations. Our cases originating at POEs are processed through the efforts of the U.S. Customs Service. Customs either makes the drug seizures from INS referrals or takes over seizure and investigation based upon an INS discovery on primary inspection. Between the ports-of-entry, where Border Patrol is the lead agency responsible for interdicting drugs, Border Patrol turns cases over to the Drug Enforcement Agency (DEA) for federal level cases, or to local enforcement agencies for non-federal level seizures. Accordingly, we do not have statistics on prosecutions or outcomes of these cases.

TERRORISM

When it comes to a potential terrorist threat to the United States, numbers do not tell the story. Much of the terrain from the Midwest to the Pacific Northwest is rugged and sparsely populated. While this deters casual illegal entrants, it also renders detection more difficult for those charged with patrolling our borders. Nonetheless, the U.S. Border Patrol is ever vigilant to the potential threat of terrorist entry across the Northern Border.

One notable case is the case of Gazi Ibrahim Abu Mezer. This Palestinian was ultimately arrested within the United States, charged and convicted for possession of pipe bombs, which he intended to detonate in the subways and other public places of New York City.

Now, you may wonder why I cite Mezer as an example of success, since he did enter the United States. But the reality of Mezer's case is that he was intercepted by INS three times as he attempted to cross illegally. After his first two attempts, Mezer, who claimed refugee status in Canada, was repatriated across the border. On his last attempt at entry he was placed in removal proceedings, and INS recommended he be held without bond. However, he was released on bond by a judge because there was no record or other indication of a criminal history or involvement in terrorism. Mezer's case illustrates both the effectiveness of the Border Patrol at the Northern Border, and the complexities of combating terrorism in a free society.

Abu Mezer is not the only terrorist who has used Canada as his portal to the United States. Other aliens with terrorist ties to such diverse groups as the IRA, HAMAS, the Tamil Tigers and various Sikh separatist groups have also done so.

In the fall of last year, the director of the Canadian Security Intelligence Service (CSIS) testified before his Senate that CSIS was investigating 50 terrorist organizations that had established infrastructures in his country. Put simply, this is because Canada, like the United States, has a long and cherished tradition of embracing immigrants and openness of expression. And, as with the United States, one of the challenges for their democracy is in striking the right balance between openness and guarding against becoming a refuge for terrorists from abroad.

In combating terrorism, in particular, the challenge for United States and Canadian officials is the rapid and timely exchange of information on such individuals, who pose a shared threat. While most exchanges of information follow established formal protocols, there is also considerable personal liaison between officers and direct communication between INS and Canadian agencies.

There are three different locations in which INS identifies suspected terrorists, and I will briefly describe them:

Ports-of-Entry: At POEs, our inspectors use the Interagency Border Inspections System, or IBIS, to verify and obtain information on applicants for admission. IBIS is made up of several information systems including: National Crime Information Center (NCIC), Treasury Enforcement Communication System (TECS). It also includes the INS' own National Automated Immigration Lookout System (NAILS), and the State Department's Consular Lookout And Support System (CLASS), as well as TIPOFF, a (non-acronym name) terrorist database. Each of these systems is capable of providing information on an applicant's past history and affiliations. TIPOFF is particularly helpful in the detection of terrorists, as it is a repository of classified information collected from the federal intelligence and law enforcement communities.

In addition to these index checks, of course, INS inspectors are continually alert to the possibility of presentation of altered or counterfeit documents. When this occurs in combination with other factors leading to a suspicion that the subject may be a terrorist or supporter of terrorist organizations, the Inspector notify the FBI, as well as others within INS's own chain of command. This results in an extensive debriefing of the suspect and a thorough search of his or her possessions. Determinations as to custody and initiation of criminal or removal proceedings are made thereafter.

Between the Ports: When Border Patrol agents apprehend an alien attempting to enter without inspection, they too conduct automated index checks and thereby have access to the same information databases. In addition, Border Patrol and Inspectors at POEs are routinely notified via "heightened security alerts" of any activities or events of which they must be particularly vigilant in their patrol duties. Standing instructions require that apprehended subjects suspected of terrorist involvement be immediately reported to INS Headquarters through regional offices. This notification triggers a chain of events, including coordination with other intelligence and enforcement agencies of the government (FBI, CIA, etc.), in order to determine the true identity and affiliations of the suspect taken into custody.

Urban Areas Proximate to the Border: In U.S. cities and populated areas under the jurisdiction of district offices, such as Detroit, INS Investigations special agents are assigned to the FBI-led Joint Terrorism Task Forces (JTTFs). By this liaison and coordination mechanism, these agents work side-by-side with other agency counterparts in proactively investigating and detecting aliens suspected of involvement with, or support of, terrorist activities. Determinations are made jointly with the FBI as to whether and when to initiate criminal or administrative enforcement actions within INS jurisdiction.

BORDER STRATEGY

Now that I've discussed these important and unique aspects of our operations at the Northern Border, I would like to address our border strategy. The INS has a national strategy for control of the border. Simply stated, that strategy is to regain control of the border by focusing new resources on those areas where most illegal crossings occur. We know that as our enforcement presence increases, crossing patterns shift. Our newest resources are assigned accordingly. In the case of the Border Patrol, we are concentrating our efforts on the area of greatest need—the Southwest Border—where we commenced deployment of new personnel in 1994 in the El Paso and San Diego areas. Further deployments have progressed to Tucson and South Texas. Future concentrations will be in the remainder of the Southwest Border, the Coastal States, Puerto Rico and the Northern Border. Our experience to date does not indicate a shift in illegal entries from the Southwest to the Northern Border. The shifts have occurred within the area of the Southwest Border, as we had anticipated in our planning.

Nationally, the Border Patrol apprehended more than 1.5 million aliens in FY 1998. Of these, about 12,000, or 1%, were apprehended near the Northern Border. Of these 12,000, only a small number were recent entries without inspection who came across the Northern Border. A statistical chart details these figures for the last three fiscal years (see attachment 1.1, 1.2). Apprehension figures of illegal entries from Canada into the United States are small when compared to those on our Southwest Border. Still, the Northern Border is an alternative gateway for illegal entry into the United States, and migrants from well over 100 countries attempted illegal entry into the United States from Canada last year.

Illegal immigration across the Northern Border has been through attempts at Ports-of-Entry utilizing traditional means, such as false claims to U.S. citizenship, misrepresented purpose for entry, and fraudulent or improper documentation, and through entry without inspection between ports. I have provided a statistical chart (attachment 2.1) that covers the last three fiscal years, and compares total numbers of persons inspected to detected illegal attempts for entry. Total persons inspected on the Northern Border for FY 1998 was 113 million, while persons refused entry was 131,793. The Southwest Border numbers were 304 million and 396,976, respectively. As with the experience of our Border Patrol, a higher percentage of inadmissible persons are encountered on the Southwest Border.

Also of serious concern is the illegal migration of persecutors. Canada, like the United States, is a responsible member of the international community. Both countries have undertaken peacekeeping responsibilities in various parts of the globe under the auspices of the United Nations or North Atlantic Treaty Organization. And, both countries have accepted their fair share of refugees fleeing war, oppression and even genocide abroad. Thus, both countries have also faced the difficult problem that emerges when human rights abusers and persecutors, fleeing justice, change their identities to merge among the throngs of persecuted seeking refuge in stable and welcoming democracies. And, when discovered by their hosts, such persecutors will again attempt to hide among the displaced. Because of geographical proximity, when such persecutors are discovered by Canadian immigration or security authorities, they often flee south to the United States. This has happened, for instance, with a number of former officials of the Siad Barre regime in Somalia. These active cases are under proceedings and we are unable to site specifics at this time.

With regard to staffing, expansion of personnel in officer occupations within the INS has been at a much slower rate than the Border Patrol increases. The national strategy for these other officer positions is to examine the individual need of each INS district and distribute new assets equitably, according to the overall analysis of each identified need. Accordingly, we have seen minimal, if any, increases in officer staffing along the Northern Border.

The INS staffing for the Northern Border for the last three fiscal years is covered in the third chart (attachment 3.1). We have allocated 22 new Border Patrol Officer positions to three of the Northern Border Sectors this fiscal year. A total of 113 million people were inspected on the Northern Border in FY 1998, and 131, 793 people were refused entry into the United States during that period. The FY 1998 figures for the Southwest border were 304 million inspections and 396,976 persons refused entry. Thus, approximately 27% of the workload is covered by a commensurate 25% of INS' Inspections staff. Thus h is staffed with 25% of the INS personnel assigned to the Inspection program. Both apprehension statistics and inspection statistics overwhelmingly indicate that our greatest need for enforcement is along the Southwest Border.

CONCLUSION

As you can see, the situation at the Northern Border presents both challenges and, because of our close partnership with Canada, unique advantages and opportunities. Through cooperation and technology, the United States and Canada have maintained our shared goal of a secure border. Clearly, there is much more to be done. But while we work in partnership on the Northern Border, we must focus the bulk of our efforts and resources toward regaining control of the Southwest Border. This is our strategy, and we believe it is sound. In closing I would emphasize that inherent in our strategy is the flexibility to respond to emerging conditions and changing tactics. As we have demonstrated in the past, INS is prepared to shift the deployment of new and existing resources to meet any threat, in any location.

TERRORISM IS A RECOGNIZED THREAT

As was made perfectly clear in this testimony, terrorism is a recognized threat along the northern border with efforts being directed specifically toward defusing the perceived threat. There is no doubt that along the Northern Border, there is a heightened awareness of the possibility of terrorists slipping into this country. Sadly, it is downplayed along the southern border. But let us go further and see what the U.S. Border Patrol has to say about the status of our northern border.

CHAPTER SIXTEEN
THE NORTHERN BORDER: THE BORDER PATROL VIEW

As stated by the INS witness before Congress, terrorism is ranked as a major effort in their enforcement efforts. However, INS is not the agency that is on the front lines day after day, that is the Border Patrol. Now let us examine the testimony of the Deputy Chief of the US Border Patrol from Blaine, Washington.

STATEMENT OF EUGENE DAVIS, DEPUTY CHIEF, UNITED STATES BORDER PATROL, BLAINE, WA

Mr. DAVIS. Mr. Chairman and members of the subcommittee, my name is Engene R. Davis. I am the Deputy Chief Patrol Agent for the U.S. Border Patrol for the Blaine Sector in Blaine, Washington. Thank you very much for this opportunity to testify on enforcement issues and concerns that exist along the U.S.-Canada border.

For the past 20 years, it has been my privilege to serve as a Border Patrol agent, supervisory Border Patrol agent and staff officer in the Blaine area of operations. It is my hope that I can convey to you an accurate synopsis of the day-to-day challenges that the men and women of the U.S. Border Patrol in the Blaine sector encounter.

The Blaine sector shares approximately 102 miles of land border with Canada plus 150 miles of water boundary. The majority of illegal smuggling activity takes place within the 35 miles between Blaine and Ross Lake, Washington. The other 65 miles, which extends to the crest of the North Cascade Mountains is mostly remote wilderness area made up of terrain, which is very difficult to enter.

The 35-mile area between Blaine and Ross Lake is diverse and very challenging to patrol. Much of this land consists of open berry fields on both sides of the border and roads in Canada and the United States that parallel each other. It is very easy to simply jump or drive across the small ditch that separates the two countries.

The U.S.-Canada border is significantly different than our border with Mexico in that most of the smuggling on our southern border is north bound, whereas smuggling along the border in Blaine sector is both north and south. In fact, it is common to have the same smugglers moving illegal contraband in both directions. Their bottom line is profit.

At the present time, Blaine Sector has 42 Border Patrol agents on duty with an additional 7 agents allocated for fiscal year 1999. These positions are spread among five Border Patrol stations and also include our sector staff positions. The present 42 agent positions also include an aircraft pilot and an intelligence agent. Currently, we have three agents on detail to the southwest border.

By far, the best strategy that has been developed along the border is the operational liaison and intelligence the sector has been able to establish with other law enforcement agencies. This includes working closely with U.S. Customs, the Drug Enforcement Administration, and local law enforcement agencies and with the Royal Canadian Mounted Police in Canada.

Each of our individual agencies has limited manpower along the border, so we have developed a unique border management posture. We have treated the border as a common entity and have made great strides in not only sharing intelligence but in actually working joint operations. We share a common radio frequency and we are in constant contact as we work along both sides of the border.

With HIDTA funding, we are in the midst of establishing an intelligence center at Blaine Sector headquarters, which will house intelligence analysts from the various agencies along the border. We anticipate in the near future most operations will be intelligence-driven.

Over the last 10 years, there has been phenomenal growth in the areas north of us in Canada. Vancouver, British Columbia has become one of the fastest growing cities in North America. It is an important link along the Interstate 5 corridor, which runs north from southern California into the Pacific Northwest and then into Canada.

We have experienced large increases in organized crime along the border. Our manpower levels during this time have been static. Ten years ago we experienced very little alien or drug smuggling activity along the border. We now know that illegal smuggling activity takes place on a daily basis. Due to limited manpower, we are able to respond to only 50 percent of the sensor intrusion alarms on any given day.

Canada has a non-visa requirement with several countries that the United States continues to require visas from. This has resulted in many smugglers being able to easily bring third country nationals into Canada and then smuggle them across the border into the United States. As an example, we have noted a large increase in the smuggling of Korean nationals during the last several years.

Over the last 3 years, the Blaine Sector has experienced an increase in drug seizures along the border. The primary drug has been high quality BC Bud marijuana that is grown in British Columbia. This high-grade marijuana has a THC level which tests between 20 and 30 percent. Most Mexican marijuana usually contains a THC level of around 5 percent. We have had reports of BC Bud going for as high as $8,000 a pound in the Los Angeles area. Blaine Sector seizures of BC Bud during the last fiscal year was 600 percent over the previous year.

Since June 1996, Blaine Sector Border Patrol agents have arrested three different individuals with terrorist ties, the most notable being Abu Mezer. A New York City Police Department police responded and shot Abu Mezer just before he planned to put bombs on the New York subway system.

In closing, I again appreciate the opportunity to address the committee. Each of us in the Border Patrol have worked on the southern border over the last decade and are aware of the terrific challenges that are there. I do not believe that we will ever have the same magnitude of problems along the Canadian border but we do have significant challenges that need to be met.

[The prepared statement of Mr. Davis follows:]

PREPARED STATEMENT OF EUGENE DAVIS, DEPUTY CHIEF, UNITED STATES BORDER PATROL, BLAINE, WA

Mr. Chairman and members of the subcommittee, my name is Eugene R. Davis. I am the Deputy Chief Patrol Agent, U.S. Border Patrol, at the Blaine Sector, in Blaine, Washington. Thank you very much for this opportunity to testify on enforcement issues and concerns that exist along the U.S./Canada Border. For the past 20 years it has been my privilege to serve as a Border Patrol Agent, Supervisory Border Patrol Agent, and Staff Officer in the Blaine Sector area of operations. It is my hope that I can convey to you an accurate synopsis of the day-to-day challenges that the men and women of the U.S. Border Patrol in the Blaine Sector encounter.

INTRODUCTION

The Blaine Border Patrol Sector shares approximately 102 miles of land border with Canada. The majority of illegal smuggling activity takes place within 35-miles between Blaine and Ross Lake, Washington. The other 67 miles, which extends to the crest of the North Cascade Mountains, is mostly remote wilderness area, made up of terrain, which is very difficult to enter. The 35-mile area between Blaine and Ross Lake is diverse and is very challenging to patrol. Much of this land consists of open berry fields on both sides of the Border and roads in Canada and the United States that parallel each other. It is very easy to simply jump or drive across the small ditch, which separates the two countries. This is the most common modus operandi for the smugglers operating along both sides of the border. The U.S./Canada Border is significantly different than our border with Mexico in that most of the smuggling on our Southern Border is northbound, whereas smuggling along the Border in Blaine Sector is both north and south. In fact, it is common to have the same smugglers moving illegal contraband in both directions. Their bottom line is profit.

Blaine Sector also is responsible for 150 miles of water boundary that separates the United States and Canada. Within these waters just south of Canada are the San Juan Islands, which number close to 200 small to medium size islands. Over the past 100 years these islands have always been a haven for smuggling activity.

In addition to the responsibility for controlling the border areas, Blaine Sector has also been tasked with various interior enforcement functions. The Sector has overall enforcement responsibility for 16 counties in Western Washington and five counties in Oregon. The majority of the work in these areas has consisted of working with other law enforcement agencies to identify and remove criminal aliens. We also have enforcement responsibility in agriculture, reforestation, and the commercial fishing industry in Western Washington, Oregon and Alaska.

MANPOWER RESOURCES

Blaine Sector at the present time has 42 Border Patrol Agents on duty. These positions are spread out among five Border Patrol Stations and also include our sector staff positions. (We also have a six member Anti-Smuggling unit and eight Detention Enforcement Officers.) The 42 Agent positions also include an Aircraft Pilot and an Intelligence Agent.

Within the past two months Blaine Sector has been given an additional seven agents that will increase our total Border Patrol Agent level of staffing to 49 positions. These additional Agents will be assigned to our Stations at Blaine and Lynden, Washington. This will increase the total Agents at Blaine Station to 21 and Lynden Station to 13.

OPERATIONAL STATEGIES

By far the best strategy that has been developed along the Border is the operational liaison and intelligence that the Sector has been able to establish with other law enforcement agencies. This includes working closely with U.S. Customs, the Drug Enforcement Administration, and local law enforcement agencies and with the Royal Canadian Mounted Police in Canada. Each of our individual agencies has limited manpower along the border, so we have developed a unique Border Management posture. We have treated the border as a common entity and made great strides in not only sharing intelligence, but in actually working joint operations. We share a common radio frequency and are in constant contact as we work along both sides of the border. With HIDTA funding, we are in the midst of establishing an Intelligence Center at Blaine Sector Headquarters, which will house Intelligence Analysts from the various agencies along the border. We anticipate that in the near future most operations will be intelligence driven.

PROBLEM AREAS

Over the last 10 years there has been phenomenal growth in the areas north of us in Canada. Vancouver, British Columbia has become one of the fastest growing cities in North America. It is an important link along the Interstate 5 corridor, which runs north from Southern California into the Pacific Northwest and then into Canada. We have experienced large increases in organized crime along the border. Our manpower levels during this time have been static. Ten years ago we experienced very little alien or drug smuggling activity along the border. We know now that illegal smuggling activity takes place on a daily basis. Due to limited manpower, we are able to respond to only 50% of our sensor intrusion alarms on any given day

Over the past several years Canada has adopted a non-visa requirement policy with many countries that the United States continues to require visas from. This has resulted in many smugglers being able to easily bring third-country nationals into Canada and then smuggle them across the border into the United States. As an example, we have noted a large increase in the smuggling of Korean nationals during the last several years.

Over the last three years, Blaine Sector has experienced an increase in drug seizures along the border. The primary drug has been the high quality "BC Bud" marijuana that is grown in British Columbia. This high-grade marijuana has a THC level which tests out to 20% to 30%. Most Mexican Marijuana usually contains a THC level of around 5%. We have had reports of "BC Bud" going for as high as $8,000 a pound in the Los Angeles area. Blaine Sector's seizure of "BC Bud" during the last fiscal year was 600% over the previous year that is 117 pounds interdicted in 1997 compared to 692 pounds in 1998.

Since June of 1996, Blaine Sector Border Patrol Agents have arrested three different individuals with terrorist's ties. The most notable being ABU MEZER. A New York City Police Department Response team shot ABU MESER just hours before he planned to put bombs on the New York Subway

System. The Canadian Government has stated that virtually every known terrorist group in the world has offices in Canada.

The Blaine Sector has no marine presence in the 150 miles of water boundary between the United States and Canada. It is suspected that there is a lot of smuggling activity taking place, but the only agency operating in these international waters on a permanent basis is the Coast Guard. They are tasked mainly with search and rescue type operations.

The last major concern that the Blaine Sector has is the continual detail of Blaine Agents to the Southern Border. At the present time we continue to send three agents south each month. This seems like a relatively small number but it reflects over 7% of our assigned manpower resources. We certainly see the need to send experienced journeyman agents to the southern Border and we have always done so when requested. However, it does affect our ability to provide coverage in our own area of responsibility.

CONCLUSION

The Border Patrol certainly recognizes the problem of terrorists slipping across our open borders. The problem is that there are a small number of agents assigned to patrol a largely deserted border region. How can we hope to keep the terrorists out of what has been described as the largest terrorist target in the world? But there is more information available to us to be used to assess our northern threat. Next we will hear form the Inspector General, U.S. Department of Justice.

CHAPTER SEVENTEEN
THE NORTHERN BORDER:
THE VIEW OF THE
U.S. DEPARTMENT OF JUSTICE

STATEMENT OF MICHAEL BROMWICH, INSPECTOR GENERAL, U.S. DEPARTMENT OF JUSTICE

Mr. BROMWICH. Thank you.

Mr. Chairman, Ms. Jackson Lee and members of the subcommittee, I very much appreciate the opportunity to appear before you to discuss the work of the Office of the Inspector General with respect to immigration law enforcement issues at the U.S.-Canadian border.

As the subcommittee is well aware, the OIG has done extensive work in investigating, auditing and inspecting programs and personnel along this country's southern border with Mexico. At this point, northern border issues have received far less of our attention and far less attention from the INS and other Federal agencies seeking to secure our Nation's borders.

There is ample work for us to do along the northern border and I am hopeful that our budget situation will improve in fiscal year 2000 such that we will be able to do more such important work.

This morning, I plan to do two things briefly. First, to describe an initiative underway in our Inspections Division to review INS' strategy and deployment of resources for securing the border between the U.S. and Canada. Second, I will discuss a special investigation we completed last year that involved a Palestinian who crossed the northern border illegally and was convicted for plotting to bomb the New York City subway system.

The U.S.-Canadian border, as other witnesses have said, extends for approximately 4,000 miles and is one of the longest land borders in the world.

Approximately 300 Border Patrol agents assigned to one of eight sectors share responsibility for controlling it.

Our inspection, which began in February of this year, will review law enforcement threats along the northern border and the Border Patrol's use of its resources, intelligence information and law enforcement relationships to address these threats. Thus far, the inspection team has reviewed considerable background information, including the Border Patrol's strategic plan, annual intelligence assessments, workload data and press reports on northern border issues. The team also has interviewed senior Border Patrol officials at INS headquarters in Washington, D.C. and senior managers at Border Patrol sectors in Spokane, Washington; Grand Forks, North Dakota; Havre, Montana; and Holton, Maine. We are just beginning the fieldwork phase of this inspection and plan to visit Border Patrol sections in Swanton, Vermont, Buffalo, New York, Detroit, Michigan, and Blaine, Washington. We expect to complete our site visits and interviews by mid-June.

While our inspection team is just beginning its fieldwork, I would like to share some preliminary observations with you. First, the Border Patrol's national strategy implemented in 1994 focuses on deterrence, that is, preventing illegal aliens from penetrating the border. This approach differs from the Border Patrol's previous operational strategy that mixed deterrence with traffic checks, farm and ranch checks and jail checks.

The current strategy has curtailed these Border Patrol interior enforcement activities significantly in favor of a greater emphasis on a show of force to prevent illegal immigration. The best-known examples—quite well known to this subcommittee—are the Gatekeeper operation in the San Diego Sector and Operation Hold-the-Line in El Paso, Texas.

The Border Patrol's national strategy includes four phases for controlling the entire U.S. border. The first three phases direct the vast majority of Border Patrol resources to the southwest border until sufficient deterrence is achieved. When this is accomplished, the Border Patrol will move to the fourth phase that calls for achieving deterrence at all remaining border areas, including the northern border. The Border Patrol is currently in the second phase of this strategy and it may be several years before Phase IV begins and the northern border is provided significant additional resources.

The nature of the law enforcement threats on or near the northern border includes alien smuggling, drug smuggling, illegal alien entry and terrorism. The intensity and type of specific threats vary from sector to sector.

Several examples: The border in western Washington is experiencing, as witnesses have already said, a marked increase in the smuggling of "BC Bud," an especially potent strain of marijuana that sells at a price as high as cocaine in southern California.

The Swanton, Vermont Sector has experienced a unique alien smuggling operation in which Native Americans have used tribal lands that straddle the border to smuggle illegal aliens from Asia into the United States.

INS and other intelligence reports indicate that terrorist groups locate in Canada, in part because of Canada's liberal visa and asylum laws, and because of the country's proximity to the United States.

I look forward to sharing the results of our inspection with the subcommittee when it is completed.

Now, on to our special investigation. A special investigation by my office was released in March 1998 and was called "Bombs in Brooklyn, How the Two Illegal Aliens Arrested for Plotting to Bomb the New York Subway Entered and Remained in the United States." That special investigation highlighted the fact that illegal aliens who enter the country through the northern border may be involved in terrorist activities.

In this investigation, the OIG examined how two aliens, Gazi Ibrahim Abu Mezer and Lafi Khalil, entered and remained in the United States before they were arrested in July 1997 for allegedly planning to bomb the New York City subway system. Mezer was subsequently convicted of the bomb plot and received a life sentence.

As the subcommittee may remember from my testimony several weeks ago, Khalil illegally remained in the United States after his visa expired. He was a visa overstay. He was acquitted of charges stemming from the bombing plot but convicted of immigration charges and was sentenced to 3 years in prison.

As our report discussed, Mezer was first apprehended attempting to enter the United States on June 23, 1996 when the National Park Service stopped him in a remote area in North Cascades National Park in Washington State. After Mezer was turned over to the Border Patrol he was returned voluntarily to Canada. During our investigation, INS officials told us that because of the unavailability of detention space, aliens who are apprehended attempting to enter the U.S. illegally along this stretch of border are typically returned to Canada voluntarily, as Mezer was, unless there are unusual circumstances such as evidence that the alien is an aggravated felon.

The vast majority of illegal aliens apprehended entering the United States from Canada, for example 723 of 794 in the Blaine Sector in fiscal year 1996, are voluntarily returned to Canada. We found that record checks are rarely done on these illegal aliens to see if they may be suspected terrorists. In addition, aliens are rarely prosecuted for the criminal offense of entry without inspection even after repeated apprehensions.

Six days later, the Border Patrol detained Mezer again trying to enter the U.S. illegally through a park next to a busy port of entry 65 miles west of where he had been apprehended the previous week. Once again, the Border Patrol voluntarily returned Mezer to Canada. Six months later, Mezer was apprehended a third time by a Border Patrol agent as Mezer was boarding a bus in Bellingham,

Washington, 25 miles south of the Canadian border. This time Canadian immigration officials told the Border Patrol that Canada probably would not accept Mezer back. The Border Patrol agent commenced formal deportation proceedings against Mezer but as is common in such cases, Mezer was released on bond. He subsequently filed an asylum application to remain in the U.S. claiming that he was persecuted in Israel because the authorities incorrectly believed he was a member of the terrorist group Hamas. He subsequently withdrew the application and was placed in voluntary departure status, meaning he had 60 days to leave the country voluntarily. A month later, Mezer was arrested in Brooklyn for the plot to bomb the subway.

Contrary to the perception that arose at the time of Mezer's arrest, he was not a known terrorist the U.S. immigration authorities allowed to travel around the United States while awaiting deportation. Although we did not find improper actions by any individual officials, our review did reveal important and systemic problems that are not unique to Mezer's case. First, his easy entry into Canada and his ability to remain in Canada despite criminal convictions for use of a stolen credit card and misdemeanor assault, coupled with his repeated attempts to enter the United States illegally, highlight the difficulty in controlling illegal immigration into the United States.

Second, Mezer's case shows the inadequacy of INS resources for preventing illegal immigration along the northwest border. With an average of four Border Patrol agents assigned to western Washington stations that cover 102 miles of the border and no coverage of the border from midnight until the morning, it is surprising that Mezer was apprehended once, much less three times.

Third, the virtual impunity from prosecution that aliens face when they are caught entering the United States illegally is also made apparent by Mezer's case. Border Patrol statistics show that most illegal aliens apprehended entering the United States from Canada are voluntarily returned without any criminal or immigration consequences. Despite twice being caught attempting to enter the U.S. illegally within 1 week, Mezer was simply returned voluntarily to Canada each time.

Fourth, Mezer's case demonstrates the significant differences of understanding as to which Federal agencies check for information regarding whether an asylum applicant is a terrorist. We found that the Immigration Court and INS Asylum Officers believe that the State Department checks its databases for information about individual terrorists. State Department officials said they thought INS and its Asylum Officers had access to such information and conducted these checks. In fact, absent unusual circumstances, the State Department does not check for terrorist information.

While we were told that the Border Patrol stations have access to the State Department's "Tipoff" system that contains information about suspected terrorists, it is not clear whether these officers check this information routinely when an alien is detained. Even more significantly, we were told that no terrorism checks are performed either by INS or by the Department of State on the vast majority of asylum applications that are submitted by asylum officers, more than 90 percent of the 150,000 asylum applications filed annually. While we have no indication that any information was available to indicate that Mezer was a terrorist, we believe that Mezer's case shows that the INS and the State Department need to coordinate more closely on appropriate procedures for accessing and sharing any information suggesting that a detained alien or an asylum applicant may be a terrorist.

Since issuance of our report last March, we have sent two letters to the Immigration Service to check on the status of their corrective actions, the first in October 1998 and the second in January of this year. INS has not responded to either letter.

It is clear to me from this case example and from the work that our inspection team has conducted to date that the northern border enforcement issues are vitally important to the security of the United States. I encourage this subcommittee's continued oversight of this issue and I look forward to sharing the results of our review of INS' strategy and deployment of resources for securing the northern border between the United States and Canada.

[The prepared statement of Mr. Bromwich follows:]

PREPARED STATEMENT OF MICHAEL BROMWICH, INSPECTOR GENERAL, U.S. DEPARTMENT OF JUSTICE

Mr. Chairman, Congresswoman Jackson Lee, and Members of the Subcommittee on Immigration and Claims:

I. INTRODUCTION

I appreciate the opportunity to appear before the Subcommittee to discuss the work of the Office of the Inspector General (OIG) with respect to immigration law enforcement issues at the border between the United States and Canada. As this subcommittee is well aware, the OIG has done extensive work investigating, auditing and inspecting programs and personnel along this country's southern border with Mexico. Up to this point at least, northern border issues have received far less of our attention and, I suspect, far less attention from the Immigration and Naturalization Service (INS) and other federal agencies charged with securing our nation's borders. While the OIG will continue to play an active role in Southwest Border States, I am hopeful that our budget situation will improve in FY 2000 to enable us to open a small field office in Detroit, MI, to handle an increasing number of northern border issues.

This morning I plan to do two things during my remarks: first, describe an initiative under way in our Inspections Division to review INS's strategy and deployment of resources for securing the northern border between the United States and Canada. Second, I will discuss a Special Investigation we completed last year that involved a Palestinian who entered this country illegally across the northern border and was convicted for plotting to bomb the New York City subway.

I. OIG[103] INSPECTION OF BORDER PATROL EFFORTS ALONG THE NORTHERN BORDER

The U.S.-Canadian border, which extends for approximately 4,000 miles (excluding Alaska), is one of the longest land borders in the world. Approximately 300 Border Patrol Agents assigned to one of eight Sectors share responsibility for controlling this vast border. Our inspection—which began in February of this year—will review law enforcement threats along the northern border and the Border Patrol's use of its resources, intelligence information, and law-enforcement relationships to address these threats.

Thus far, the inspection team has reviewed considerable background information, including the Border Patrol's Strategic Plan, annual intelligence assessments, workload data, and press reports on northern border issues. The team also has interviewed senior Border Patrol officials at INS headquarters in Washington, D.C., and senior managers at Border Patrol Sectors in Spokane, Washington; Grand Forks, North Dakota; Havre, Montana; and Houlton, Maine. We are just beginning the fieldwork phase of this inspection and plan to visit Border Patrol Sectors in Swanton, Vermont; Buffalo, New York; Detroit, Michigan; and Blaine, Washington. We expect to complete our site visits and interviews by mid-June.

While our Inspections team is just beginning its fieldwork, I offer several preliminary observations:

The Border Patrol's national strategy implemented in 1994 focuses on deterrence—i.e., preventing illegal aliens from penetrating the border. This approach differs from the Border Patrol's previous operational strategy that mixed deterrence with traffic checks, farm and ranch checks, and jail checks. The current strategy has curtailed these Border Patrol interior enforcement activities significantly in favor of a greater emphasis on a "show of force" to prevent illegal immigration. Perhaps the best-known examples of this strategy are the "Gatekeeper" operation in the San Diego Sector and "Operation Hold-the-Line" in El Paso, Texas.

---

[103] Office of the Inspector General

The Border Patrol's national strategy includes four phases for controlling the entire U.S. border. The first three phases direct the vast majority of Border Patrol resources to the Southwest border until an appropriate level of deterrence is achieved. When this is accomplished, the Border Patrol will move to the fourth phase that calls for achieving deterrence at all remaining border areas, including the northern border. The Border Patrol is currently in the second phase of this strategy and it may be several years before Phase IV begins and the northern border is provided significant additional resources.

The nature of the law enforcement threats on or near the northern border includes alien smuggling, drug smuggling, illegal alien entry, and terrorism. The intensity and type of specific threats vary from sector to sector. A few examples:

- The border in western Washington is experiencing a marked increase in the smuggling of "BC Bud"—an especially potent strain of marijuana—that sells for as much as cocaine in Southern California.

- The Swanton, Vermont, Sector has experienced a unique alien smuggling operation in which Native Americans have used tribal lands that straddle the border to smuggle illegal aliens from Asia into the United States.

- INS and other intelligence reports indicate that terrorist groups locate in Canada in part because of Canada's liberal visa and asylum laws and the country's proximity to the United States.

I look forward to sharing the results of our Inspection with the Subcommittee when it is completed.

III. SPECIAL INVESTIGATION: BOMBS IN BROOKLYN

A. Investigative Findings

A Special Investigation by my office released in March 1998—"Bombs in Brooklyn: How the Two Illegal Aliens Arrested for Plotting to Bomb the New York Subway Entered and Remained in the United States"—highlighted the threat that illegal aliens who enter the country through the northern border may be involved in terrorist activities. In this investigation, the OIG examined how two aliens, Gazi Ibrahim Abu Mezer (Mezer) and Lafi Khalil (Khalil), entered and remained in the United States before they were arrested in July1997 for allegedly planning to bomb the New York City subway system. Mezer was subsequently convicted of the bomb plot and received a life sentence. As the Subcommittee may remember from my testimony several weeks ago, Khalil illegally remained in the United States after his visa expired—a visa overstay. He was acquitted of charges stemming from the bombing plot but convicted of immigration charges and sentenced to three years in prison.

As our report discussed, Mezer was first apprehended attempting to enter the United States on June 23, 1996, when the National Park Service stopped him in a remote area in North Cascades National Park in Washington state. After Mezer was turned over to the Border Patrol, he was returned voluntarily to Canada. During our investigation, INS officials told us that because of the unavailability of detention space, aliens who are apprehended attempting to enter the United States illegally along this stretch of border are typically returned to Canada voluntarily, as Mezer was, unless there are unusual circumstances, such as evidence that the alien is an aggravated felon.

The vast majority of illegal aliens apprehended entering the United States from Canada—for example, 723 of 794 in the Blaine Sector in FY 1996—are voluntarily returned to Canada. We found that record checks are rarely done on these illegal aliens to see if they may be suspected terrorists. In addition, aliens are rarely prosecuted for the criminal offense of entry without inspection, even after repeated apprehensions.

Six days later, the Border Patrol detained Mezer again trying to enter the United States illegally through a park next to a busy port of entry 65 miles west of where he had been apprehended the previous week. Once again, the Border Patrol voluntarily returned Mezer to Canada.

Six months later, Mezer was apprehended a third time by a Border Patrol agent as Mezer was boarding a bus in Bellingham, Washington, 25 miles south of the Canadian border. This time, Canadian immigration officials told the Border Patrol that Canada probably would not accept Mezer back. The Border Patrol agent commenced formal deportation proceedings against Mezer, but, as is common in such cases, Mezer was released on bond. He subsequently filed an asylum application to remain in the United States, claiming that he was persecuted in Israel because the authorities incorrectly believed he was a member of the terrorist group Hamas. Mezer was later arrested in Brooklyn for the plot to bomb the subway.

B. Systemic Weaknesses

Contrary to the perception that arose at the time of Mezer's arrest, he was not a known terrorist who U.S. immigration authorities inappropriately allowed to travel around the United States while awaiting deportation. Although we did not find improper actions by any individual officials, our review did reveal important and systemic problems that are not unique to Mezer's case.

First, his easy entry into Canada and his ability to remain in Canada despite criminal convictions for use of a stolen credit card and misdemeanor assault—coupled with his repeated attempts to enter the United States illegally—highlight the difficulty in controlling illegal immigration into the United States.

Second, Mezer's case shows the inadequacy of INS resources for preventing illegal immigration along the northwest border. With an average of four Border Patrol agents assigned to Western Washington stations that cover 102 miles of the border—and no coverage of the border from midnight until the morning—it is surprising that Mezer was apprehended once, much less three times.

Third, the virtual impunity from prosecution that aliens face when they are caught entering the United States illegally is also made apparent by Mezer's case. Border Patrol statistics show that most illegal aliens who are apprehended entering the United States from Canada are voluntarily returned without any criminal or immigration consequences. Despite twice being caught attempting to enter the United States illegally within one week, Mezer was simply returned voluntarily to Canada each time.

Fourth, Mezer's case demonstrates significant differences of understanding as to which federal agencies check for information regarding whether an asylum applicant is a terrorist. We found that the immigration court and INS asylum officers believed that the State Department checks its databases for information about individual terrorists. State Department officials said that they thought that INS and its asylum officers had access to such information and conducted these checks. In fact, absent unusual circumstances, the State Department does not check for terrorist information. While we were told that Border Patrol stations have access to the State Department's "Tipoff" system that contains information about suspected terrorists, it is not clear whether these offices check this information routinely when an alien is detained.

Even more significantly, we were told that no terrorism checks are performed either by INS or by the Department of State on the vast majority of asylum applications that are submitted by asylum officers—more than 90 percent of the 150,000 asylum application filed annually. While we have no indication that any information was available to indicate that Mezer was a terrorist, we believe that Mezer's case shows that the INS and the State Department need to coordinate more closely on appropriate procedures for accessing and sharing any information suggesting that a detained alien or an asylum applicant may be a terrorist.

Since issuance of our report last March, we sent two letters to the INS to check on the status of their corrective actions—the first in October 1998, the second in January of this year. INS has not responded to either letter.

IV. CONCLUSION

It is clear to me from this case example, and from the work that our Inspection team has conducted to date, that northern border enforcement issues are vitally important to the security of the United States. I encourage this subcommittee's continued oversight of this issue, and I look forward to sharing the results of our review of INS's strategy and deployment of resources for securing the northern border between the United States and Canada.

CHAPTER EIGHTEEN
THE NORTHERN BORDER:
THE VIEW OF THE
UNITED STATES CUSTOMS SERVICE

STATEMENT OF ROBERT TROTTER, ASSISTANT COMMISSIONER, UNITED STATES CUSTOMS SERVICE

Mr. TROTTER. Good morning, Mr. Chairman and members of the committee. It is a pleasure to appear here today before you.

We appreciate being invited to this hearing. I think you well know that the U.S. Customs Service handles about one-half of the primary processing on the northern and southern land borders, so we are right there next to the Immigration Service. We also are in charge of cargo inbound and outbound. So that is part of our role along the borders.

In February of this year, Commissioner Ray Kelly of the Customs Service named me as the new Northern Border Coordinator, a position that has never been held before in the Customs Service. I think this shows the importance of the northern border to the new Commissioner. I am wearing two hats right now. I am Assistant Commissioner for Strategic Trade as well as U.S. Customs Northern Border Coordinator. I travel a great deal on the northern border, look at the operations up there and meet routinely with the Canadians. In fact, I was in Ottawa just this Monday with Citizenship and Immigration Canada and Revenue Canada (their customs service), talking about new methods for work along the border as well as enforcement efforts.

We, in the U.S. Customs Service, have found it extremely important to look at what is going on on the northern border. We have faced southward for many years looking at the southern border. Not to diminish the importance of the southern border, but we are also quite aware of the importance of the northern border. The Canadians are our number one trading partner and very important people with which to deal.

We are working with the Immigration Service, Citizenship and Immigration Canada, and Revenue Canada on a number of programs to actually look at what we are doing, to measure how well we are doing it, and then to develop new programs, after deciding whether to use technology or additional resources. We also are in the throes of looking at resource needs throughout the entire Customs Service. The Commissioner has gone outside to a private contractor to build an allocation model of resource needs in the Customs Service.

We know that this subcommittee is interested in the enforcement activities along the border with respect to narcotics. Just to name a few of the instances that have occurred on the border, we summarize them in actual contraband seized. In fiscal year 1998, the U.S. Customs Service seized a total of 4,413 pounds of drugs along our northern border. In terms of types of drugs, we seized a little over 615 pounds of cocaine, 3.84 pounds of heroin and 3,800 pounds of marijuana. We also have a concern about narcotics interestingly enough going northbound and southbound both.

As was mentioned, in the Vancouver, Seattle, Blaine corridor, BC Bud, the very high potent marijuana that is being grown out there is a concern for us. It is a concern that, as was mentioned by the Border Patrol, the people who are engaged in smuggling drugs often are engaged in smuggling currency as well.

We also know that some of the best opportunities we have in dealing with the growth along the border, not only the enforcement risks as they come to us, but also just the general passenger and cargo flow along the border, is the use of information sharing. We work very hard with the other agencies—Immigration, DEA, the FBI and other Federal, State and local agencies—on information sharing. We are working very closely with the Canadians on data and information sharing. These are important issues to us.

As mentioned earlier, we need to know as far in advance as possible those risks that are coming at us. Our job is to separate out the low risk traveler, the low risk cargo and concentrate our efforts in the high-risk areas. One thing that we are very interested in which was talked about a little bit is the weapons of mass destruction. We are certainly concerned about the movement of weapons of mass destruction along our borders coming from Canada as well as through the seaports and airports.

We have recently trained many of our inspectors and many have a detector they wear on their belts to determine if they are being exposed to any nuclear or atomic release at least small enough to know that would give them advanced warning. We are working very closely with the DEA, FBI and Immigration through the Department of Justice on forming an intelligence group that has been in existence for some time in Buffalo, New York. Speaker of the House Hastert has asked us to relook at that group and see if it is as viable as it could be, to see if we have to reenergize that. That is one of the issues we are looking at for not only continuing the information exchange but also taking that next step.

I have cut my presentation short as you asked. Because most of these gentlemen have covered everything else, we stand by to answer any questions you may have.

[The prepared statement of Mr. Trotter follows:]

PREPARED STATEMENT OF ROBERT TROTTER, ASSISTANT COMMISSIONER, UNITED STATES CUSTOMS SERVICE

Mr. Chairman and Members of the Committee, it is a pleasure to appear before you today to discuss the emergence of a new focus that the U.S. Customs Service is placing on its activities along the Northern Border.

In February of this year, Customs Commissioner Kelly took a major step towards placement of a new focus on the Northern Border by naming me as U.S. Customs first Northern Border Coordinator. In addition to examining our passenger, cargo and enforcement activities and initiatives along the border, I am charged with the following:

- Identifying opportunities and take steps to improve service through the use of technology;

- Engaging in the development and implementation of both bilateral and U.S./Canadian Accord initiatives; and

- Consulting with a broad spectrum of U.S. and Canadian government officials, to identify and exchange ideas relative to Northern Border issues.

Since assuming my new role, I have been traveling to border sites, educating myself and others, and building relationships with U.S. and Canadian border enforcement agencies. I have met with senior representatives of Revenue Canada with Citizenship and Immigration Canada representatives, and with U.S. Ambassador Giffin and his staff in Ottawa.

I hope the following facts will help to highlight the enormity of our task but also the magnitude of the economic relationship we have with Canada:

- Canada is our oldest and largest trading partner. In terms of area, it is the second largest country in the world.

- Our common border from Maine to Blaine and North to Alaska is some 5,500 miles in length.

- Most Canadians live within 100 miles of the U.S. border with more than half the population concentrated in the eastern provinces of Ontario and Quebec.

- The U.S. Customs Service supports 125 Northern Border crossings with 27 Commercial Centers that are open 24 hours each day. At these 125 crossings, we have 83 ports of entry and 42 stations, including 5 seasonal crossings.

- The total trade in goods between the United States and Canada in 1998 was $330 Billion.

- U.S. exports to Canada equaled $153.2 Billion or 22% of total U.S. exports to the world ($682 Billion); and, U.S. imports arriving from Canada equaled $176.7 Billion or 20% of our worldwide imports ($897 Billion).

- By value, almost 56 percent of our imports from Canada move through three of our 83 Northern Border ports of entry—namely—Detroit, Buffalo and Port Huron.

- In addition to processing cargo at the Northern Border, U.S. Customs processes passengers, busses, trains and trucks. In Fiscal Year 1998, we processed almost 101,700,000 passengers and close to 44 million conveyances that crossed our border with Canada.

We are working with the Immigration and Naturalization Service, Citizenship and Immigration Canada, and Revenue Canada on a number of programs to improve the processing of travelers and merchandise across our common border. The Remote Video Inspection System (RVIS) is an example. It expands service at small locations and relies on the agencies working together to approve applications, monitor crossings and conduct compliance checks. In another initiative, Immigration officers on a collateral duty basis have been added to our Intelligence Collection and Analysis Team in Buffalo.

A significant amount of time is being expended by U.S. Customs on the "Canada/US Accord on our Shared Border," which is the foundation for enhancing the management of our shared border with Canada to meet future enforcement, trade and facilitation needs. This Accord, announced by Prime Minister Chretien and President Clinton on February 24, 1995, contributes to fulfilling the expectations of the traveling public and business community for better service. Recognizing successes that have been achieved under the Accord umbrella, U.S. Customs, Revenue Canada, INS, and Citizenship and Immigration Canada agreed during a meeting in Buffalo in early March, to support ongoing joint efforts. In June, the Accord Coordinating Committee with representatives from each of the aforementioned agencies will meet in Halifax, Nova Scotia to discuss and focus our Accord-related efforts.

A decision in the spirit of mutual cooperation Accord cooperation was U.S. Customs and Revenue Canada's agreement to exchange "Liaison Officers" to focus on specific issues. This past Monday, I traveled to Ottawa with our first "Liaison Officer" to discuss a 30-day temporary assignment that he is undertaking in Ottawa with Revenue Canada. This individual will be working with the Canadians on passenger programs. His primary focus will be on CANPASS, a Canadian approach to expediting the movement of legitimate U.S. and American travelers into Canada. Next Monday, Revenue Canada will send a representative to Washington to perform a similar detail focused on trade automation.

As I am sure the members of this subcommittee know, drug smuggling activities along our Northern Border are markedly different from that of the Southern Border. Nevertheless, we cannot lose sight of the fact that trade patterns are constantly shifting and as these shifts occur, new opportunities for the smuggling of drugs and contraband will occur. In Fiscal Year 1998, U.S. Customs seized a total of 4,413 pounds of drugs along our Northern Border. In terms of types of drugs, we seized 614.77 pounds of cocaine, 3.84 pounds of heroin, and 3,794.63 pounds of marijuana (including from South East Asia) We are concerned about and we are attempting to address potential shifts in trade patterns that could accelerate the flow of illegal drugs and other contraband via Canada into the United States.

Among the other enforcement challenges we face on the Northern Border are:

- Prohibited imports from Iran including Iranian rugs, which are the nation's second largest export.

- Drug proceeds entering the United States.

- Cigarette and liquor smuggling.

- Telemarketing fraud.

- Precursor chemicals used to manufacture illicit drugs entering the United States.

- Stolen vehicles.

To help address these ever present threats, U.S. Customs has an excellent relationship with Revenue Canada, the Royal Canadian Mounted Police and provincial authorities across Canada.

Similarly, we are concerned with and involved in the fight to combat international terrorism. We have two broad goals in combating international terrorism:

Protect the American public from the introduction of Weapons of Mass Destruction (WMD) and other instruments of terror into the U.S. from abroad; and, Prevent international terrorists from obtaining WMD materials and technologies, arms, funds and other support from U.S. and foreign sources.

To achieve these goals, Customs employs its unique border search and law enforcement authority in processing international passengers, conveyances and cargo to detect and pursue violations related to international terrorism. Our overall objectives are to disrupt illegal trafficking of WMD materials and technologies, arms, and other instruments of terror through interdiction of illicit shipments; and to dismantle trafficking organizations supplying and supporting rogue states and international terrorists.

During the past fiscal year, we provided training on radiation detection and assigned radiation detectors to our Customs Inspectors. Additionally, Customs uses various other technological devices to assist in the detection of terrorist-related devices and materials. Included are x-ray vans, portal radiation detectors and particle detectors. Currently, we are in the process of developing satellite broadcast training for the detection of illegal importations of chemical and biological warfare agents to curb the threat of illegal proliferation of weapons of mass destruction.

Thank you again for the opportunity to appear before the Subcommittee to address the new emphasis that the U.S. Customs Service is placing on the Northern Border. The border is changing and we are working both here and in Canada to modernize and streamline our processes. Our intent is to meet our obligations while taking into account the needs of our "customers" and the needs of the American public. This concludes my statement and I am happy to answer any questions you may have.

CHAPTER NINETEEN
THE NORTHERN BORDER:
THE VIEW OF THE
STATE OF MICHIGAN

PREPARED STATEMENT OF JOHN CONYERS, JR., A REPRESENTATIVE IN CONGRESS FROM THE STATE OF MICHIGAN

I want to thank the Chairman for holding this hearing on law enforcement problems at the border between the United States and Canada. No member is more concerned about this is than I am. We can see Windsor, Canada from my District. Each day, thousands of people cross the Ambassador Bridge in and out of Detroit and Windsor. More commerce crosses this bridge than is involved in all of the U.S. exports to Japan. I need to hear from the witnesses first hand on what the border crossing problems are and what is being done to correct them.

I want to extend a special welcome to Mark Hall, President of the Detroit National Border Patrol Council, Local #2599. I look forward to his testimony and the other panelist who are in the day-to-day work of protecting our borders. I am pleased the U.S. Customs Service is here to testify to share with us their multifaceted responsibilities in enforcing criminal laws but if we *really* want an understanding of how law enforcement is combating terrorism and drug trafficking, I believe receiving testimony from Drug Enforcement Agency and the Federal Bureau of Investigation, the federal agencies responsible for criminal laws, is warranted.

Drug and alien smuggling can only be curtailed and eliminated by cooperation between Canadian and United States law enforcement agencies.

Although hearing the problem first hand is critical, it is also important to hear the Canadian and United States criminal law enforcement perspective. I request unanimous consent to insert in the record a letter from the Canadian Ambassador, which sets forth the cooperation between the two country law enforcement agencies. I am also requesting that the record remain open to receive testimony from the FBI and the DEA on their efforts on the northern border.

Mr. Chairman, I hope that we do not have to deal today with argument that we need to implement Section 110 of the 1996 Illegal Immigration Reform and Immigration Responsibility Act of 1996. This section requires an automated system to document every "alien" entering and leaving the United States. Clearly, section 110 will not assist law enforcement in identifying or apprehending drug smugglers or terrorists because it would do nothing to limit "movement" once the individual has recorded his or her entry. Furthermore, although it will provide the Immigration and Naturalization Service with better statistics, it will not help the INS remove non-immigrant aliens who have stayed longer than permitted. The information produced by this system will not tell the INS where to find the overstays. Section 110 is "an expensive guest book" and creating this entry/exit system will divert funding from legitimate law enforcement programs. This tells you what Section 110 won't do, let me tell you what is will do:

Cause unnecessary delays and traffic jams at land borders. Eighty per cent of U.S. exports to Canada and 70 per cent of total bilateral merchandise trade is shipped by truck. Any delays at the border would have a serious impact on the buyers and sellers of goods in both countries. Deliveries in border state industries are required on a "just-in-time" basis. Delays would have an immediate economic impact, particularly on the automobile industry.

Hurt commerce, trade, and tourism. The United States trade more than one billion U.S. dollars a day with Canada. In 1996, Canadian visitors spent at total of $7.3 billion in the United State. Over 10 million Canadians take overnight trips to the United States each year. Implementation of Section 110 would greatly jeopardize U.S./Canada trade relations.

In closing, Mr. Chairman, I believe that we should examine and solve the problems on the northern border. But I want to reiterate that Section 110 is not the answer. It is bad for our economy, a burden to U.S. citizens, and inefficient enforcement tool. It is my hope that this hearing is not just an attempt to resurrect Section 110 for immediate implementation, as if, it is an answer to any of the border problems.

Mr. SMITH. Mr. Pearson, let me direct my questions first to you and say that I appreciate your being candid in your prepared statement. Let me read a couple of phrases from it and I will base my first question on those.

You mentioned the use of Canada as "a staging area for terrorists seeking entry to the United States." You mentioned that "The northern border is a favored transit point for aliens from Asia, particularly China." You say that "Canada's asylum law permit persons to enter Canada, claim asylum and be free while their cases are processed. Some of them attempt entry to their real destination, the United States." By the way, that is a theme that we are going to hear from a number of witnesses today, that we have a situation where, because the Canadian immigration laws are more relaxed, it is easier to enter Canada and get to the United States or cross our northern border than some other direction. You also mentioned that the number of prosecutions for smuggling cases has been increasing dramatically along the northern border.

That all might lead to an obvious question which is, if these kinds of problems exist and if, in fact, they are increasing in many instances, why are not we providing more Border Patrol agents and other law enforcement officials along the northern border, not at a loss of such personnel along our southern border but in addition to what we are doing along our southern border?

Mr. PEARSON. Yes, Mr. Chairman. Thank you for that question.

You took a number of things there that are absolutely accurate. We do have concerns on the way that some people are coming in, some we suspect are terrorists, and that they are using the Canadian laws to get into that country more easily and not be incarcerated so that those who want to seek entry to the United States have an opportunity to do so. That is why we have increased our investigations, why we have put more focus in this area.

I know this is a northern border issue but it really gets down to a matter of how we are spreading our resources, the resources that we do have.

Mr. SMITH. Actually, that was not my question. I was not assuming a fixed amount of resources. Maybe I will ask more directly. It is my understanding that the INS did request 1,000 new Border Patrol agents from the White House and the White House vetoed those requests. What are you doing to convince the White House that more Border Patrol agents are necessary, if you feel that they are?

Mr. PEARSON. Mr. Chairman, we do need more Border Patrol agents, that is clear Commissioner Meissner said that, and we have said that all along. We do need more on the northern border.

Specifically what we are doing through the Department of Justice and OMB, I am not prepared to tell you at this point because I have not been involved in those specific discussions, but clearly, we do need more resources on the northern border and we know that.

Mr. SMITH. Thank you for that answer.

This was not something we warned you we were going to ask about, but

I am just curious if you know. How many terrorists has the INS known about who have crossed from Canada into the United States? I mentioned in my opening statement that we had public records of I think 14 altogether. Are there more than that of which we are not aware? What is the total number of terrorists who might have entered across the northern border?

Mr. PEARSON. Mr. Chairman, I do not have that number handy. I asked for the numbers I looked at since 1993 and the number is not significantly off the number that you used that we have reported.

Mr. SMITH. If you can get those to us, if possible by the end of the hearing, we would be interested because it is my understanding there have been half a dozen in the last year so.

Mr. Bromwich, in his testimony in his prepared remarks, said "We found that record checks are rarely done on those illegal aliens to see if they may be suspected terrorists. In addition, aliens are rarely prosecuted for the criminal offense of entry without inspection even after repeated apprehensions." Why is that? How do you justify a policy that does not prosecute repeaters and how do you justify a policy where you do not check to see if illegal aliens are suspected terrorists?

Mr. PEARSON. We do have several policies to check on these people. We have the IDENT system that is deployed; we have run people through that to find out who they are and to have a record of who is coming through.

Mr. SMITH. So you are saying that you do check illegal aliens to see if they are suspected terrorists?

Mr. PEARSON. I said that we have policies that do so.

Mr. SMITH. Ah, semantics here. I know you have a policy. Why do you not do it if you have the policy? That is even more damaging that you have the policy and do not use it.

Mr. PEARSON. I understand what you are saying and part of it has to do with workload as we spoke about earlier and what is going on at the time; with the number of people we have on the northern border, how many apprehensions are made and how much time we have them. I think Mr. Davis can probably answer that question better and how it works in Blaine Sector.

Mr. SMITH. My time is up and we will have another round of questions. I will pick this up then.

The gentle lady from Texas is recognized for her questions.

Ms. JACKSON LEE. Thank you very much, Mr. Chairman.

Let me also thank the panelists for their very instructive testimony.

Just to emphasize my understanding of this hearing as an oversight hearing dealing with drug smuggling, illegal immigration and terrorism, but as I am listening to the problems, I know that it is also important to keep in mind what may ultimately be the resolution. So my referral to 110(a) was to acknowledge that if that was a possible solution, we might want to ensure that we have a complete feasibility study to ensure that it would, in fact, answer some of these very important concerns that have been expressed.

Mr. Bromwich, let me thank you for your report and query you on several points. Though you might not want to pose yourself as an expert, I think having done the study; you can be very helpful to us.

For example, I noted your comment about the need to collaborate between States and INS, the procedure of checking on asylum applications. How would that work? How would you see that working, at least a check on asylum applications?

Mr. BROMWICH. My understanding is that the databases are available. It is not just a matter of routine practice for those databases to be queried to determine whether there is any information connecting an individual with terrorist organizations. We have not done a lot of work in this area. The inspection I described in my prepared testimony is just in process and the special investigation that I summarized, those are really the only pieces of work that we have done. So this is new territory for us. My understanding is that partly because this is a new phenomenon, there needs to be an emphasis in the Immigration Service and the State Department, a greater degree of collaboration. The State Department needs to provide training and information to INS making INS more aware than apparently people in the field are of the databases that exist that can be queried and INS needs to train its people to do so on a routine basis

My impression, Congresswoman, is that the tools and the data are there. It is a matter of better collaboration between the State Department and INS on the one hand, and better training for INS and Border Patrol personnel to make themselves use those tools.

Ms. JACKSON LEE. That is very helpful. Existing infrastructure, existing data that could be utilized in a more effective manner is certainly one step.

In looking at the border and its size, correct me if I am wrong, did you mention or where do you see the piece of the Border Patrol portion playing on the northern border? I say that in the context of the fact that obviously Canada and the United States maintain very friendly relations. Of course there are the Royal Mounties who are very committed to law enforcement. Where do you see the nexus on the Canadian border between what we do in the United States and what they do?

Mr. BROMWICH. I think the Immigration Service witnesses have been clear, they do not have adequate resources right now to patrol a vast northern border. There is simply too much land across which terrorists, drug smugglers and alien smugglers can work for the Border Patrol to really have an effective deterrent affect right now. It is an enormous task they have right now. I think they clearly do need additional resources in order to provide more of a deterrent. I think it is a major problem right now.

Ms. JACKSON LEE. You would agree with them.

Let me go right to the gentleman on the front line, Mr. Davis. Tell us what you need.

Mr. DAVIS. I think obviously manpower is one of the areas that we do really need. I think for a number of years we have needed more technology and right now, we are getting that technology. As Mr. Pearson stated, we are in the process of getting a camera system, which will be a tremendous help to us. Instead of having to respond to a sensor and not know what is there, it will give us the opportunity of hooking the sensor to the video to actually see if we have a vehicle coming, and to have a description of that vehicle. Technology is coming, but with the technology, we are still going to have to have sufficient number of agents in order to back it up.

Ms. JACKSON LEE. Would you venture a guess for me, Mr. Davis, as to how many agents would aid you along, may not give you all that you want? Maybe you want to give me a second place prize and a first place prize in terms of numbers? I am told you have 300 now. Maybe that is a correct number or not. What would help you out?

Mr. DAVIS. In the Blaine Sector, right now we have 42 agents. I can only address the needs of the Blaine Sector, but in order to effectively work the area in which we have responsibility, we would need a minimum of an additional 74–75 agents.

Ms. JACKSON LEE. In your area?

Mr. DAVIS. In our area alone.

Ms. JACKSON LEE. Mr. Chairman, I see my light has come on. Let me also indicate that I am going to leave. I have a meeting to go to and I will be returning and hopefully will be in time for the second panel.

Thank you very much.

Mr. SMITH. Thank you.

Mr. Pearson, let me return to the question I asked before and read the statement I read a minute ago by the Inspector General and one other in addition. He said, "We found that record checks are rarely done on those illegal aliens to see if they may be suspected terrorists. In addition, aliens are rarely prosecuted for the criminal offense of entry without inspection even after repeated apprehensions." Later on, the Inspector General says, "We were told that no terrorism checks are performed either by INS or by the Department of State on the vast majority, about 90 percent of the asylum applications that are submitted by asylum officers."

You were saying that the INS has a policy of checking to see if illegal aliens and asylum seekers are suspected terrorists but you have not been able to implement that policy. You said we need more Border Patrol agents. If we do not get those additional Border Patrol agents, are we increasing the risk that we will be allowing terrorists to come into our country and perhaps even perform deadly deeds?

Mr. PEARSON. Mr. Chairman, I was aware of the Inspector General's report and since my arrival at INS, we have put out guidance and talked with the Chief of the Border Patrol and the Northern Chiefs to ensure that the weaknesses described in his report of not doing these checks were overcome. So we do have policies now to ensure the checks are done.

Mr. SMITH. Can you implement those policies completely with the current number of Border Patrol agents or is the reason you said you needed more to help implement those policies?

Mr. PEARSON. We did not ask for more in order to implement the policies, but you are right, there is a totality in this. There is a nexus in doing all of this.

Mr. SMITH. So again, you said we need more Border Patrol agents. I suspect one of the reasons we need more Border Patrol agents is to prevent terrorists from coming into the country?

Mr. PEARSON. Yes, sir.

Mr. SMITH. Also, in the Inspector General's statement, and he mentioned it verbally a minute ago, he said he had sent two letters to the INS to check on the status of their corrective actions, the first in October 1998 and the second in January of this year. The INS has not responded to either letter. Is that true as we sit here right now?

Mr. PEARSON. Mr. Chairman, I am embarrassed to say I was not aware of either of those letters, but I will certainly check on that. Also, on a previous question you asked about the number of terrorists and I do have the numbers. My records go back to 1978, 22 terrorists suspected encounters along the northern border by the districts and the sectors and Canadian authorities. The majority of the encounters, 19, have been since 1990. Of the 22 encounters, 5 were confirmed to be terrorists or affiliated with known groups and the remaining were only suspected or self-proclaimed.

Mr. SMITH. That is helpful. Thank you, Mr. Pearson. Mr. Davis, you mentioned a minute ago, "The same smugglers moving illegal contraband operate in both directions." I think that is an important point, which is to say that both American citizens and Canadian citizens have much at stake and much to benefit from a more secure border. Certainly Canadians do not want more drugs coming into their country from the United States and the United States certainly does not want more drugs coming this way either. Again, we sometimes lose sight of the fact that both countries benefit by stopping the flow of drugs, which, unfortunately, is a two-way street. You mentioned this in your prepared remarks, that there are large increases in organized crime along the border. You say "Our manpower levels during this time have been static. We know now that illegal smuggling activity takes place on a daily basis but due to limited manpower, we are able to respond to only 50 percent of our sensor intrusions or alarms on any given day." A minute ago, the Ranking Member asked you what you needed. If you are only responding to half the indications you get of illegal activity of one sort or another, and if there have been increases in organized crime, what is the number of Border Patrol agents and other backup staff you think is needed either in your area or along the entire northern border?

Mr. DAVIS. Again, sir, the entire northern border, I cannot speak for, but I know for Blaine Sector, as I stated, in the last 10 years, the growth north of us has been phenomenal. We find the BC Bud coming in and our intelligence sources tell us that two main organized groups that have involvement with the drugs are one, Hell's Angels out of BC, and the second is organized Asian crime. This is a problem that just continues to escalate. I do not know what the future holds, but every year for the last 4 years, we have seen an increase.

Mr. SMITH. Let me follow up on that. I know you need the increase and I will not push you on the exact figures because clearly you need more. You and another witness today also said you had absolutely no individuals to help along the water boundaries between the two countries. In your case, you have 150 miles and in another case, it is slightly less. I presume you need more agents to protect the waterways. How much of a problem is it, do you think, that alien smugglers or drug smugglers use the waterways?

Mr. DAVIS. I believe that there is a major problem. The 150 miles of waterway we have that goes from Blaine Sector's area out through the Straits of Juan de Fuca historically has always been an area that has been a problem of smuggling into the United States. You have Canada, you have Vancouver Island, which is a huge area, and a lot of that area is very remote. South of there you have the San Juan Islands, which is in the United States. There are over 200 islands along this route.

Mr. SMITH. And yet you have no one along that 150-mile border?

Mr. DAVIS. We have no presence whatsoever on the water.

Mr. SMITH. You and others have mentioned that you believe the drug and alien smugglers actually monitor agents' schedules and then when the agents are off duty, the smugglers see an open border and they come in. That is so incredible. Do you know that is the case? What is your basis for saying that?

Mr. DAVIS. Several years ago, we had a very interesting case that we worked along with Customs and DEA that involved a group of local people who were involved in the smuggling of BC Bud. They actually were surveilling our units. They sat across the street with cellular phones, watched when our people went home and were actually doing surveillance on us.

Mr. SMITH. It occurs to me while you are saying that, we have a little fewer than 300 Border Patrol agents on the close to 4,000 mile northern border. If you divide that into three 8-hour shifts that means at any time you only have 100 agents for close to 4,000 miles. It is no wonder that can be taken advantage of one way or the other, whether it is agents' schedules or lack of agents altogether. You mentioned something that other individuals mentioned as well. You said "Over the past several years, Canada has adopted a non-visa requirement policy with many countries that the United States continues to require visas from. This has resulted in many smugglers being able to easily bring third country nationals into Canada and then smuggle them across the border into the United States." Is that one reason you think the illegal alien and illegal drug traffic is increasing on the northern border?

Mr. DAVIS. I think certainly it is a factor. We have noted from South Korea the last several years an increase of people being flown from Seoul into Vancouver, held somewhere overnight and then the next day simply walk across the border.

Mr. SMITH. Mr. Davis, a last question, and that is, you now are getting ready to finish 30 years with the Border Patrol, is that correct?

Mr. DAVIS. Yes, almost 30 years.

Mr. SMITH. When is it going to be 30 years?

Mr. DAVIS. One more year.

Mr. SMITH. One more year. Let me say to you personally what I have said to many other Border Patrol agents who have testified and that is, I have never met a Border Patrol agent who has not been completely professional, completely dedicated to their job, and wanting to act in the best interest of the communities they, quite frankly, protect. I thank you for all that and for your testimony as well. My final question is, with 29 years of hindsight and practical experience and expertise, what do you think generally we can do to solve some of the problems we have with illegal immigration and illegal drugs?

Mr. DAVIS. I really appreciate that question. My 29 years of service with INS is not only within the Border Patrol; I have also spent time as an immigration inspector; I spent time as a special agent. Just a quick example. In September 1994, I had the opportunity of reading the report of the Select Commission on Immigration that was chaired by Barbara Jordan. I am usually not a letter writer but when I read this particular report that was put together by this bipartisan committee and they talked about the problems with immigration, it was my opinion that they hit the nail right on the head with the area where they talked about verification.

Interestingly enough, several months later, I had the opportunity when Barbara Jordan and her committee came to Canada of attending a luncheon and actually speaking to them and briefing them on the problems that were unique along the northern border. I will always remember as I went in to meet Barbara Jordan, here was a woman in a wheelchair, incapacitated, in chronic pain and I said you probably do not know me but I wrote you a letter because I want you to know that when you talked about the need for verification based on Social Security, as far as I am concerned, that has to be an important element. To me that is the key, to shut off the magnet. As I said this to her, she said, come over here, would you, and she reached up out of her wheelchair, she put her arms around me and gave me a hug. She said, Mr. Davis, I do not know if you know how much that means to me to have somebody from Immigration say that.

I guess what I would like to say to you, sir, as someone from Immigration, I really believe that it is important. It is very important that we put agents along the border. This is needed; there is no doubt about it. But from all of my years of experience, the thing that brings people to this country is jobs. Documentation shows us that only 50 percent of the people in the country illegally came across the border; others, who came here strictly as visitors, did not go home because of jobs.

I believe the only way to do this is through verification based on Social Security and then we go from there. If we need to make other adjustments such as a guest worker program or other things, we need to do it.

The thing that really disappoints me about this is this report was prepared by Congress. I met with my own congressman several years ago and we talked about this issue. He had never even seen a copy of the report.

My hope is that the torch Barbara Jordan carried on this thing—she was exactly right—that when she died, this does not die as well.

Mr. SMITH. Thank you, Mr. Davis.

I will not ask you a question about what you think of the current INS policy about reducing the number of work site enforcement efforts, but I agree with you and let me say also that Barbara Jordan's legacy continues. I do not think I am exaggerating when I say that 80 or 90 percent of what this Immigration Subcommittee does is based upon the recommendations made by the Barbara Jordan bi-partisan commission, whether it is legal or illegal immigration reform. We continue and try to implement her good recommendations. I appreciate your testimony to her.

Mr. Bromwich, I have already quoted you a couple of times today. Maybe you are going to get those letters from the INS after all. We hope Mr. Pearson will make sure that happens.

You mentioned early in your testimony the problem areas. You mentioned western Washington, Vermont and you said "The INS and other intelligence reports indicate that terrorists locate in Canada in part because of Canada's liberal visa and asylum laws and the country's proximity to the United States." How serious of a problem is that? It seems to me it is an open invitation for people to take advantage of both the Canadian immigration system and our system or lack of system along the northern border. What is the potential for problems   there?

Mr. BROMWICH. I think the potential is high. Again, our work in this area has been quite limited but my experience has always been you learn a lot of general things about a problem by looking at a specific case. We learned a lot from looking at the Mezer case.

It is quite clear, based on statements that he made both to Immigration officials and others, that the reason he came to Canada was to come to the United States. The United States all along was his ultimate destination, but he was aware that it was more difficult to get here so he went to Canada as his first step. Once there, he then tried to come to the United States by applying for a visa. I am happy to report that application was denied as a so-called routine refusal by the State Department. That is when he had to resort to trying to come across the border illegally multiple times.

Oddly, the Mezer case is a case study in which various aspects of the system worked reasonably well. The State Department denied his visa application, the Border Patrol apprehended him three different times, even with terribly inadequate resources. So we did not find any individual misconduct at all. We found systemic issues and problems which we think the Immigration Service, together with the State Department and Customs, needs to address, which is why we harp on the letters because we think corrective action needs to be addressed and the Immigration Service needs to focus on the specific findings we have made.

Mr. SMITH. One more question. You found there were no record checks or rarely were there record checks on illegal aliens and their background and there was rarely prosecution of individuals who had repeated crossed illegally. Do you think there are sufficient numbers of Border Patrol agents now to rectify that problem?

Mr. BROMWICH. No, I do not think there are sufficient numbers of Border Patrol agents. I think they definitely need more. The non-prosecution policies that exist along the northern border really mirror, to some extent, the policies that have existed along all of our borders for quite some time. Those have been changed recently in San Diego and in other locations along the southwest border such that there are administrative consequences on the second entry and frequently, if not always, criminal prosecution on the third.

So one of the things I think, not just the Immigration Service, but the U.S. Attorneys' Offices in those northern border States need to consider is whether to put more of their resources into providing a credible criminal deterrent to illegal aliens who come over the border repeatedly.

Mr. SMITH. I could not agree more.

Let me just add that the Administration's own drug czar, General McCaffrey, has said that we felt we needed about 20,000 Border Patrol agents. We have close to 9,000 today, so even he is recommending twice as many as we have today which would certainly be of great help and it help would stop the flow of illegal drugs and the threat of terrorism as well.

As I have done before, I will put that in perspective for those who do not know it. Compare the 9,000 Border Patrol agents we have today with the 30,000 police officers just in the City of Chicago alone and you get a feel for why we need more Border Patrol agents.

Mr. Trotter, we have a vote coming up but let me ask you a question or two. You said in your prepared testimony, but maybe not in your verbal testimony, that "In 1998, Customs seized a total of 4,400 pounds of drugs along our northern border." That was in 1998. How does that 4,400 pounds of drugs on the northern border in 1998 compare to five or 10 years before? Give us a sense of whether it is increasing or decreasing?

Mr. TROTTER. It is certainly increasing. I do not have the facts right at my finger tips to say how much but there is no doubt about it—on the border we continue to refer to and where the Border Patrol Chief is from, Blaine, WA, is pumping more drugs into our country.

Also, oddly enough I was up in Champlain, New York to look at the other side of the equation, and one of our inspectors actually stopped a truck that was what we would consider a rather routine shipment of textiles coming down from Canada, though the driver looked a little bit out of sorts, nervous perhaps. Our inspector opened the truck and on the back of it he found 100 pounds of marijuana stored there.

What we are seeing is that these trends, although the preponderance tends to be on the West Coast and that connection is out there, it may be spreading, especially the ability to grow marijuana indoors. That has really changed. The Canadian climate, for the most part, is not too receptive to growing marijuana outdoors and we are seeing that.

Mr. SMITH. That is not stopping them. They go indoors?

Mr. TROTTER. That is correct. We do have some new technologies to help fight that we do exercise with the RCMP, MP and others.

It is increasing. We have to put it in somewhat of a picture. I know we do not want to talk too much about the southern border.

Mr. SMITH. That is all right.

Mr. TROTTER. For example, we seized a million pounds worth of narcotics last year. So 4,000 pounds is less than .4 of a percent of what we seized, so just some perspective.

Mr. SMITH. Thank you, Mr. Trotter.

Let me say again, and correct me if I am wrong, if anyone else thinks I am wrong, but it seems to me that every witness today has said the problem is increasing on the northern border, both in regard to the quantity of illegal drugs coming across, as far as illegal immigration goes and as far as our inability to check the backgrounds of individuals who might be known terrorists. You wouldn't disagree with that?

Mr. TROTTER. No, sir.

Mr. SMITH. Thank you, Mr. Trotter.

Thank you all for testifying today.

CHAPTER TWENTY
THE NORTHER BORDER:
THE VIEW OF WHATCOM COUNTY, WASHINGTON

STATEMENT OF DALE BRANDLAND, SHERIFF, WHATCOM COUNTY, WASHINGTON STATE

Mr. BRANDLAND. Thank you, Mr. Chairman.

My name is Dale Brandland. I am the Sheriff of Whatcom County, Washington State. I have been in law enforcement for 23 years and I have been the sheriff for the past seven. I would like to thank you for the opportunity to appear before your committee and testify on law enforcement issues at the northern border.

Whatcom County is located in the northwest corner of Washington State, just south of Vancouver, British Columbia. Our northern border is shared with Canada and the population of greater Vancouver just across our border is 1.5 million. Because of our proximity to the border, Whatcom County has several Federal agencies that are in some way involved in controlling the transportation of drugs to and from Canada. It is a pleasure to report to you that we enjoy a high level of cooperation among local and Federal agencies.

We encounter the full spectrum of drugs seen throughout the country but in a very general sense, as you have heard, much of our attention is focused on high grade marijuana being exported from Canada and cocaine that is being imported into Canada. I cannot tell you the number of cases that are generated by our Federal agencies but I can tell you that almost all of their cases are handled at the local level. Most Federal cases taken to the U.S. Attorney's Office in Seattle are declined because they do not meet the minimum weight threshold for prosecution. The case is then referred to our local agencies.

It is handled by our prosecutor, processed in our courts and eventually those arrested are housed in the Whatcom County Jail or sent to the State Department of Corrections. If we did not handle these cases, they would not be prosecuted at all.

We have watched the threshold for prosecution climb over the years and as things have gotten worse and the quantity of drugs seized increases, so does the threshold. The reality is that the Whatcom County criminal justice system is doing most of the Federal Government's work after the initial arrest is made.

Our friends to the north, the Canadians, are good neighbors but I must tell you that I too am troubled by their liberal immigration policies. Anyone that has a passport can enter Canada and there is very little to stop them from entering the United States once they get there. Mr. Abu Mezer is a prime example.

Local Border Patrol personnel in Whatcom County had apprehended Mr. Abu Mezer on three separate occasions after attempting to enter the country illegally. He was finally held pending formal deportation but was able to post bond and be released. Approximately 7 months later, he was shot by the New York City Police Department just prior to planting a bomb that would have blown up the subway system. There have been more recent incidents involving suspected terrorists entering the country at Blaine, so I do not think that this is an isolated incident. The front line to stop this type of person from entering our country is the U.S. Border Patrol and as you well know, our front line is relatively nonexistent.

As you may well imagine, the Whatcom County Sheriff's Office and the U.S. Border Patrol have a close working relationship. Both of our agencies have a limited number of people to work in a very large area and we regularly depend on one another for backup. Unfortunately, our relationship at the local level does not extend to the regional level.

I would like to say that I take strong exception to the decision that minimizes the Border Patrol's presence here. The attitude at higher levels seems to be that all of their resources should go to the southern border. I certainly agree that the problem is greater there, but to ignore the problems facing us at the northern border is courting disaster.

The Blaine Sector now has 49 people assigned to it. Those 49 people cover all of Alaska, western Washington and all of Oregon. They do not have enough people to adequately cover the border 24 hours a day, 7 days a week and that does not address the fact that they do not have any personnel to cover our coastline.

Several years ago, the Border Patrol implemented a policy that diverted manpower from the northern border to the southern border. This was said to be a temporary measure because of an increased threat at that time. This practice is still going on today. Of the 49 people assigned to the Blaine Sector, 3 are regularly sent south to bolster southern manpower. I believe that a cost benefit analysis would show that there is far greater benefit to the Border Patrol by leaving them there.

I would like to conclude by saying that I am aware that our problems at the northern border cannot compare with those at the south, but I do feel that we have distinct needs and those needs are not being properly addressed at this time. I do not expect the Border Patrol to shift its entire focus but I would appreciate it if they would at least acknowledge that there is a problem.

[The prepared statement of Sheriff Brandland follows:]

PREPARED STATEMENT OF DALE BRANDLAND, SHERIFF, WHATCOM COUNTY, WASHINGTON STATE

Mr. Chairman and members of the subcommittee, my name is Dale Brandland and I am the Sheriff of Whatcom County in Washington State. I have been in law enforcement for 23 years and have been the Sheriff for the past 7 years. I would like to thank you for the opportunity to appear before your committee and testify on law enforcement issues at our northern border.

DEMOGRAPHICS

Whatcom County is located in the northwest corner of Washington State. We are just south of Vancouver, British Columbia. Our county has just over 2000 square miles and the population is approximately 160,000. Our northern border is shared with Canada and the population of greater Vancouver, just across our border is 1.5 million.

DRUGS AT OUR BORDER

Because of our proximity to the border, Whatcom County has several agencies that are in some way involved in controlling the transportation of drugs to and from Canada. It is a pleasure to report to you that we enjoy a high level of cooperation among the local and Federal agencies. We meet on a regular basis and information sharing is the norm. We also enjoy working relationships with our counterparts in British Columbia. We encounter the full spectrum of drugs seen throughout the country. But, in a very general sense, much of our attention is focused on high-grade marijuana being exported from Canada and cocaine that is being imported into Canada.

I cannot tell you the number of cases that are generated by our Federal agencies but I can tell you that almost all of their cases are handled at the local level. Most Federal cases that are taken to the U.S. Attorneys Office in Seattle are declined because they don't meet the minimum weight threshold for prosecution. This means that they will not prosecute the case. The case is then referred to our local agencies for prosecution. It is handled by our prosecutor, processed in our courts and eventually those arrested are housed in the Whatcom County Jail or sent to the State Dept. of Corrections. If we did not handle these cases they would not be prosecuted.

We have watched the threshold for prosecution climb over the years. As things have gotten worse and the quantity of drugs seized increases . . . so does the threshold. The reality is that the Whatcom County criminal justice system is doing most of the Federal government's work, after the initial arrest is made.

Another unfortunate consequence of our proximity to the border is warrant arrests. It is not uncommon to have out of state fugitives apprehended at the border. They rarely agree to immediate extradition so we have to absorb the cost of prosecution, public defender, court infrastructure and, of course their time in jail.

LIBERAL IMMIGRATION POLICIES IN CANADA

Our friends to the north, the Canadians, are good neighbors but I must tell you that I am troubled by their liberal immigration policies. Anyone that has a passport can enter Canada and there is very little to stop them from entering the United States once they get there. Mr. ABU MEZER is a prime example.

Local Border Patrol personnel in Whatcom County had apprehended MR. ABU MEZER on three separate occasions, after attempting to enter the country illegally. He was finally held, pending formal deportation, but was able to POST BOND and be released. Approximately 7 months later he was shot by the New York City Police Department just prior to planting a bomb that would have blown up the subway system. There have been more recent incidents involving suspected terrorists entering the country at Blaine so I do not think that this is an isolated incident. The front line to stop this type of person from entering our country is the U.S. Border Patrol and as you well know, our front line is relatively nonexistent.

THE ROLE OF THE BORDER PATROL

As you may well imagine the Whatcom County Sheriff's Office and the U.S. Border Patrol have a close working relationship. Both of our agencies have a limited number of people to work in a very large area so we regularly depend on one another for back up. Our personnel monitor each other's radio frequencies and it is not uncommon for both of our agencies to be involved in the same event. In fact, in March of 1998 two border patrol personnel apprehended a homicide suspect within minutes of the incident because they were monitoring our frequency. Had they not done this it is very likely that we would not have been able to resolve the case. Unfortunately, our relationship at the local level does not extend to the regional level.

I would like to say that I take strong exception to the decision that minimizes the Border Patrols presence here. The attitude at higher levels seems to be that all of their resources should go to our Southern border. I certainly agree that the problem is greater there but to ignore the problems facing us at the northern border is courting disaster.

The Blaine sector now has 49 people assigned to it. That brings them up to the level that they were at 4 years ago. Those 49 people have to cover all of Alaska, Western Washington and all of Oregon. They do not have enough people to adequately cover the border 24 hours a day, 7 days a week and that does not address the fact that they do not have ANY personnel to cover our coast line of that area of water that separates us from Canada.

Several years ago, the Border Patrol implemented a policy that diverted manpower from the northern border to the southern border. This was said to be a temporary measure because an increased threat at that time. At the start, 50% of the sectors manpower was sent south. This practice is still going on today. Of the 49 people assigned to the Blaine sector, 3 are regularly sent south to bolster southern manpower. I believe that a cost benefit analysis would show that there is far greater benefit to the Border Patrol by leaving them here. It would have a big impact locally and I doubt that anyone would notice their absence down south.

POINT ROBERTS

In Whatcom County we have a unique situation in that you have to enter Canada in order to get to one part of our county. I am referring to Pt. Roberts. Pt. Roberts is a small two square mile peninsula that is only accessible by driving into Canada. After you enter Canada at Blaine, you have to drive 26 miles to the North and West before you can reenter the U.S. at Pt. Roberts. The population is about 750 and I have two deputies that live there full time. If they arrest someone, we need to have the Coast Guard remove them by boat because we cannot drive them through Canada. Pt. Roberts has a port of entry but it is relatively easy to smuggle contraband or drugs in by boat and then walking into Canada. This is another area where we see very little of the Border Patrol

CONCLUSION

Mr. Chairman, I would like to conclude by saying that I am aware that our problems at the northern border do not compare with those in the south. But, I do feel that we have distinct needs and that those needs are not being properly addressed at this time. I don't expect the Border Patrol to shift its focus but I would appreciate it if they would acknowledge that there is a problem.

CHAPTER TWENTY-ONE
THE NORTHERN BORDER:
VIEW OF THE
NATIONAL BORDER PATROL COUNCIL

STATEMENT OF MARK HALL, PRESIDENT, NATIONAL BORDER
PATROL COUNCIL LOCAL 2599, DETROIT, MI

Mr. HALL. Good morning, Mr. Chairman.

My name is Mark Hall. I am President of the National Border Patrol Council, Local 2499 in Detroit, Michigan. I have been a Border Patrol agent for over 14 years. Currently, I work as a senior Border Patrol agent in the Detroit, Michigan Station on the Canadian Border. I have been working in the Detroit station for 12 years.

In the past few years, enhancements on the southwest border are much needed but during the same period, resources on the northern border have actually decreased. In 1988, there were 21 field agents in the Detroit Sector; today, there are only 19 field agents to cover over 800 miles of border.

The most recent staffing numbers I was able to obtain are from September 1998. They show there are 7,357 agents on the southwest border to patrol 1,900 miles of border. The northern border has 289 agents to patrol 3,987 miles of border. That is more than twice the border with 25 times less the manpower.

The Canadian Government immigration laws make it simple for citizens of numerous countries to enter Canada with only a passport. We see these individuals using Canada as nothing more than a stopover on their way to the United States. This is highlighted by an incident that occurred last month.

I arrested two Mexicans entering the United States illegally. They stated to me they entered Canada from Mexico with only their passports. They claimed under NAFTA they no longer needed visas. They said, the southwest Border Patrol enhancements have escalated the risk of apprehension and the fees that smuggler's charge. They said they could buy an airline ticket to Canada, then cross into the United States. They said they knew the number of Border Patrol agents on the northern border was small. They knew if caught, we had no money to return them to Mexico or any money to detain them. They were right. They were released and sent on to their final destination in the United States after a short processing period.

In the Detroit Sector, we have no money to detain criminal aliens, let alone the illegally entering alien. Our funding for detaining aggravated felons allows us to only detain two per week. This is very frustrating and it makes us feel that we are nothing more than a bump in the road for these criminals.

The tongue and cheek acronym, CARP, which stands for catch and release program is now a common usage on the northern border. The Detroit Sector has 19 field agents for 5 stations. Not one station in this sector has 24-hour coverage. We have to respond to details to the southwest border, oral hiring boards and training details at the Academy. There are days when nobody is even on duty.

Detroit Sector's border is totally comprised of water. Last year, the station's patrol boat logged only 20 hours due to manpower shortages.

When we look at terrorism, terrorist experts have identified terrorist organizations with ties to the metro Detroit area. During the Gulf War, we had information of possible terrorist smuggling efforts in our area from Canada. Our manpower was so low, we could not even muster up enough agents to put one agent in one patrol car for 24 hours a day.

Securing our southwest border is essential, but the resources needed on our northern border must be addressed. The number of arrests on the northern border in Detroit are greater than they have ever been in my 12 years, 44 percent greater this year compared to last year for the same period. I believe this corresponds directly with the pressure being placed on the southwest border. This will only worsen as more pressure is placed on the southwest border.

Last year in Detroit Sector, a jet skier was stopped on his personal watercraft and arrested going into Canada with four kilos of cocaine as he departed the United States. The stakes in the illicit smuggling activities are great; the profits are far too high for all of the smugglers to abandon their lucrative activities.

A strategy to bring the southwest border under control without dedicating any resources and manpower to the second front line is fatally flawed. Prioritization is absolutely essential to any well-run organization. However, to declare you only have one priority is patently unsound and impractical. This jeopardizes the safety of the men and women whose duty it is to protect the integrity of our borders.

[The prepared statement of Mr. Hall follows:]

PREPARED STATEMENT OF MARK HALL, PRESIDENT, NATIONAL BORDER PATROL COUNCIL LOCAL 2599, DETROIT, MI

Mr. Chairman and members of the Subcommittee, my name is Mark P. Hall. I am the President of the National Border Patrol Council, Local 2499 in Detroit, Michigan. I have the honor of being employed as a Border Patrol Agent and proudly serving my country for over fourteen years. I currently work as a Senior Border Patrol Agent on the U.S./Canada border and have done so since 1987. Thank you for this opportunity to testify on the law enforcement problems at the border between the United States and Canada, focusing on the issues of illegal immigration, terrorism, alien and drug smuggling.

INTRODUCTION

There has been a call from Congress and the American people to focus greater attention on controlling our borders. The additional resources to the southwest border over the past few years are much needed. But during this period the resources on the northern border actually declined. This lack of attention to our northern border undermines the enforcement efforts on our southern border and will simply divert the flow of illegal activity across our borders.

RESPONSE

The past several years the Border Patrol has seen an increase in resources/manpower never seen before in the 75 years of proud history. The Border Patrol has gone from about 3,500 agents to approximately 7,600 as of September of 1998, a dramatic increase in just a few years. The increases in technical equipment such as, state of the art infrared cameras, sensors and communications equipment have made the job of controlling our borders more manageable and safer for my fellow agents. These unprecedented increases were in response to the overwhelming call by the American people for us to get control of our borders. The southwest border was out of control. Alien and narcotics smuggling were rampant; the risk of arrest was far outweighed by the opportunities of the illicit activities transpiring on our borders. These increases in the Border Patrol resources have helped to stem this illicit flow and bring our southwest border under some form of control.

As of September 1998 approximately 7,357 Border Patrol Agents protect our 1,945 miles of southwest border with Mexico. Our northern border with Canada is 3,987 miles long with 289 to protect it. The northern border is more than twice the size of the southwest border. But yet the southwest border has a more 25 times the manpower than the northern border with less than half the border.

ILLEGAL IMMIGRATION

The Canadian government's immigration laws make it simple for citizens of numerous countries to enter with nothing more than a passport. We see these individuals using Canada as nothing more than a stopover on their journey to the United States. Almost every year since my transfer to the northern border in 1987, our apprehensions have increased. Last year the Detroit Border Patrol Sector's apprehensions were at a five-year high. So far this year our arrest numbers are over 40% greater than last year for the same time. Ironically, amount of agents that work the field for this period has actually decreased. Though there has been a net decrease in available manpower, arrests continue to rise. Request from local, state and federal law enforcement have steadily increased as well. As the southwest border is brought under control, there is a corresponding increase in apprehensions on the northern border. The strategy to bring the southwest border under control without dedicating any resources and manpower to the other second frontline of defense is fatally flawed. The stakes in the illicit activities are great. The profits are too high for all of the smugglers to abandon their lucrative illicit activities. We have seen this, assault on agents have increased as the frustrations of the smugglers increase. Others have simply changed how they operate.

This is highlighted by an incident that occurred last month. I apprehended two Mexican nationals as they entered the United States illegally from Canada. After a lengthy interview and examination of their documents I discovered an emerging trend. The Mexicans flew from Mexico with their passports into Canada. They claim that under NAFTA (North American Free Trade Agreement) Mexicans no longer need visas to enter Canada, simply a passport. Then can just come to the United States by way of our northern border. They told me why they chose the northern border route because the Mexican border is more difficult to cross into the United States because of the large Border Patrol presence. This has escalated both the prices the smugglers and the risk of apprehension and returned to Mexico much greater. The aliens said they can buy and airline ticket to Canada, travel to the border and cross into the United States. They said they knew the number of Border Patrol Agents on the northern border was very small. Even if they were caught by the Border Patrol they said they knew we had no money to return them back to Mexico or detain them. They were right. We have very little money to detain criminal aliens let alone the undocumented border crosser.

This fiscal year funding for the detention of undocumented aliens is all but non-existent. What little we have seen has trickled in and is quickly gone. Agents here in Detroit have been told the only detention funding available is to be used for aggravated felon aliens. INS Deportations branch maintain the detention funding. We have been told we can arrest and detain only two aggravated felons per week. This has to be done during the hours that Deportations is "open", Monday through Friday during day shift; otherwise these individuals are not detained because Border Patrol has no detention money. We have no I&NS detention facility in the Detroit Metro area, therefore we must rely on local jails and pay for the use of their facilities

In March of this year, a local police department arrested five foreign nationals involved in a $45,000.00 jewelry store robbery. These subjects claimed to have been from five different countries. Investigation revealed these subjects were members of a highly organized interstate robbery/fraud ring operating in at least five states. One subject had a photo-altered passport. A fingerprint check revealed two were listed with the FBI as having previous felony theft convictions. Due to lack of detention funding these subjects were processed for a deportation hearing at a future date and released on their own recognizance with not so much as a dollar posted for bond.

Border Patrol Agents are dedicated to performing their duties in the highest tradition of the Agency. Unfortunately, we all know the duties of a Border Patrol Agent can call for the ultimate sacrifice. Last year, sadly we lost the greatest number of Agents ever within a year period. At one point in the Detroit Station, 50% of the Agents had been involved in a shooting. Personally, I have been involved in two shootings on the northern border. When Border Patrol Agents answer the call to protect our nation's borders, only to have the violators of law show little concern for arrest, because we have no money for detention or repatriation, has a devastating effect on our morale. This frustrating dilemma is taking its toll on agents. The tongue in cheek recently this frustrating dilemma is taking its toll on Agents. The acronym, C.A.R.P., which stands for Catch and Release Program, is common usage on the northern border.

One of the Border Patrol's biggest problems on the northern border is lack of resources. There is not one station within the Detroit Border Patrol Sector that has agents on duty 24 hours a day. There are days when not a single agent is on duty. Often days go by without an agent even coming close to patrolling our sector's northern border area. The manpower shortage is alarming. Agents have to respond to other law enforcement agency's requests concerning foreign nationals in an area responsibility of four states with only 19 field agents. Agents must also participate in oral hiring boards, academy details, and details to the southwest border. At one point, the Detroit Station had three agents detailed to the southwest border for 30 days, thus leaving only four of seven at the station for the day to day patrol duties. Last summer the manpower shortage was so great and calls from other agencies were high, the station's patrol boat had less than 20 hours of service logged. With such shockingly low actual border patrolling hours we cannot even get an idea of what is happening on our northern border.

In the Detroit Sector it is not uncommon for an agent to travel 200 miles one way to pick up an alien from another law enforcement agency only to process the individual and then release him. The Detroit Sector has only one Detention Enforcement officer to transport these individuals. Over the past two years the Detroit Sector's only Detention Enforcement Officer travels over 200 miles per day on average. More support personnel are needed to free Border Patrol Agents to do their regular duties.

As stated earlier the Detroit Sector has 19 field agents. This year the Detroit Border Patrol Sector's management/union partnership council drafted a proposal of what they felt would meet the sectors manpower needs for 24 hour on duty coverage. The *minimum* number was an astounding *additional* 104 Border Patrol Agents or 5 1/2 times as many field agents currently in the sector. This I believe would have to be done over several years. It is my firm belief that northern border agents should transfer from the southwest border for a number of reasons. First, to obtain the foreign language skills needed to do the job, which someday could save that officer's life. Another reason is to gain the unique skills necessary to work the southwest border so that when they are detailed to the southwest border for short periods of time, they are effective. Finally, and be no means the least importantly, employees from the southwest border should be allowed to transfer to the northern border for morale purposes and to help stem an alarming rate of attrition on the southwest border.

TERRORISM

The FBI has identified several Mid-East organizations as known terrorist groups. The Detroit Metro area has the largest mid-east population on the globe outside of the mid-east. The Detroit area also has a significant Serbian and Albanian population. Although it is true, there are many other groups through out the world that are known and acknowledged terrorists groups, I am going to address our situation here locally in Detroit. Terrorism experts indicate that Canada has become an assembly point for potential terrorists seeking U.S. targets.

During the Gulf War the Detroit Border Patrol was in a high state of security. We received intelligence almost daily of potential terrorist smuggling efforts from Canada in our area of operation. The intelligence indicated that smuggling of terrorist across the border to transit to "safe houses" in our area was a very real probability. Due to extremely low staffing levels, vigilance on the border was minimal to none. This was the best we could do with the dismal manpower we had at that time. Our staffing today is less than it was then.

In the mid-1990's an environmentalist group sailed by vessel up the St. Lawrence Seaway to the Detroit River. They anchored off the shore of a local nuclear power plant located on the international boundary waterway. They then surreptitiously and illegally entered the grounds, scaled the cooling towers and held security, police, and FBI at bay for 6 hours. The nearest on duty Border Patrol Agent responded from another state after being requested by the FBI. This group transited more than 100 miles of our international waterways unmolested, unchallenged by any law enforcement. We can only be thankful that this group did not have more of a destructive motive. Our role is to protect and secure our national sovereignty, but we are unable to do so effectively because of the lack of personnel and resources.

In summer 1995 Detroit Border Patrol had received reports that a group of more than 20 Serbians at an unknown location in the Windsor, Ontario, Canada area. These individuals, at least some were thought to have terrorist ties, were suspected to attempt entry into the United States via the Detroit River. One evening while no agents were on duty, we received a call from the U.S. Coast Guard. They had apprehended six of these subjects, only after their boat broke down in the Detroit River in front of the Coast Guard Station. Witnesses stated this boat was seen traveling back and forth from Canada to the U.S. all day, always loaded with people. All six subjects in the boat were listed on our "lookout" bulletin. Suspiciously, only the operator of the boat had a sunburn. I cannot tell you how many made of the other 20 individuals made it to our shores, or how many were suspected terrorists.

DRUG SMUGGLING

We know drug smuggling is prevalent on our Canadian border, but to the actual extent is unknown for all of the previously mentioned reasons. Over the past several years Detroit Sector Border Patrol has been involved in several millions of dollars worth of narcotics seizures. We have arrested Canadians buying drugs to resell them in Canada. Agents have arrested Americans taking drugs to sell in Canada. We have stopped watercraft on our border and found hidden compartments with drug dogs alerting on these empty spaces, indicating there had been drugs in them. I stopped watercraft with specially designed PVC type containers that could be tethered underwater to a boat for surreptitious transport of contraband. Again a police drug dog alerted to the presence of a controlled substance.

We have detained individuals coming from Canada via the Detroit/Windsor freight train tunnel (this tunnel runs under the Detroit River from Canada). We have stopped known gang members with empty duffel bags making return trips from Canada, persons with pending criminal drug cases, pending weapons smuggling cases to name a few. This tunnel has been a hot bed of illicit activity ever since prohibition.

Intelligence indicates that the increasing Asian gangs in Toronto, Ontario are smuggling heroin into the United States across our northern border and smuggling back cocaine. Intelligence tells of increased marijuana smuggling from Canada into the United States because of an increasing trend of hydroponics production in Ontario, British Colombia, and Quebec.

Confidential Sources of Information tell us that contraband smuggling across the waterways is rampant. We are told that individuals run contraband by boat with little fear of being stopped due to the meager law enforcement presence. We are told they would rather travel unchallenged by boat as opposed to car and face questioning at a traditional vehicle Port of Entry.

This past year we were so short of manpower it was difficult to get two agents on duty at the same time to run the Detroit patrol boat. Border Patrol agents rode with Coast Guard in order to have some coverage. On one such night last fall while stopping and boarding boats crossing the international waterway from Canada, three boats ran at high speed and evaded apprehension by "blacking out" and out-running federal law enforcement. This was just one night! This past year a "Jet Ski" type personal watercraft was stopped on the St. Clair River and four kilograms of cocaine were seized as it entered Canada from the United States.

LACK OF PHYSICAL RESOURCES

The Detroit Sector sorely lacks the resources to assist its agents. Its patrol vehicles are older and have high mileage. Boats are the basic tool for patrolling a border entirely comprised of water. Only four of our five stations in the Detroit Sector have a boat. Two of the boats we have, one at Trenton Station and the other at the Port Huron Station are cast off equipment from other sectors. These two boats were old and headed for the surplus pile, but were fixed up and put into service in the Detroit Sector.

The Detroit Sector two-way radio system, as most on the northern border is outdated, and easily scanned by smugglers. When agents leave their patrol vehicles their walkie-talkies are useless in all but a few locations. We see agencies such as the Michigan State Police receiving huge federal funding (rightfully so) to replace their out of date two-way radio system with a state of the art 900 MHz. Digital systems.

Intrusion sensors and cameras in the sector are decades behind in current technology. Intrusion cameras don't even project a "real time" picture. They simply "click" a picture and send it over a phone modem, thus valuable time and information is lost. Thereby the risk of escape by offenders is greatly increased.

CONCLUSION

The resources needed on our northern border must be addressed. I believe that the increased flow of illicit traffic across the northern border that we have already seen will only worsen as more pressure is placed on the southwest border. Prioritization is absolutely essential to any well-run organization, however, to declare that you have only one priority is patently unsound and impractical. To declare the Border Patrol has only one priority jeopardizes the safety of the men and women whose duty it is and threatens the integrity of our borders.

Mr. Chairman and members of the Subcommittee, I thank you for this opportunity and I am pleased to answer any questions you might have.

Mr. SMITH. Thank you, Mr. Hall.

CHAPTER TWENTY-TWO

THE NORTHERN BORDER: THE VIEW OF A CANADIAN

STATEMENT OF DAVID HARRIS, PRESIDENT, INSIGNIS STRATEGIC RESEARCH, OTTAWA, ONTARIO

Mr. HARRIS. Mr. Chairman, members of the subcommittee, my name is Dave Harris. I am with INSIGNIS Strategic Research in Ottawa, Canada. I was formerly Chief of Strategic Planning with the Canadian Security Intelligence Service. Through academics and other undertakings, I maintained my interest in terrorism and counterterrorist issues.

Canada is often thought of and frankly flatters itself as being a peaceable kingdom. That is the historic label Canadians are often brought up with. Others talk about us as being a land of milk, toast and honey. We are considered masterly inoffensive on any number of levels and we have been kind of proud of having kept it that way for a good deal of our history.

While the United States has had the agonies of Vietnam and various nuclear and conventional force balance concerns to worry about, Canada has focused increasingly internally on priorities like Medicare, bilinguals and multiculturalism and of course, peacekeeping.

We are a population of 29 million people. We have relatively few obvious enemies, unlike many other countries familiar to you. Altogether, you could say that we have a remarkably unthreatening profile.

One of the problems that we who have been involved with our intelligence community and concerned about terrorism in Canada and links of terrorism is Canada is the fact that perception I described of a completely nonthreatening, almost a non-player in the terrorism world is now tremendously dated. I think it is tremendously important that we come to recognize the potential for political violence in Canada, the risk of it spreading through the

United States and other friendly nations, and indeed, the lack of national resolve found in Canada for confronting this potential terrorism and violence.

I would like to review quickly certain highlights of the 1980's and 1990's in Canada, a period when we first began to see the clearest possible evidence of the spread and manifestation of terrorist activity. I think the message in all of this is that we are seeing in this the tip of a few very unpleasant icebergs.

We have had several incidents in Ottawa and elsewhere in Canada involving Armenian-related violence, including the assassination of a Turkish diplomat. We have had invasion of the Turkish Embassy and a series of matters of this general sort implying the presence, among other groups, of the BKK.

The world's biggest single terrorist toll was linked to Canada in 1985 when over 300 passengers died in the Air India Boeing 747 bombing. This has been linked to Sikh extremists, themselves desirous of an independent country or state in India.

Another airliner at that time was also bombed and both of these bombs were put on board in Canada it is believed, by Canadian residents or people with extremely close ties to Canada. We have also seen in the 1980's an assassination attempt on a Cabinet minister from India in British Columbia, this again linked to similar sources.

In 1992, the Mujahedin-E-Khalq made their presence violently known in Ottawa as part of a coordinated worldwide response to an Iranian attack on an MEK base in Iraq. They invaded the Iranian Embassy, there was some violence involved there, and there were more questions about the extent of coordination of the Mujaheddin group in Canada and around the world.

Hassan al-Turabi, who may be known to subcommittee member as Sudan's power beyond the throne and not himself far removed from concerns about terrorism was wounded in an assassination attempt at Ottawa International just a month after the Mujaheddin attack in Ottawa and the resident Sudanese exile was charged in that.

Zaire's Ottawa High Commission was invaded by Congolese representatives in 1993 and at about that time an IRA-linked individual, an Irish-born Canadian, was arrested for involvement in major IRA weapons and technology networks.

Perhaps quite dramatic, beginning in the early 1990's has been developing evidence of a Hizballah network in Canada. We have in the form of the Federal Court of Canada documents and transcripts, proof accepted by the Federal Court of Canada that there is and are such networks in Canada.

A proceeding that occurred about 2 years ago featuring Mr. Al Sayegh resulted in his being reviewed for possible deportation and other concerns relating to security certificates. He was implicated, as you are well aware, I believe, in the Al Khobar Towers bombing in Saudi Arabia.

We had a Molotov cocktail attack on the U.S. Consulate in Toronto only weeks ago and we had similar confrontations relating to consulates and other such establishments in Montreal and Toronto recently.

All in all, this is to at least suggest, I would say highlight in vigorous terms, the fact that terrorism is now alive and well and living in Canada. It is the obligation of the Canadian Government and the Canadian people to emphasize that fact and begin to adjust.

[The prepared statement of Mr. Harris follows:]

PREPARED STATEMENT OF DAVID HARRIS, PRESIDENT, INSIGNIS STRATEGIC RESEARCH, OTTAWA, ONTARIO

Mr. Chairman, Ms. Jackson Lee and Members of the Subcommittee, thank-you for your invitation to testify on important Canadian aspects of the northern boundary security situation. My name is Dave Harris. I am a Canadian citizen, President of *INSIGNIS* Strategic Research, and formerly served as Chief of Strategic Planning of the Canadian Security Intelligence Service (CSIS). I continue to pursue my specialties in intelligence, counterterrorism and international affairs as a lecturer and commentator in Canada and abroad.

Americans often tell me that it is difficult to think of Canada and international terrorism in the same context. Canadians themselves have the same problem. But the largely untold truth is that Canada and terrorism *do* go together. A failure to see this stems from a failure to realize that Canada is simply not the country it used to be.

Abroad, Canada is often regarded as a land of milquetoast and honey. Even with the occasional French-English tiff, Canadians are considered a well-intentioned and largely harmless species of North American, awash in crystalline lakes, grizzly bears and mounted police. We almost revel in the historical label, "the peaceable kingdom."

To be sure, Canada has seen history's sharper edges. Its losses in the First World War were greater *per capita* than those of the United States. In WWII, Canada had the world's third largest navy, and Canadian forces suffered through the Korean stalemate with the rest.

But, in the half-century following all this, much changed in the Canadian experience and attitude. Canada drifted far from the concept of a threat-aware, front-line nation. While the US, for example, was in the agony of Vietnam, strategic nuclear doctrine and European force balance, Canadians were largely removed from such concerns, living under America's protective nuclear and conventional force "umbrella". Indeed, Canadians practically liquidated their military, and have developed an essentially inward-looking national self-image embracing peacekeeping, medicare, bilingualism, multiculturalism, and—our national sport—constitutional debate. At 29 million in population, the country recently boasted the highest standard of living among OECD nations.

All this explains something of Canada's unthreatening profile on the world scene and Canadians' belief that they are almost innately free from international political violence. However, although the myth has largely endured, it is increasingly misleading. For, the last decade or two have seen quiet shifts in the country and its society, with the development of pronounced undercurrents that highlight both the potential for political violence, and the lack of national resolve in confronting this potential.

Let me highlight just a few examples from the 1980s and 1990s of signs pointing to the engaging of Canadian territory and residents in internationally related violence. It is crucial to bear in mind that international political violence—terrorism and its networks—had been practically non-existent in Canada before this period. These examples therefore represent a new trend, which finds Canadians, and their contacts engaged in planning, fundraising, arms' transfer and storage, and execution of international terrorism. In short, these episodes should be viewed as the tip of a variety of icebergs and reflective of a disquieting trend.

EXAMPLES OF GROWING VIOLENCE

In separate incidents in Ottawa in the mid-1980s, Armenian-related violence resulted in the assassination of a Turkish diplomat and severe injury to another. The Turkish embassy itself was invaded.

The world's single biggest terrorist toll was linked to Canada in 1985 when over 300 passengers died in the bombing of an Air India Boeing 747. The explosive was planted in Canada by Sikh extremists working for an independent Sikh state in India. Another was placed at about the same time in Canada on another airliner, exploding later than planned, after the aircraft landed in Japan, and killing baggage handlers. In British Columbia in the 1980s a visiting cabinet minister from India was wounded in an assassination attempt linked to Sikh extremism.

In April 1992, members of the Iraq-backed Mujahedin-E-Khalq invaded the Iranian embassy in Ottawa as part of a coordinated worldwide response to an Iranian attack on an MEK base in Iraq.

A month later, Hassan al-Turabi, Sudan's power-behind-the-throne, was wounded in an assassination attempt at Ottawa International Airport. A resident Sudanese exile was charged.

In 1993, Zaire's Ottawa high commission was invaded by Congolese. At about this time an Irish-born Canadian was arrested for involvement in a major IRA weapons and technology network.

By the late 1990s, immigration proceedings brought several revelations. In one, the Federal Court of Canada considered a security certificate issued by

Canada's Solicitor General and Minister of Citizenship and Immigration against Mr. Mohamed Husseini al Husseini under s. 40 of the *Immigration Act*. Mr. Al Husseini confirmed that Hizballah members were in Canada. Two years ago, a similar proceeding was undertaken in the Federal Court with respect to Mr. Hani Abd Rahim Al Sayegh, a suspect in the June 1996 Al Khobar Towers bombing in Saudi Arabia. The Court accepted as proved, government evidence that Mr. Al Sayegh was a member of Saudi Hizballah, that Hizballah has networks in Canada, and that these are directed from south Lebanon.

Only weeks ago, Serbian-Canadians Molotov-cocktailed Toronto's US consulate. Days before, in response to Turkey's capture of a Kurdish guerilla leader, Kurdish supporters invaded a Montreal consulate and attacked an Ottawa embassy with Molotovs.

All of this underscores the potential in Canada for "homelands"-related terrorism.

A major element in this situation is immigration. For about two decades roughly a quarter of a million immigrants have entered Canada yearly, making the country the biggest recipient of immigrants, by proportion, in the western world. Every year immigration adds another percent to the national population.

The composition of immigration reflects a dramatic shift from the regional—many would say European-based—preferences of 40 years ago. Four decades ago, 80% of each year's immigrants were coming from relatively stable European regions. Today, and for some years now, 80% of our quarter-million annual immigration intake has been coming from Africa, the Middle East, Asia and other regions thought to include trouble spots. A great many of these trouble spots are areas where, as counterterrorist specialists would say, "homelands" disputes predominate.

It is trite, of course, to say that the overwhelming mass of our immigrants are peaceful, productive citizens. But it is also undeniable that a small portion have imported with them the issues and hostilities—the resentments—from foreign homelands. The result of this influx has been Canada's growing engagement in world terrorism. From the limited, relatively minor Quebec terrorist activity that petered out in the early 1970s, we have now progressed to more expansive and ominous activity on a variety of fronts connected with global political violence. Intelligence highlights the use of Canadian territory and resources in the planning, funding, recruiting and provision of cover for international terrorist activity.

In the face of this situation, Canada's security and intelligence community have done heroic work. But Government reaction at the political level has not been adequate to the counterterrorist task, and is reflected in a number of ways.

One serious area of concern involves the collecting of funds destined for terrorism, by groups benefiting from charitable tax status. Mr. John Bryden, a highly respected Member of Parliament and author, has condemned the fact that, under Canada's antiquated accountability regime for "charitable" organizations, tens of millions of dollars in tax-free donations are channeled to groups supporting international terrorism. Thus Canadians, through their tax system, inadvertently subsidize terrorism and send abroad the message that Canada is a soft source for the soft money of terrorism. Mr. Bryden points out that "the only law on the books as far as Revenue Canada is concerned that actually describes what charities are supposed to do is an Elizabethan statute of 1601." Little has been done to make legislative adjustment.

Nor has Canada any statutes comparable to the US terrorism legislation that allows the government to declare certain countries and groups "terrorist" in nature, with the triggering of derivative sanctions, measures and intelligence targeting.

And security and intelligence budgets have been cut at a very dangerous time. As an example, the Canadian Security Intelligence Service (CSIS), with major counterterrorism responsibilities, has had staff reduced 26 percent, from 2760 in FY 1992–93, to a current level below 2000. Depending on its calculation, the CSIS budget will have fallen by between 21 and 37 percent over the period 1993–94 to 1998–99.

What is the answer? At bottom, the problem is that Canadians lack an attitude appropriate to the severity of the threat and our responsibility for guarding against it. Having been beneficiaries of their peaceful history, Canada and Canadians are becoming victims of it. Canadian political leadership must bring home the message that "it can happen here" and act appropriately on the several fronts noted earlier. This means more in counterterror funding and research. It also means a decisive change in attitude, especially in the framework and ethos underlying immigration.

Observers point out, for example, that federal politicians' delay in taking action against terror funding in Canada arises from the growing political clout of expanding immigrant groups and their lobbyists. The auguries are not good, and to understand this it is important to appreciate the concept of Canadian multiculturalism.

Federally supported, that is, funded, multiculturalism has meant a lack of real integration of newcomers into Canadian society and values. Public policies and pronouncements have made government-funded multiculturalism untouchable, giving recent immigrants a reasonable expectation that they need not sacrifice allegiance to foreign groups and interests with whom they, as a matter of ideology or other sentiment, might associate themselves. Growing immigration numbers and lobbying power have moved Canada's political leadership further from integration and from dealing directly with related terror potentialities.

Perhaps indicative of the resulting malaise and inaction was a report made a week or two ago by the Canadian Broadcasting Corporation—CBC Television—as Canadian aircrew were risking their lives in combat over

Yugoslavia. The CBC interviewed a few Serbian Canadians who were condemning Canada's action in support of NATO, essentially swearing allegiance to Yugoslavia, and, in one case, baldly declaring his intention to return to his homeland to fight for the Milosevic government *against Canadian forces if necessary*. (Recall, incidentally, that in the Yugoslav conflict three years ago, a Serb-Canadian participated in chaining United Nations—including Canadian—peacekeepers to NATO targets as human shields.)

Despite the quasi-wartime situation, Canadian authorities have neither condemned nor taken action against such "patriots". This is a telling comment on the *laissez-faire* attitude of Canada's federal politicians and public in the face of major issues of international security and terrorism.

Mr. SMITH. Thank you, Mr. Harris, for your excellent testimony.

CHAPTER TWENTY-THREE
THE NORTHERN BORDER:
VIEW OF CARNEGIE
ENDOWMENT FOR PEACE

STATEMENT OF DEMETRIOS G. PAPADEMETRIOU, SENIOR ASSOCIATE, INTERNATIONAL MIGRATION POLICY PROGRAM, CARNEGIE ENDOWMENT FOR INTERNATIONAL PEACE

Mr. PAPADEMETRIOU. Thank you, Mr. Chairman and Ms. Jackson Lee for your leadership on this important issue. Ms. Jackson Lee, I also want to thank you for giving the thrust of my testimony in your opening remarks.

What my colleagues at the Carnegie Endowment and I have tried to do is basically sit back the last few days and reflect on some preliminary ideas and findings from a project that is about one-third of the way to completion. It basically looks at border issues and how different countries or different borders within different countries handle the challenges that are implicit in every single border.

My colleagues at the Endowment and I have focused our efforts on the northern border. That is what we are trying to do, giving you an idea of some of our initial thoughts on that.

We have spent quite a bit of time, maybe 20 days, on the northern border, three parts of the northern border—Detroit, Windsor and Port Huron, Buffalo, Fort Erie, Niagara, Seattle, Bellingham, Surrey and Vancouver. We have done that in the last 6 months.

What we have found after about 70 or 80 interviews and speaking with maybe 150 or so people, many of whom are the types of people you have had in this hearing, Border Patrol agents, INS district directors, Customs district directors, as well as businesses and NGOs. We have, in sense, concluded a number of things that I am going to read for you.

First, we think we should not inconvenience everyone and interfere with economic interests and local community dynamics in the hopes of catching a few additional violators. There are more effective and efficient ways to deal with the bad guys, in our view, and we can perhaps discuss some of those in our Q and A period after this.

Secondly, we think we should be working more closely with our Canadian counterparts at every level, institutionalizing contacts, enhancing cooperation and sharing information on matters small and large. Our respondents made clear to us time and again that interagency cooperation across the border is extremely effective and that, in fact, is taking place quite routinely among officials in both countries, if only informally and intermittently because it is not yet formally sanctioned by the two central governments.

Cooperation of this nature should be actively encouraged by the governments of both countries. In doing so, neither country should shy away from unconventional ways of solving problems. Among these might be the physical sharing of buildings and facilities, cross-training, joint operations and the like.

In all the sites we visited along the border, we heard nothing but positive comments about the Canadian consulates and their effectiveness in pulling together a variety of interested parties on border issues and being catalysts for change and forward thinking. Interestingly enough, the Mexican consulates play a similar role along the southern border quite effectively, especially given the nature of their challenges.

If indeed these are shared concerns, in other words the concerns of this hearing as we believe they are, our U.S. consulates in Canada and Mexico where appropriate should do no less.

Third, we believe that we should be making much greater investments in intelligence gathering and gradually focus ever-larger parts of that effort at the initial entrance into the North American continent. For those who are so inclined, a fortress North America may in fact be easier to create than a fortress USA.

We should be making far greater investments in infrastructure and technology, both at ports of entry and the corridors leading to such ports. Both types of investments are critical components of any comprehensive effort at improving the management of the border. Such investments must proceed, we believe, from a reconceptualization of the current inspection methodology to rely much more on risk assessment and random inspections and less on inspecting every person.

Under the current methodology, as you know, Mr. Chairman, an inspector, whether Customs or INS, must speak with every crosser. They must also focus most directly on targeting resources toward preclearance programs for both people and cargo. The fifth recommendation is that we should work more closely with private sector interests whose thinking is often ahead of the curve, ahead of our thinking.

Whether these interests have a financial stake in making the border work more smoothly and predictably or simply are community-based organizations committed to better border management, better treatment by border officials and more efficient travel, their ideas should be solicited and listened to systematically.

Finally and most importantly, we believe that the Federal Government should make a habit of working more closely with the communities that are affected by these issues on a daily basis. Their input, including soliciting ideas and providing feedback on others' ideas, should be incorporated at an early stage in the policy process.

Thank you, Mr. Chairman.

[The prepared statement of Mr. Papademetriou follows:]

PREPARED STATEMENT OF DEMETRIOS G. PAPADEMETRIOU, SENIOR ASSOCIATE, INTERNATIONAL MIGRATION POLICY PROGRAM, CARNEGIE ENDOWMENT FOR INTERNATIONAL PEACE

ABSTRACT

This testimony is based on preliminary impressions from fieldwork along the U.S.-Canada border that aims to catalogue existing local initiatives, understand and explain similarities and differences, pull out and contextualize "best practices" in local self-management, and share these with a variety of stakeholders. The project's point of departure is a widely shared concern that policy-making and discussion about borders and their management occurs primarily in national capitals. We start from a working hypothesis that at the local level, communities on both sides of a common border are thinking creatively and often collaboratively about common problems and interests and, to the degree they are allowed to do so, develop processes and institutions that give substance to the concept of devolution. After extensive fieldwork along the U.S.-Canada border, we have become convinced that local officials, in partnership with business interests, worker organizations, and community-based and other relevant group, should play a much more significant role in the ongoing discussions about and the implementation of policies that affect their lives.

We would like to summarize our observations with the following six statements:

1. We should not inconvenience everyone and interfere with economic interests and local community dynamics in the hopes of catching a few additional border violators. There are more effective and efficient ways to deal with the bad guys.

2. We should be working with our Canadian counterparts at every level, institutionalizing contacts, enhancing cooperation, and sharing information on matters small and large. Our respondents made clear to us time and again that inter-agency cooperation across the border is extremely effective and that it in fact is taking place quite routinely among officials in both countries—if only informally and intermittently because it is not yet formally sanctioned by the two central governments. Cooperation of this nature should be actively encouraged by the governments of both countries.

3. We should be making much greater investments in intelligence gathering and gradually focus ever-larger parts of that effort at initial entries into the North American continent. For those who are so inclined, a Fortress North America may be easier to create than a Fortress U.S.A.

4. We should be making far greater investments in infrastructure and in technology (both at ports-of-entry and the corridors leading to such ports). Both types of investments are critical components of any comprehensive effort at improving the management of the border. Such investments must proceed, we believe, from a reconceptualization of the current inspection methodology to rely much more on risk assessments and random inspections and less on inspecting every person.

5. We should work more closely with private sector interests whose thinking is often ahead of the curve. Whether these interests have a financial stake in making the border work more smoothly and predictably or are simply community-based organizations committed to better border management, better treatment by border officials, and more efficient travel, their ideas should be solicited and listened to systemically.

6. Most importantly, perhaps, the federal government should make a habit of working more closely with the communities that are affected by these issues on a daily basis. Their input (including soliciting ideas and providing feedback on others' ideas) should be incorporated at an early stage of the policy process.

I. INTRODUCTION

Mr. Chairman, Ms. Jackson Lee, Members of the Subcommittee. My name is Demetrios Papademetriou, and I am the Co-Director of the International

Migration Policy Program at the Carnegie Endowment for International Peace. Thank you for asking me to testify today regarding the U.S.-Canada border.

I am submitting this testimony on behalf of myself and my colleagues at the Carnegie Endowment, Deborah Meyers, and Nicole Green. It reports on the preliminary impressions from extensive fieldwork along the U.S.-Canada border. That fieldwork is part of an ambitious comparative international project that seeks to advance understanding of how communities that straddle an international border, and at times form a single economic and cultural entity, manage common challenges, and particularly the migration relationship. The project looks at five different international border regions—U.S.-Canada, U.S.-Mexico, Germany-Poland, Russia-China, Russia-Kazakh. It aims to catalogue existing local initiatives, understand and explain similarities and differences, pull out and contextualize "best practices" in local self-management, and share these with a variety of stakeholders, including central governments.

The project's point of departure is a widely shared concern that policy-making and discussion about borders and their management occurs primarily in national capitals. We started from a working hypothesis that at the local level, communities on both sides of a common border are thinking creatively and often collaboratively about common problems and interests and, to the degree they are allowed to do so, develop processes and institutions that give substance to the concept of devolution. After extensive fieldwork along the U.S.-Canada border, we have become convinced that local officials, in partnership with business interests, worker organizations, and community-based and other relevant group, should play a much more significant role in the ongoing discussions about and the implementation of policies that affect their lives.

Although our project is looking at several borders, my remarks today are based upon our own work in three different regions along the U.S.-Canadian border, as well as on our understanding of circumstances along the U.S.-Mexican border. We have made five extensive visits to three areas along our Northern border (Detroit/Windsor/Pt.Huron, Buffalo/Ft. Erie/ Niagara, Seattle/Bellingham/Surrey/Vancouver) over the last five months. During these Northern border trips, we have visited nine different ports-of-entry. We have conducted well over 70 interviews in both countries with local government officials, business leaders, federal immigration and customs officials, bridge operators, community-based non-governmental organizations, researchers, and local residents. We will be happy to share additional information from this project with you in the fall, once we have received initial reports from the teams that are doing similar work along the other four international borders.

II. GENERAL OBSERVATIONS

A. "One Size Fits All" Strategy Doesn't Fit Both Borders

Our overall impression from our own work is that a single policy and set of rules does not, and will not, work for managing both of our land-borders. The principle of treating our two NAFTA partners equally is crucial; our policies, however, must be sensitive to three factors that distinguish our relationship with Canada from that with Mexico: 1) The history of special bonds between the U.S. and Canada; 2) The reality that access to each other's countries has been a long established and accepted practice; and 3) The geography (and topography) of the Northern border.

Let me give you some examples of what I mean by these. Regarding the special, historical links between the United States and Canada, these include a shared language (mostly) and historical tradition; similar emphases on the rule of law, democratic principles, etc.; a tradition of cooperation in matters large and small; and long-term alliances and partnerships in regional and global matters. It also includes virtually identical immigration traditions and similar levels of social and economic development, particularly in the border regions. Well before NAFTA, many industries along the Canadian border already related to both countries in a seamless manner (the auto industry became fundamentally a single industry with the Auto Pact of 1965) and viewed their proximity to the border as an advantage. The NAFTA simply accelerated the pace and added depth to the level of such seamlessness. Finally, the two countries have a number of unique agreements in place, such as the International Joint Commission which acts as an independent advisor to both governments, resolves disputes under the 1909 Boundary Waters Treaty, and helps protect the transboundary environment.

On the issue of access between the two countries, the communities themselves frequently view themselves as one, with Windsor residents working in Detroit and fervently cheering for the Detroit Red Wings (rather than the Toronto Maple Leafs) and Detroit residents viewing Windsor as just another suburb and taking routine weekend trips to Windsor restaurants or Toronto theaters. Similarly, Buffalo residents frequent their summer cottages in Ft. Erie, Ontario, and Canadians fill up the parking lot at the Ellicottville, NY ski resort.

Despite many similarities, however, border traffic varies along the Northern border.

The Detroit ports-of-entry, for instance, receive many visitors from Asia and Europe because the Detroit airport is a major entry point for nonstop flights from Asia and Europe. As one might expect, commercial traffic there relates primarily to the auto industry and much of the other traffic consists of the region's residents.

The Buffalo region sees an extremely large number of international tourists because of Niagara Falls, while from a commercial standpoint, it is located along a high tech, fiber optics, and medical research and development corridor.

Crossings at Point Roberts, Washington (a peninsula below the 49th parallel that has 1,000 year round residents and is surrounded on three sides by water and on the fourth by Canada) consists almost exclusively of local residents (and summer tourists). As a result, the same few inspectors see the same cars and passengers numerous times each day, every day, every week, every month— crossing through Canada to get to Bellingham or to Blaine on the American side for work or for school or for shopping or for whatever else they may need that is not available on Point Roberts.

Regarding geography, the length of the Canadian border is at least double that of the Mexican border and approximately 90% of the Canadian population lives within 60 miles of the American border. This makes the border an extremely relevant issue for Canadians. (Only a small proportion of the U.S population lives close to a border.) In many of these areas, such as Detroit and Windsor, the crossing infrastructure (e.g. the Detroit-Windsor tunnel that runs underneath the Detroit River) cannot be enhanced without enormous investments of additional funds.

B. "One Size Fits All" Strategy Doesn't Fit Even One Border

Differences among ports-of-entry in terms of needs, challenges, priorities, etc., make it difficult to generalize even about the entire length of a single border, much less about both borders. Border policy must thus be sensitive to the "facts-on-the-ground" in each border area.

For instance, in some ports-of-entry in the Eastern half of the U.S., the primary problems (e.g. long lines and long waits because only two out of ten booths may be staffed) can be alleviated with additional staffing. More inspectors can translate into greater facilitation and better enforcement while also addressing such collateral issues as the additional environmental pollution resulting from trucks awaiting inspection. In ports-of-entry in the Pacific Northwest, there is a sense that U.S. border inspectors must try to prevent the entry of high quality marijuana produced in British Columbia (and apparently valued highly among U.S. users), that Canadian inspectors must redouble their efforts to deter weapons smuggling, and that both countries must work harder to prevent the entry of goods that are fraudulently labeled so as to make them tariff free under NAFTA.

How, then, should we treat our borders? In our view, the idea would be to have a single national border policy that treats both borders equally, but allows different regions and ports-of-entry along both borders to set their own priorities and to develop and apply tools that respond to the challenges and opportunities that the region presents (by "region" we mean a space that may include both sides of a border). Of course, while local flexibility and innovation should be encouraged and rewarded, it must be accomplished in a manner that makes arbitrary actions or the arbitrary interpretation of fundamental rules unacceptable. We spoke with many people in our fieldwork who were extremely frustrated with inconsistent (and often seemingly improper) behavior by staff of the inspection agencies. Most people told us they would be happy to comply if they knew what the rules were and if the rules didn't seem to change all the time.

Another way of looking at the issue of how much uniformity we should insist upon—particularly when it comes to managing both of our borders—might be to think of Mexico and Canada as situated on a continuum whose two end points are sealed borders and no borders. Canada and Mexico, for the reasons we discussed in our listing of the similarities between Canada and ourselves, are at different points along that continuum—although we envision that eventually, they will be moving toward the direction of fewer, rather than more border formalities. Clearly, such progress is likely to occur at different speeds. By acknowledging that the *ultimate* aim of our policy will be the equal treatment of both countries, we give ourselves the flexibility to treat both of our NAFTA partners within a single framework while dealing in practical ways with the fact that they are located at different points on that continuum.

With Canada, we can experiment with policies and test ideas that are specific to a locality and, if they prove successful, can then be "exported" to other localities along that border. And with regard to the Southern border, we can offer Mexico the prospect of importing those among those innovations that prove useful *as soon as it can replicate the conditions that made them succeed in the Northern border*. Such an open-ended, "learning by doing" approach, is likely to serve broad U.S. interests best while acknowledging both the different realities of each border (and port-of-entry) and the need to be sensitive to the optics of treating Canada and Mexico too differently.

Our research has also identified several good ideas and initiatives that already are taking place. We outline them here without much discussion because we believe that they should be widely publicized across the entire border and that the federal government should start taking them into account as its thinking evolves in these matters.

Private sector initiatives

The Canadian-American Border Trade Alliance is a border wide public/private binational partnership that works to improve the efficient flow of goods and people across the U.S.-Canadian border.

The Canada-U.S. BorderNet Alliance is a cross-border regional network of business organizations focused on the development of trade, tourism, and investment in the Niagara Region.

Academic initiatives

The University of Windsor offers a special NAFTA tuition rate for U.S. and Mexican students who want to study in Canada. That rate is almost the same as what Canadian students pay and only about one quarter of the tuition paid by other international students.

The Golden Horseshoe Educational Alliance is a coalition of academics at over twenty colleges and universities in the region ranging from Toronto to Rochester.

Tourism-related initiatives

The Convention and Visitors' Bureaus in Washington State and British Columbia are marketing the Two-Nation Vacation in Cascadia.

The Chambers of Commerce in Niagara, Ontario, and Niagara, New York, and the Greater Niagara Partnership are doing the same for Niagara Falls. In fact, the two chambers are thinking regionally in even more substantive ways by undertaking joint overseas trade missions and promoting the economic development of the region.

Government initiatives

The Pacific Northwest offices of the two principal border inspections agencies, Customs and INS, are experimenting with some innovative ideas with regard to staffing and technology that should be of interest to other regions. Among them are multi-agency international border enforcement teams working against organized crime, pre-clearance of certain types of cargo for particular companies, the use of transponders, the re-routing of late-night passenger traffic to truck lanes to permit staff from the lightly used car traffic lanes to reduce the long truck backups.

Some local county governments and planning organizations are working together to secure funds for significant improvements to the infrastructure of trade corridors (such as I–94 in Detroit which connects to the 401/QEW in Ontario). In the Pacific Northwest, the Whatcom County Council of Governments has organized a bi-national regional planning group with stakeholders from both countries, including representatives of localities, federal government agencies, Chambers of Commerce, etc. The resulting International Mobility and Trade Corridor (IMTC) group meets monthly; it shares information, discusses challenges and solutions, and has made a joint proposal for funding for international border crossings from the Transportation Equity Act for the 21st Century (TEA–21).

These are only some of the many ideas we heard on our visits.

III. CHALLENGES

U.S. Customs and the INS do the work of over 20 federal and state government agencies as they inspect goods and people at the border. The challenge clearly is to balance effectively all the major interests and actors—

facilitating access by the legal traffic, preventing entry of illegal goods and turning back all unauthorized traffic, appropriately responding to asylum claims, etc.

I would like to make three general points regarding the challenges that are intrinsic to performing this critical inspection function.

First, the growing trade and commercial relationship between the United States and Canada is so important that interfering with it is simply foolish. Canada is our number one trading partner with $329 billion in two-way trade in 1998, which means that almost $1 billion in goods and services crosses the border daily. Estimates are that 45 percent of U.S.-Canada trade goes through a Michigan/Ontario Port-of-Entry and that 30 percent goes through the Buffalo/Ft. Erie/Niagara region. The Ambassador Bridge in Detroit, in fact, accommodates the largest commercial exchange in the entire United States (almost 11 million vehicles in 1997, including over 2.5 million trucks).

On the passenger side, traffic also has significantly increased. All indications are that it will continue to do so. In recent years, over 30 million people went through the Detroit ports-of-entry each year, followed by almost 30 million crossings in the Buffalo district, and over 20 million in the Seattle district. Considering the sheer size of these numbers, the Congress should be thinking of ways to encourage federal agencies and assist local agencies and private sector organizations to further enhance facilitation, rather than creating obstacles.

Second, the threats of illegal immigration, drugs, and terrorism, are indeed real in the following sense: every port-of-entry is vulnerable to penetration by undesirable elements. And, as experience has taught us, this vulnerability extends to the issuance of visas—making entry through the front gate perhaps the easiest route of entry by most intending criminals. The rest of them, and especially the more "serious" criminals, have ample space—*and the resources*—to bypass port-of-entry controls without much effort. Indeed, we all told that the evidence from a variety of ports-of-entry seems to indicate that entry attempts by criminals who are potential threats to our society are rather rare and isolated, particularly relative to the huge number of crossings. In fact, in town-hall and focus-group meetings in Detroit, Michigan and Point Roberts, Washington, both of which included both Americans and Canadians, not a single person put forward serious security concerns about the entry of Canadians or Americans into their respective countries or argued that a more open or differently managed border would lead to less security.

The lesson, we think, is obvious: we should not abandon common sense and overreact to occasional violations of our laws by inconveniencing the 98 or 99 percent of compliant traffic while trying to pursue the remaining one or two percent who are non-compliant. On the immigration side, many of those who are non-compliant seem to be neither deliberately nor meaningfully non-compliant. (Primarily, they are Canadians who are only in technical violation of the rules).

On the drug side, some port-of-entry Customs officials acknowledge that most of those who are not compliant seemed to be "mom-and-pop" types carrying small amounts of marijuana—rather than serious drug smugglers.

We do not mean to belittle the importance of the drug and people smuggling interdiction efforts. But, outside of the Washington State/British Columbia crossings, nobody even suggested to us that such smuggling was a serious problem. Furthermore, *we have seen no evidence and have heard of no claim that, even in places where the anti-smuggling/drug effort is most dedicated, the inspection system currently in place at either border intercepts most would-be violators.* A number of people even suggested to us that a random inspection method would probably be as effective as the current inspection methodologies. And under questioning, even those most committed to the anti-alien smuggling/ anti-drug effort acknowledged that most of their good "busts" occur as a result of tips and good, old-fashioned, human intelligence work, and through seamless on-the-ground cooperation with the Royal Canadian Mounted Police.

The recommendation that flows from this analysis is obvious: more attention and resources should be devoted to intelligence gathering and information sharing regarding third country nationals and drug, alien, or weapons smugglers (the serious threats), than on "thickening" the current system of inspections. (The inspector corps of both main inspection agencies should increase, however, if we hope to keep up even minimally with increased traffic.)

Controlling illegal immigration, drugs, and terrorism are of concern to all of us and a proper priority for the government. The method being proposed in IIRAIRA Section 110, however, seems unwarranted and unlikely to achieve additional results *absent extraordinary new investments in human and physical infrastructure.* Failing that—and many people in fact argue that even *with* that— we will find ourselves in the unenviable positions of shooting ourselves in the foot both economically and in terms of our relations with one of our closest partners—and all that while looking for the perfect solution to a near non-problem (or, more accurately, to a problem that can be handled more effectively and efficiently through other initiatives).

We want to emphasize again that this does not mean that we propose that we should be doing nothing more. Violators and potential violators need to be targeted through other means, including intelligence and cooperation with the Canadians, who are not likely to be any less interested in keeping out of Canada the same types of terrorists, and organized drug and alien smugglers, who are of concern to us. In fact, one idea whose time seems to us to have arrived, is engaging in open-ended negotiations with Canada about increasing the level of harmonization between U.S. and Canadian policies on such matters as cargo and passenger pre-clearance programs, law enforcement programs of all types, and, in due course, even the issuance of visas.

Pre-clearance for regular commuters, for instance, could be harmonized so that Canadians and Americans who register with the program and who qualify for it could enter both countries from any port-of-entry in an expedited manner. Similarly, on cargo inspections and anti-alien and anti-drug smuggling efforts, why not start from the premise that both we and the Canadians want to keep out the same persons and goods? (We found little argument anywhere with that premise.) Then, why not work together more closely to agree on who can enter (and facilitate those entries), to share as much information as possible about matters of common interest, and to keep out those who should not be admissible to or welcome in either country? And although we cannot expect identity of views with Canada on all matters up front, enough agreement exists to make negotiations on the issues on which we disagree worth the effort.

Finally, we need to start thinking about the border as a system. With NAFTA pushing all three partners inexorably toward a fully integrated region, such practices as just-in-time production and the ability to move goods and people across *all three countries* (in an efficient if still regulated way) become critical elements of regional competitiveness. The prosperity of all of us relies on such competitiveness. Intelligent inspection strategies that are realistic and can inspect without unnecessary hassles of delays throughout the NAFTA space must thus be given priority.

At present, our Southern border seems to be reeling under the weight of efforts that try to bring it under control while the U.S.-Canadian border may be suffering partly from the malady of inattention (reflected in large part in understaffing). The results, however, are in some ways similar. In neither border are the goals of facilitating all the commercial, commuter, and visitor traffic (while doing an effective enforcement job) being met satisfactorily.

Good enforcement and good facilitation go hand-in-hand; you can't do one without paying attention to the other. Absent concurrent and roughly equivalent efforts to do better along all borders, undesirable border crossers will indeed look for and exploit the weak links. Since we don't believe that any of us is thinking seriously about "leak-proof" borders, the changes in effectiveness and efficiency must come from *thinking differently* about the inspection function.

Thinking about the border as a system allows us to think prospectively about the greatest challenges an inspections-based border effort faces while addressing issues of smuggling before smugglers and their cargo reach the border—where they might or might not be intercepted. It also compels us to think differently about the infrastructure necessary to execute whatever inspection methodology is relied upon. Infrastructure—which includes not only the crossings themselves (be they land crossings, bridges, or tunnels), but also the inspection space for both countries, the immediately surrounding roads, and the highways leading into and away from them—is already bursting at the seams along the Northern border. Before we make massive new investments on building more of the same, why not think first about how we want to see borders operate in the future and then build the infrastructure that can take us there?

IV. CONCLUDING PRINCIPLES

We leave you, then, with the following six general principles about how to handle the U.S.-Canadian border, which summarize many of the items we have discussed above.

We should not inconvenience everyone and interfere with economic interests and local community dynamics in the hopes of catching a few additional violators. There are more effective and efficient ways to deal with the bad guys.

2. We should be working with our Canadian counterparts at every level, institutionalizing contacts, enhancing cooperation, and sharing information on matters small and large. Our respondents made clear to us time and again that inter-agency cooperation across the border is extremely effective and *that it in fact is taking place quite routinely among officials in both countries—if only informally and intermittently because it is not yet formally sanctioned by the two central governments.* Cooperation of this nature should be actively encouraged by the governments of both countries. In doing so, neither country should shy away from unconventional ways of solving problems. Among these might be the physical sharing of buildings and facilities, cross-training, and joint operations. In all U.S. sites that we visited along the border, we heard nothing but positive comments about the Canadian consulates and their effectiveness in pulling together a variety of interested parties on border issues and in being catalysts for change and forward thinking. Interestingly enough, the Mexican consulates play a similar role along our Southern border quite effectively, especially given the nature of the challenges they face. If indeed these are shared concerns, as we believe they are, our Consulates in Canada (and Mexico), where appropriate, should do no less.

3. We should be making much greater investments in intelligence gathering and gradually focus ever-larger part of that effort at initial entries into the North American continent. For those who are so inclined, a Fortress North America may be easier to create than a Fortress U.S.A.

4. We should be making far greater investments in infrastructure and in technology (both at ports-of-entry *and the corridors leading to such ports*). Both types of investments are critical components of any comprehensive effort at improving the management of the border. Such investments must proceed, we believe, from a reconceptualization of the current inspection methodology to rely much more on risk assessments and random inspections and less on inspecting *every* person. (Under the current methodology, an inspector must speak with every crosser). They must also focus more directly on targeting resources toward pre-clearance programs for both people and cargo.

5. We should work more closely with private sector interests whose thinking is often ahead of the curve. Whether these interests have a financial stake in making the border work more smoothly and predictably or are simply community-based organizations committed to better border management, better treatment by border officials, and more efficient travel, *their ideas should be solicited and listened to systemically.*

6. Most importantly, perhaps, the federal government should make a habit of working more closely with the communities that are affected by these issues on a daily basis. Their input (including soliciting ideas and providing feedback on others' ideas) should be incorporated at an early stage of the policy process.

Thank you again, Mr. Chairman and Ms. Jackson Lee for inviting me here today.

Mr. SMITH. Thank you, Mr. Papademetriou.

CHAPTER TWENTY-FOUR
THE NORTHERN BORDER:
QUESTIONS FROM CONGRESS

Sheriff Brandland, let me direct my first question to you. You mentioned in your testimony, "I must tell you I am troubled by the liberal immigration policies of Canada. Anyone that has a passport can enter Canada and there is very little to stop them from entering the United States once they get there." Does that contribute significantly to the problem in your judgment or is that something that could be remedied perhaps by some changes in the law? How do you feel we should address that problem?

Mr. BRANDLAND. I guess, Mr. Chairman, my own feeling seems to have been backed up today by the fact that it is just so easy to get into Canada that something needs to be done at that level, I feel. There is nothing to stop these people once they get into Canada. So if I am hearing you correctly, I would say my first response would be to deal with the issue at the Canadian level, if that is possible, and then more enforcement on the northern border to deal with those that do manage to get in.

Mr. SMITH. To go from immigration policy to crime policy, it is my understanding that Canada has relatively lenient criminal penalties for drug offenses, whether it is trafficking or possession. Is that the case and can you elaborate on that?

Mr. BRANDLAND. That is true. We have actually seen that. We do not have marijuana-growing operations in my county. They have all moved north across the border. As I have said, it is all primarily being funded and sponsored by the Hell's Angels motorcycle gang. That is pretty well documented. So from that perspective, we feel, yes, their lenient drug policies have actually moved the problem out of my county and into theirs.

Mr. SMITH. Lastly, you say in your testimony that "The lack of a sufficient number of Border Patrol agents is courting disaster." What do you mean by "courting disaster"?

Mr. BRANDLAND. I think that Mr. Abu Mezer is a classic example. I truly do believe that as important an issue as drugs are in our country, I believe that a stronger presence on our border to deter terrorists from entering our country is a very, very important issue. It will only take one incident like we saw in Oklahoma City to create the disaster that I am talking about.

Mr. SMITH. Thank you, Sheriff Brandland.

Mr. Hall, you used an acronym that I have actually heard before on the southern border and you tell me now that it is in common use on the northern border and that is CARP which stands for "catch and release program." That is not, I do not think, a compliment to the procedures that are sometimes used in regard to illegal immigration or illegal drugs. Tell me what you mean by CARP and how bad you think the situation is and also, why does it come about? Where did the term come from and how did you arrive at that particular description of the procedures?

Mr. HALL. It is just frustrating for myself and the other agents. We are out in the field working and arresting these individuals. You may end up in a fight with one of them because a lot of times they do not want to be placed into custody. You take back these individuals only to have no money to detain them. Like I said, we are simply a bump in the road. We catch them, we process them and release them and they continue on their way, many times never to be seen again by the Immigration Service. We process them, serve them with documents that say they must report for Immigration Court and there is nothing there. They do not even have to post a bond. There is no incentive to make them come back for their immigration hearing and down the road they go. This is extremely frustrating for us.

Just recently within the past 2 weeks, we were involved in an operation where there were five foreign nationals that robbed a jewelry store of $45,000 of precious gems. When these individuals came into our custody, we did not know and today we do not really know who they were. We processed their fingerprints, FedEx them off to the FBI, and two of them had prior criminal records. We are still not sure what countries they were from. They had photo-altered passports. We processed them with the best information we had and released them with not a penny of bond being posted. They are gone today to continue on in their criminal activities and to perpetrate them against our communities.

Mr. SMITH. You mentioned also two trends, and I am going to try to link them together, and you tell me if you think I am correct.

You mentioned the emerging trend of individuals particularly from Mexico choosing not to cross the southern border but to come around to the northern border, it being oftentimes less expensive in many ways. Tell me if this is really accurate, that you are literally being told by the INS to detain only two aggravated felons per week and when you do detain them, they can only be during the times that the office is open Monday through Friday during the day shift? Is that right?

Mr. HALL. As shocking as it sounds, yes, that is correct. These Mexican citizens that I detained freely admitted the fear of being arrested by me was almost a joke to them. They were laughing and joking as they were in custody in my station, and I had a candid conversation with them and there was no hesitation on their part whatsoever.

Mr. SMITH. How do you account for an immigration policy, an INS policy, that puts a quota on the number of criminal aliens you can stop? Is that contrary to the national interest and to the safety of our citizens?

Mr. HALL. It is shocking. I cannot justify a policy of that nature at all. This information on the aggravated felons came to me from a fellow agent just as of Friday. He is involved in the high intensity drug trafficking task force and comes across criminal aliens and aggravated felons on a regular basis.

He says now he has to schedule his work day as to when he can arrest these individuals because the Border Patrol itself locally has no detention funds to speak of whatsoever and we have no local detention facility so we have to rely on individuals like the Sheriff here to house our prisoners at an expense to the Border Patrol. We have no money, we cannot detain them, so the Immigration Detention Section in Detroit has funding but we have to present those individuals for detention to them during the hours they operate which is Monday through Friday, 9 a.m. to 5 p.m.

Mr. SMITH. I like your one word description of "shocking" describing that policy. Thank you, Mr. Hall.

Ms. Jackson Lee is recognized.

Ms. JACKSON LEE. Thank you very much, Mr. Chairman.

Mr. Hall, I would like to follow up with that line of questioning. Can you articulate for me, other than the generic term more resources, how could we be more effective with respect to that particular problem of arresting and then having the place to incarcerate?

Mr. HALL. Ideally, if the INS were able to provide us with a local detention facility where INS could maintain it and run it, we would have the bed space available to house these individuals. That would be the most perfect world. Shy of that, just the money to apprehend and take these aliens that are criminals, that are a threat to society and at least detain them until they can have an immigration hearing to determine by a judge whether they should be released or whether they should be returned to their home country. That would be the minimum, just so we have the funding to take these people that are threats or perceived threats out of circulation until the case can be adjudicated.

Ms. JACKSON LEE. What is the facility that you use now?

Mr. HALL. We beg, borrow and steal.

Ms. JACKSON LEE. So you are taking beds where they are available?

Mr. HALL. Wherever we can get them.

Ms. JACKSON LEE. What about the opportunity to utilize space in the Federal Bureau of Prisons in a larger or more consistent manner?

Mr. HALL. Wherever I can get a bed to put a person who is a criminal, I will take them there myself. I have no problem with that.

Ms. JACKSON LEE. If you had a consistent number of beds available to you by the Federal Bureau of Prisons and were knowledgeable that they existed, would that be helpful to you?

Mr. HALL. That would be helpful as opposed to nothing right now, yes.

Ms. JACKSON LEE. The facilities that you are using are they mostly local governmental facilities or are you using any private prisons?

Mr. HALL. I do not believe there are any private ones to my knowledge that exist in the area.

Ms. JACKSON LEE. Just the local governmental?

Mr. HALL. Yes, city, county.

Ms. JACKSON LEE. Being a union representative, give me a guesstimate of how many more agents you think you could use along the northern border?

Mr. HALL. With the Partnership Council in Detroit, the Union Management Partnership Council, we sat down and we addressed this, management and myself with other members and we came up with five stations that we have now, for 800 miles of border, we felt 109 additional agents would give us sufficient manpower to cover our border 24 hours a day with minimal staffing.

Mr. SMITH. Would the gentlewoman yield for just a minute?

Ms. JACKSON LEE. I would be happy to yield.

Mr. SMITH. Just to put that into perspective, is that about five times the number you have now?

Mr. HALL. We have 19 now, so yes, it would be about five times what we have now.

Mr. SMITH. Thank you.

Ms. JACKSON LEE. What area are you speaking of?

Mr. HALL. The entire Detroit Sector, Sault Ste. Marie, Detroit, Port Huron, Trenton, and Grand Rapids.

Ms. JACKSON LEE. And you would need 109, an extra 109 or total?

Mr. HALL. An additional 109 agents.

Ms. JACKSON LEE. Thank you very much for that.

Let me also acknowledge your service and I appreciate very much what you do for us. Let me direct my questions to Mr. Harris first and then I want to direct my questions to Mr. Papademetriou to answer some concerns.

Mr. Harris, I have both listened to your testimony and indicated I had a meeting. I believe you might have started as I came in, but in any event, I read it. What strikes me is that you seem to be quarreling with the foreign policy of Canada, which to my knowledge, my Constitution does not allow me to tamper with the foreign policy of Canada. You also seem to be dealing with the basic gentility, if you will, or gentleness of the Canadian people. To my knowledge, I do not have any authority to deal with that as well. Let me cite some of your testimony.

"At the bottom is the problem that Canadians lack an attitude appropriate to the severity of the threat and our responsibility for guarding against it. Having been beneficiaries of their peaceful history, Canada and Canadians are becoming victims of it." Then you note, "Federally supported, that is funded multiculturalism has meant a lack of real integration of newcomers into Canadian society." You also make note of the fact that "The new newcomers are African, African-based people of color." How am I to respond to that and what relevance does that have to what we are talking about today?

Mr. HARRIS. I have think we have to respond to it with rationality and reasonableness and these are extremely good and important questions that have to be asked and have not been asked in the past.

What I was talking about was a problem that we have attitudinally in Canada, the Canadian citizens and the political level in particular. We have a tremendous, almost fabulous level of immigration. For a country of 29 million people, we bring in about a quarter of a million people each year. That is a full 1 percent of the population increase.

Some years ago, 40 years ago, most of these people came from relatively stable European environments. Now they are coming from areas that involve the Middle East, Africa and so on where we have trouble spots and it is the factor of the trouble spots that is relevant, not any real or imagined racial or other ethnocultural aspect. That is a very key thing to recall.

Ms. JACKSON LEE. May I ask the chairman for an additional minute so that Mr. Harris may finish but my questions to the other witnesses complement his.

Mr. SMITH. We are going to have another round of questions.

Ms. JACKSON LEE. I may not be able to stay. I would like to have him finish. Would you continue?

Mr. HARRIS. I guess the point is an attitudinal one.

Ms. JACKSON LEE. Let me do this. I note the letter that John Conyers submitted into the record by the Ambassador from Canada, which I appreciated, focused more on collaboration between the United States and Canada along the borders, DEA, the Royal Mounties, and so forth. How is your testimony instructive on working along the border to alleviate some of the problems that we have?

Mr. HARRIS. I guess the basic point to make is that our two sides work with exceptional close cooperation and always have. While we are at it, I would just like to support what you said and what the Canadian Ambassador has said, that although we may need strong action at policy levels in dealing with our immigration law, this is not to say that Section 110 as currently proposed is appropriate to the challenge.

If I may, just from the record of the Ambassador's statement, such controls, he says, would be of no use in preventing the movement of terrorists or drug smugglers because they would not add any screening value in terms either of improving the quality or quantity of intelligence available or applying it through lookouts at visa offices and border crossing points. So my large thrust in this is that we need to take some kind of real rational control of our immigration situation, give our immigrants a reasonable expectation that their allegiance is to be to Canada, that we are not to bring into Canada our homeland's problems and as a result, we are to then be the civil neighbors to the United States and other countries that would be expected of us in our tradition in the global community.

Ms. JACKSON LEE. Thank you, Mr. Chairman. Because I have so much for my last witness, I will wait for the second round and make some further comments.

Mr. SMITH. Thank you.

Mr. Harris, I think you made an excellent point which is you need to get to the root of the problem and the major cause.

Mr. Hall, in your testimony about drug smuggling, let me mention a couple of examples you talked about because I think detailed examples are helpful to highlight the problems that we are looking at.

You say, "Intelligence indicates that the increasing Asian gangs in Toronto, Ontario are smuggling heroin into the United States across our northern border and smuggling back cocaine, again, a problem that involves both countries." You say, "Confidential sources of information tell us that contraband smuggling across the waterways is rampant." We have heard testimony today that the waterways are basically unsecured. Then you said, "This past year, we were so short of manpower, it was difficult to get two agents on duty at the same time to run the Detroit patrol boat."

All that points to a problem that has been a thread that has run through almost all the testimony today which is we need more Border Patrol agents, we need better security if Americans and also our Canadian friends are going to benefit.

Let me give you a slow ball over home plate. This goes to the issue of pay for Border Patrol agents. Do you think, compared to other similar professions, the Border Patrol agents are adequately paid and if not, why not, and if not, what should they be paid?

Mr. HALL. I feel the pay does need to be increased across the board for Border Patrol agents when we look at other law enforcement agencies of similar size and similar duties. The problem is there are a lot of people interested in the job of a Border Patrol agent, it is an exciting, rewarding career at times, but the lack of pay, of salary, forces a lot of people to go other places where maybe the job is not as exciting or rewarding but the pay is there. We have to pay our bills. I believe a GS–11 across the board for Border Patrol would help stem the attrition.

Mr. SMITH. What is the salary level of a GS–11?

Mr. HALL. It varies up to Step 10 somewhere in the neighborhood, base pay, I think about $55,000.

Mr. SMITH. What is it now?

Mr. HALL. I am a GS–11. That is a promotion-type position. The regular field agent, which would be a Border Patrol agent, would be a GS–9. Do not quote me exactly on this but I think that is somewhere in the neighborhood of about $40,000 a year.

Mr. SMITH. Is that starting salary?

Mr. HALL. No, that would be after reaching a journeyman level.

Mr. SMITH. What do they start at?

Mr. HALL. I think $22,000, $26,000 a year starting for a college graduate coming out of college with a 4-year degree coming into the profession.

Mr. SMITH. Which is less than 200 percent the poverty rate. You gave me my answer. I appreciate that.

Mr. Harris, your testimony was very credible, very candid. Just for the record, are you still a Canadian citizen?

Mr. HARRIS. Yes, sir. At least I was.

Mr. SMITH. You speak with both authority and credibility. Let me read a statement from your prepared testimony. You said, "Canada and terrorism do go together. A failure to see this stems from a failure to realize that Canada is simply not the country it used to be."

I will go to three points you made later on in your testimony and I do not think you got around to making them all a few minutes ago. I think they bear dwelling on for just a minute. You pointed to three different aspects of Canada's policies that you think contribute to the problems we have. These are new to me but I think they are instructive.

You say, first of all, "Under Canada's antiquated accountability regime for charitable organizations, tens of millions of dollars in tax-free donations are channeled to groups supporting international terrorism. Thus, Canadians, through their tax system, inadvertently subsidize terrorism and send abroad the message that Canada is a soft source for the soft money of terrorism."

You also say, "Secondly, nor has Canada any statutes comparable to the U.S. terrorism legislation that allows the government to declare certain countries and groups terrorist in nature with the triggering of derivative sanctions measures and intelligence gathering." That goes to the criminal laws.

Lastly, you say, "Security and intelligence budgets have been cut at a very dangerous time." You point out they have been cut between a quarter and a third over the last 4 or 5 years.

That seems to me to be some suggestions for the Canadian Government to consider from at least your point of view. Is it fair to say that you think those three types of policies do contribute to terrorism and the flow of illegal drugs in both directions as well?

Mr. HARRIS. Yes, Mr. Chairman, I think that is a reasonable conclusion. We have it on very detailed authority that Canada is in fact subsidizing world terrorism inadvertently through its income tax legislation and policy. We need to have action taken by the government on that, not just more of the talking shots with which we in Canada have been familiar on the subject.

Mr. SMITH. Thank you, Mr. Harris.

Ms. Jackson Lee is recognized.

Ms. JACKSON LEE. Thank you very much, Mr. Chairman.

We are having this hearing somewhat in the backdrop of a very obvious and tragic situation in Kosovo. One of the things I have noted about America is our willingness, albeit that we have not been successful all the time, is to challenge and not accept levels of intolerance.

Mr. Harris, that is not anyway a suggestion that your comments are in any way a suggestion or reflection of your philosophy. It is for you to understand my questioning. I have had individuals suggest that I raise the points constantly about the treatment of minorities in particular, maybe African Americans and Hispanics, maybe the Portuguese, or that another group came in and argued against or maybe the Irish of long years back.

I make the point because I do that because I frankly that we should recognize that we are a country, particularly the United States—I do not know what Canada's philosophy is—of immigrants, but we are a country of laws. So it concerns me when a testimony is presented that reflects negatively on one particular ethnic or religious group.

I cite, for example, the immediate reaction of Americans at the time of the Oklahoma bombing. In fact, an Arab-looking individual was stopped. It happened to be an American that perpetrated the most heinous terrorism domestic act that we have ever seen.

So for the record I will continue to be the agitator on not categorizing individuals because of their race, color or creed. I would hope Canada would continue to do that as well.

I want to go to my witness, and I do not want to call you that, but in any event.

Mr. HARRIS. May I have an opportunity to respond at some point?

Ms. JACKSON LEE. Maybe the chairman will allow you to do so. I want to use my time to have Mr. Papademetriou answer my question.

For fear then for your testimony and maybe my concepts to be considered totally abandoning concern about terrorism and drug smuggling, would you help me answer how we could best respond to that because I am concerned about terrorism, drug smuggling, and alien smuggling and I would not want to have the impression that a representative from the Carnegie Endowment for International Peace abandons all caring about the protection of the borders of the United States or of the United States. How can you help us wade through this problem? What kind of solutions should we be looking at?

Mr. PAPADEMETRIOU. I think the chairman and you and I are essentially on the same page as to the importance of doing all of the things, taking all of the necessary steps to try to manage better, and if we can, to prevent, terrorist, alien smugglers and anybody else from entering our territory.

Where we begin to diverge, where we begin to have a disagreement is with the methods, the means, perhaps. I do not necessarily think that we disagree on the means but we are focusing on a different set of means than the ones the chairman is focusing on, although I do not necessarily disagree that we may need more resources in the places where you and the chairman actually are focusing.

We believe, this is the thrust of my testimony, that what we need is more cooperation of interagencies in the United States and intercountry cooperation, more investment in intelligence, more investment in technology, and more investment in infrastructure. All of them are aiming for the same goals of allowing people who belong, who have a right or should have a right to come to the United States to do so in the simplest manner and trying to keep out those people who do not belong here.

I am suggesting that it is a better approach in tandem with the approach that you are suggesting here, such as additional resources to the Border Patrol; it is a better approach, a better overall approach to handling these issues. Let me give you some examples of what we heard from the same types of people that have testified today—INS senior officers as well as people who staff the booths, as well as Customs, and community leaders on both sides of the border.

Most of the credit for whatever drug or other hits they have had were the result of tips of human intelligence. It seems to me if we have a limited number of resources—I assume that you do not have unlimited resources to double or triple the Border Patrol even if you became persuaded that we should do extraordinary things in that regard.

If we really want to invest strategically, I would invest in more cooperation with the Canadian authorities, on encouraging the formal structures of the two countries—our Foreign Affairs Ministry and their Foreign Affairs Ministry to begin conversations of how we can institutionalize these kinds of contacts.

The Mounties, everywhere we went, we were told they are extraordinarily helpful in terms of sharing their information and giving tips. People in the field, on the ground are already working quite effectively together. I would like to see that institutionalized. I would like to see some of the diplomatic resources of this country begin to focus on more cooperation.

On intelligence, I mentioned that most of the things happen because of intelligence tips. There is an awful lot of technology out there and I do not mean smart cards. I am talking about technology that allows people, our inspection agencies, to find out who is coming to the border well before they even are within shouting distance of the border. That goes back to the issue of intelligence and goes back to the issue of cooperation, and of course, the investments in infrastructure.

It seems to me that if you have visited the Detroit area and the various ports of entry over there, you will realize the limitations that exist at the level of the local infrastructure in order to do many of the things we are talking about here. So that is the thrust of my testimony today.

Ms. JACKSON LEE. Thank you very much.

I think the point I would like to leave with you is that we do not suggest that those who have a certain coloration or come from a certain area are in fact above the law and that they cannot be as well part of terroristic acts or other acts that may violate the law. However, someone from Saudi Arabia may have a different history than someone who may come from another country that is known for its terroristic activities.

So I would hope that as we look at this very severe problem, that we could look at some of the solutions you are talking about. Mr. Hall has spoken to the question and he needs more resources, how we can effectively assist him, but we can get away from and stay away from what I am concerned about always, the constant stereotyping of who it is and what.

You are suggesting that the human intelligence collaboration will help us mount an effective response to that along with the police resources that we have. I am committed, Mr. Hall, and I know the chairman is, to pushing INS on this issue. I think it is extremely important to emphasize we do a great disservice to continue to offer the stereotyping.

Mr. SMITH. Mr. Harris, you would like to respond I think to the Ranking Member's comments a while ago?

Mr. HARRIS. One point that is quite clear to understand and is one I tried to make in the Canadian media and public and with politicians as well, is that among the biggest victims of network development are the very minorities who are so often at the mercy of these networks when it comes to pressure and intimidation for recruitment, for funding money, the disruption of houses of warship and other related places.

We count among some of our greatest heroes in the counterterrorism struggle in Canada members of minorities who have come forward frankly, and begged the security and intelligence community and individuals in it for assistance.

Thank you very much, Mr. Chairman,

Mr. SMITH. Thank you, Mr. Harris.

Mr. Papademetriou, given what Ms. Jackson Lee said about Mr. Harris' testimony a while ago, let me quote some of your testimony. You probably saw this coming.

You said, "We should not have a single policy and a single set of rules to apply to both the northern and southern borders." You talk about the fact that Canada and Mexico are different. You mention with Canada we have a shared language mostly and historical traditions, similar emphasis on the rule of law, democratic priorities and similar levels of social and economic development.

I hope, and do not believe you are saying we should treat individuals differently because they do not speak English and because they are poorer than our neighbors from another part of the world. I thought I would give you an opportunity to clarify that part of your testimony.

Mr. PAPADEMETRIOU. Not only did I see it coming, maybe I put it there for you! But if you would read the subsequent paragraphs, I discussed that we should have a single policy in terms of the overall objectives and the eventual end points of our policy but in getting there, it would be legitimate to treat one border as being slightly ahead of the other in terms of what kind of experiments we might use.

Later on in my testimony, I use the concept of a continuum. One the one end of the continuum, you have the sealed borders idea. On the other end, you have the open border idea. I suspect like every other border in the world, of the two countries, Mexico may be at this point of the continuum and we seem to be trying to go this way and Canada is at this point of the continuum, more toward the open borders as long as we have all of these other kinds of things in place.

What I wanted to suggest there is that one size fits all is not really a proper approach if you are going to take things the intelligent way.

Mr. SMITH. I understand that point of view. My point, and I do not know if you clarified it or not, is that you should not necessarily treat people differently just because they do or do not speak English or just because they do or do not have a high or lower socioeconomic development as you called it.

Mr. PAPADEMETRIOU. I am in full agreement with Ms. Jackson Lee and I believe fundamentally with you, sir.

Mr. SMITH. I think both you and Mr. Harris were saying the same thing and I am glad you clarified that.

One last question. I am looking at the clock because we have two votes coming up almost immediately. You mention in your testimony the "inconvenience of sometimes having the 98 or 99 percent go through a process of border checks or whatever it might be just to try to apprehend the 1 or 2 percent that might be doing something wrong."

It seems to me that is an argument, for example, for doing away with airport security where we now check for bombs or guns because 99 or 98 percent of people are not carrying bombs or guns and yet we still go through this process because the 1 or 2 percent is important. So it is not just a question of percentages, I do not think. I think you also have to take into consideration the severity of the danger and the risk involved as well.

Mr. PAPADEMETRIOU. Precisely, Mr. Chairman, and you will notice that later in my testimony, I have talked about a different methodology, an enforcement methodology that focuses more on risk assessment and those kinds of things. I am talking about a more intelligent way of using our resources. It only takes one bomb to do whatever damage that bomb will do.

Mr. SMITH. As far as more intelligence goes, as far as greater cooperation, as you said earlier, we are on the same page and I could not agree more. Do you have any other questions?

Ms. JACKSON LEE. No. I simply want to thank the members and thanking you for letting Mr. Harris conclude his remarks. I do not have any opposition to you making your point, Mr. Harris, at all and welcome your insight. I maintain my point that some of the comments you made were attributable more to Canadian foreign policy and I sort of respect that. I hope that you will take my remarks for what they are, which is my philosophy that we work well with collaboration and working to solve the problems.

Mr. SMITH. Thank you, Ms. Jackson Lee.

Let me thank all the witnesses. Once again, this has been extremely informative. I think we have gotten good suggestions and I think we have gotten a handle on some solutions that we can point to both in the United States and Mr. Harris can point to in his country as well.

We thank you all and we will look forward to seeing you in the future.

[Whereupon, at 12:50 p.m., the subcommittee was adjourned.]

APPENDIX

Material Submitted for the Hearing Record

PREPARED STATEMENT OF THOMAS C. LEUPP, CHIEF PATROL AGENT, SWANTON BORDER PATROL SECTOR

Thank you for the opportunity to provide testimony on Swanton Sector operations. My name is Thomas C. Leupp, the Chief Patrol Agent of the Swanton Border Patrol Sector.

The Swanton Sector area of responsibility encompasses the six northern tier counties of the State of New York, all of Vermont and the northern half of New Hampshire. The Sector is bounded to the west by the Buffalo, New York Sector and to the east by the Houlton, Maine Sector. The area includes 261 miles of the international boundary with Canada and its provinces of Ontario and Quebec. One hundred seventy-three miles are land border and 88 miles are water, mainly the St. Lawrence River. Most of the topography is hilly, wooded, or divided into farms, which in some locations straddle the border. There are unguarded open roadways and ports-of-entry that are open only part time. To the north is Montreal, with a population of 3.3 million, the third largest city in Canada and to the west is Toronto, with a population of 4.4 million, Canada's largest city. The percentage of foreign-born population in Montreal is 20% and for Toronto, 28%.

The Sector is manned with four stations in New York and four in Vermont, with the Sector Headquarters located in Swanton, Vermont. Of the 84 authorized Border Patrol Agent positions, approximately 2/3 are assigned to New York Stations. Additionally, there are seven anti-smuggling unit positions and 20 support positions.

Over the past two fiscal years, an average of 1,832 deportable aliens were apprehended by the Swanton Sector. Fifty percent of those we apprehend are from Canada and the other 50% originate from over 80 different countries. Last year the five leading source countries were China, Pakistan, India, Costa Rica, and Sri Lanka. An average of 25% of those apprehended are criminal aliens. Over the past 4 years there have been at least 9 encounters documented at this office of persons believed or known to be associated with terrorist groups or involved with terrorist activities, as identified by various offices along the U.S./Canada border. Some incidents date back to 1978, with a member of the German Beider-Meinhoff group, and 1987, with three Lebanese Nationals attempting to smuggle in a bomb, both of which were encountered within this Sector.

While our ability to control the border is limited by our authorized force, the effectiveness of those agents is enhanced through the use of a matrix of surveillance and sensor devices along the land boundary. Twelve slow-scan video cameras placed at ports-of-entry for activation during closed hours and at unguarded roadways are connected to sensors that activate the cameras. When tripped, an image is transmitted through the telephone lines to the Communications Center where the operator can identify the intrusion and relay the information to an officer on duty in the area. There are also four real time cameras permanently in place for surveillance of surreptitious attempts of aliens to circumvent the Champlain, NY port-of-entry. This visual identification of intrusions enables officers to avoid unnecessary response to the area and also to intercept vehicles at locations removed from the border area. Additionally, over 140 ground sensors are strategically placed at other land boundary locations. We are also engaged in a joint ground sensor operation with the Royal Canadian Mounted Police (RCMP) that enhances both our operations. We share weekly sensor reports showing entries into Canada, as well as having direct radio communications with their base stations and mobile units.

The Swanton Sector Anti-Smuggling Unit focuses on commercial organizations that are involved in smuggling aliens into the United States. Last year, nine cases (21%) were joint investigations conducted by both the RCMP and Swanton ASU. In the past two years, three alien smuggling cases have been prosecuted in Canada under the Canadian Criminal Code, Conspiracy to Violate United States Law. This effectively shut down these three organizations on both sides of the border.

There is a unique opportunity to work on our northern border because of the shared culture and language we have with our northern neighbors. The Swanton Sector has not only established an outstanding rapport with the RCMP but with Canada Customs, Surete du Quebec, Ontario Provincial Police (OPP), Toronto Metro Police and the Montreal Police as well.

A recently completed joint operation between the U.S. Border Patrol, RCMP, Ontario Provincial Police (OPP) and Canada Customs resulted in the dismantling of a major Korean alien smuggling organization (U.S. vs. Han). This investigation resulted in 14 prosecutions and successfully dismantled the organization, which had been in operation since 1993. Prior to this joint effort, the organization had been successfully operating through the Detroit, Michigan and Buffalo, New York areas before setting up their operations in the Swanton Sector's area of responsibility.

Our rapport with other federal, state and local law enforcement authorities is also outstanding. In the last two fiscal years, Swanton Sector Border Patrol turned over to the U.S. Customs Service 159 separate cases of U.S. citizens or aliens who had failed to report for inspection, a violation under Customs law, for a total of $335,000 in penalties. This is also illustrated by Operation Over the Rainbow 11, an investigation into Chinese alien smuggling through the Akwesasne Indian Reserve and controlled by the Buffalo INS District, resulting in the indictment of 46 subjects.

The unique boundary composition of the Akwesasne Territory, which straddles Ontario and Quebec Provinces and New York State, has presented many challenges to law enforcement personnel. In an effort to address these problems additional personnel have been assigned to the Massena, New York station. In consideration of sovereignty issues, traditional border control operations are limited on a reservation. Operations on the Reservation are conducted in concert with the St. Regis Mohawk Tribal Police Department. Various other operations are also pursued under control and direction of this office off the Reservation. With their recent ability to expand to 24 hours a day, seven days a week coverage, the St. Regis Mohawk Tribal Police has been outstanding in assisting the U.S. Border Patrol by locating alien smugglers on the Akwesasne Territory.

The St. Regis Mohawk Tribal Police have been recognized for their achievements and assistance by being awarded the INS Commissioner's Inter-Agency Cooperation Award. The United States Attorney in the Northern District of New York is a true partner and is aggressive in prosecuting all alien smugglers involved in smuggling through the Reservation. Under the guidance of the U.S.

Attorney's Office there are also several task forces, OCDETF and strike force operations in affect. A report published by the U.S. Attorney's office ranked the Akwesasne Smuggling Group and Warrior Society as the largest organized crime threat in the Northern District of New York. From an immigration standpoint, it is the most significant source of alien smuggling across the northeast border.

The Canadian Border Intelligence Center (CBIC) is located at the U.S. Border Patrol Sector Headquarters in Swanton, Vermont, and is under the guidance and direction of this Sector. While the emphasis is on the Northern Border, intelligence is collected and processed from throughout the United States and Canada. CBIC analyzes raw intelligence data relating to alien smuggling activity, criminal aliens and suspected terrorists. CBIC assists numerous U.S. law enforcement agencies in identifying suspected criminal co-conspirators by obtaining subscriber information and linking telephone numbers common to the suspected conspirators. Telephone toll analyses have been completed by CBIC personnel for various INS offices throughout the United States in places such as Phoenix, AZ, Philadelphia, PA, New York City, NY and Newark, NJ. CBIC also processes record checks for both domestic and Canadian agencies.

Last year, CBIC shared information with approximately 15 Canadian agencies at numerous locations across Canada, from Vancouver, British Columbia to St. Johns, Newfoundland. The majority of these requests concern the U.S. Immigration status and criminal history for individuals seeking either refugee status or resident alien status in Canada. Additionally, we have provided information to the Quebec Government regarding individuals who had entered the United States illegally and were receiving social assistance from Canada. This information saved the Quebec government approximately $78,000 last year.

A Northern Border Report, compiled annually by CBIC, consists of more than 250 pages of statistics, analysis and comparisons from both the United States and Canada. These reports are disseminated to all Sectors and Districts along the Northern Border and provide a working reference of activity at other border locations.

In closing, I would again like to thank you for the opportunity to provide information on the Northern Border to the committee.

PART IV

THE NEW THREAT

CHAPTER TWENTY-FIVE

WEAPONS OF MASS DESTRUCTION

Just as society in general has progressed over the last few decades, so too, have the weapons at the disposal of a terrorist group progressed. We think of terrorists as little men skulking in the shadows waiting to shoot us or throw a bomb. Well, this stereotype is strictly from the movies. The modern terrorist is a true professional and their weapons reflect this professionalism. The destruction caused by the terrorists seen on our televisions on 9/11 was the result of a fluke. They had hoped to destroy the World Trade Center using the planes as flying bombs, but apparently had no idea how much damage the super hot aviation fuel would cause as it flowed into the building.

When I discussed the concept for this book with a retired military officer of my acquaintance, he snorted and said *"Hell, son, the borders have been wide open since this country was founded in the 1700s. So the terrorist groups send in a hundred or a thousand or ten thousand fanatics with their guns and their bombs. What can they do? They don't have nuclear weapons and after 9/11, we're ready for them!"*

It was clear to me that his mind was made up, who in their right mind would try to invade the United States of America? The majority of those that I talked too, in addition to my military friend, all seemed to believe that after 9/11, a major attack in this country would be quickly dealt with. However, after reviewing the situation in some detail, I know that they were almost all wrong in their assessment of the world situation and I still believe that we are even more vulnerable to terror attacks in this country than ever.

There has been much talk in the news media about weapons of mass destruction. The average individual associates this phrase with missiles and nuclear weapons. However, in this modern age, a weapon of mass destruction capable of wiping out all life in New York City could fit in the palm of your hand. I am of course, talking about chemical and biological weapons.

That is not to say that nuclear weapons should be completely discounted for a large number of countries have working nuclear weapons. In spite of the babblings of Congress about the inspectors not finding stockpiles of weapons of mass destruction if Iraq, Iraq did have nuclear weapons and a very large, robust chemical agent program[104] and weapons of mass destruction were found[105].

In spite of media stories to the contrary, several key assertions by US Intelligence that led to our invasion of Iraq have now turned out to be true, but this fact has been lost in the rush to vilify President Bush and the War on Terror. The Iraqi Survey Group, ISG, a highly trainined group of Intelligence analysts are managed by Charles Duelfer, a former State Department official and deputy chief of the U.N. led arms inspection teams, has found hundreds of cases of activities that were prohibited under U.N. Security Council resolutions. In virtually every case, whether it was chemical, biological, nuclear weapons or ballistic missiles, the United States did find the weapons and the programs that the Iraqi dictator had successfully concealed for over 12 years[106]. In fact the ISG found that Iraq had a clandestine network of laboratories and safe houses with equipment that was suitable to continuing its prohibited chemical and biological weapons program. They also found a prison laboratory where it was suspected that these agents were tested on human subjects[107].

The existence of these weapons is not science fiction; they are a deadly reality and have been used in warfare since time immemorial.

DEADLY EXAMPLES

The very concept of something that you cannot see being so deadly is mind boggling to most civilians who have never spent any time in the military or spent a fun afternoon sitting inside a gas chamber being exposed to CS gas and other crowd control agents. However, the power of chemical and biological weapons and the ease of use of these weapons by terrorist groups have been shown in a number of recent incidents.

- In 1989 in Iraq, Saddam Hussein used chemical weapons containing mustard gas and the nerve agents Sarin, Tabun and VX against his own people. He had chemical weapons containing these agents dropped from aircraft and helicopters on the Kurdish people living in the towns of

---

[104] Hamza, Khidhir with Jeff Stein, Saddam's Bombmaker, Touchstone Books, Simon & Schuster, New York. 2000
[105] Timmerman, Kenneth R., *Saddam's WMD Have Been Found*, Insight/News World Communications, Inc. 2004
[106] Ibid
[107] Ibid

Halabja, Khormol, Dojaileh. These weapons killed more than five thousand people living in and around these towns.

- In Japan, the cult Aum Shinrikyo[108] conducted several assassinations using nerve agents. The leader of the cult, Shoko Asahara, believed that through a wide spread use of these agents he would topple the Japanese government and establish a new global society led by his followers. Beginning in 1993, the cult began to manufacture Sarin gas in small quantities. Not being satisfied with the results, the cult established a major nerve gas production facility outside of Kamikiushiki which became fully operational in early 1994. Other manufacturing facilities were established in Naganohara, at Mount Aso and on a sheep ranch in Australia owned by the cult. Testing of the manufactured agents was also carried out on the animals at the Australian ranch.

  In June of 1994, the cult launched its first attack using weapons of mass destruction. Using a modified truck spray system such as many cities use to spray for mosquitoes, members of the cult drop through the sleeping city of Matsumoto, Japan spraying Sarin nerve gas. This attack killed 7 and injured 253. However, think of the potential number of casualties in a city such as New York, where a large number of people sleep with their windows cracked for the night breeze.

  Later, the cult conducted a major attack on the Tokyo subway system that killed 12 and injured 5,510 others. In this attack, the group used a diluted solution of Sarin that had been developed n house by chemists employed by the AUM cult. Bags of the agent were dropped into subway cars and punctured with the tips of umbrellas to release the gas. How much damage could such an attack do in the New York Subway system?

- In September 1950, the Army secretly used a Navy Ship to test our vulnerability to chemical attacks. This ship cruised just outside the Golden Gate and sprayed, a supposedly, harmless bacteria over the entire city. The winds from the ocean carried the bacteria over 117 square miles of the Bay Area. Eleven people became ill as a result and one of them died.

- During the heyday of the CIA's MK-ULTRA program, the CIA sent agents to test the effects of such drugs as LSD and synthetic mescaline on the people in San Francisco, Mill Valley and other US cities. Many of those exposed to these drugs became ill and two died.

---

[108] This name translates as Supreme Truth.

- It is not just governments and foreign cults that are indulging in the use of chemical and biological weapons, In Oregon, in 1984, followers of an Indian religious cult put Salmonella in restaurant salad bars in The Dales, Oregon in an attempt to divert attention of some of their other activities. Over 700 people became ill with Salmonella.

MANUFACTURE OF CHEMICAL OR BIOLOGICAL WEAPONS

There is no question that these weapons are deadly and in the wrong hands have the potential to wreck massive death and destruction. Some of these agents only take a drop to kill and others merely incapacitate. However, even enough of a harmless chemical agent, such as CS can kill those either unusually susceptible or who suffer from respiratory problems.

However, there are questions of dispersal of these agents. Most people that I talked to seemed to feel that it would be difficult to disperse these agents in a wide enough area to do much damage and all of them seemed to feel that there was no way that a few terrorists could inflict mass casualties no matter what chemical or biological weapons they chose to use.

The unfortunate fact is that most of those I talked to, and most of the strategic planners whose works I have read, seem to look at the potential immediate effects of these weapons and base their assumptions on these. However, with chemical and biological weapons, the effects are not just immediate, there are also linger effects that can be potentially devastating.

Others point to the difficulty of turning these agents into weapon systems as one of our main defenses against wide spread usage of these types of weapons. So let's look at this aspect from the point of view of a potential terrorist. How easy is it to use chemical and biological weapons against a civilian population?

Chemical and biological weapons must be processed in order for them to be used as an effective weapon. This process, called weaponization, results in these agents either being produced as a liquid or a dry powder. The liquid is relatively easy to prepare and also easy to disperse. The dry powdery form is difficult to create and requires expensive equipment but as a benefit, if successfully created, the dry form tends to be more easily dispersed.

DISPERSAL

Chemical or biological weapons are dispersed in two primary methods:

- Line source distribution – where chemical or biological agents are carried by the wind. The agents dispersed in this fashion are naturally sensitive to weather changes and climate extremes.

- Point source distribution – where agents are released in small packages such as envelopes, small bombs, or exploding containers. The attack on the Congressional Offices would be considered a point source distribution.

This technical sounding language used to disguise the distribution methods, does not carry with it the full realization for the listener of just how dangerous these agents can be. Perhaps examples would be more effective –

We have already discussed the use of chemical agents by Saddam Hussein against the Kurds by dropping the agents from helicopters or aircraft. This would be a point source distribution system. Attempts have been made to use this type of dispersal system to conduct a biological assassination attempt on United States Senators. On September 17, 2001, a series of four letters were mailed to government leaders and news media personalities. In the process of these biological bombs arriving at their destinations, several facilities of the United States Postal System were also infected.

The letters addressed to Senators Tom Daschle (D-SD) and Patrick Leahy (D-VT) contained a highly sophisticated variant of weapons grade anthrax. While the press really did not go into detail on the elements of this crime and the government certainly downplayed the dangers, the anthrax used in this attack contained ten times more spores per gram than any grade of anthrax previously made in either the U.S. or the Russian bio-weapons program during the Cold War[109]. The amount of anthrax sent to the Senate Office Building to Senators Daschle and Leahy was sufficient to not only kill the Senators, but also an additional 100,000 people. Luckily, the potential danger was contained and dealt with, but what if it had not been quickly recognized? Just how dangerous was this anthrax attack? Let's look at something that happened in the 1950s in order to get an idea of the true danger of this anthrax attack.

ANTHRAX OUTBREAK AT ARMS TEXTILE MILL

In September 1957, there was an outbreak of anthrax at the Arms Textile Mill in Manchester, New Hampshire[110]. In this outbreak, four mill workers died, all displaying what are now known to be symptoms of anthrax exposure. This incident is called the "America's Only Anthrax Epidemic" by the Center for Disease Control.

---

[109] Nance, Malcolm, The Terrorist Recognition Handbook, Lyons Press, Guilford, Connecticut. 2003.

[110] Albarelli, Jr., H.P., *Biological War-Fear: Did Army Cause Anthrax Outbreak in Mill?*, Worldnetdaily.com, 2002.

A major activity at the Arms Textile Mill through the decade of the 1950s was the processing of goat hair imported from Pakistan, Iraq and Iran. The goat hair, once processed was used for the lining of expensive suits and overcoats for m en manufactured at the mill. At the time of this outbreak of anthrax, the Arms Textile Mills employed over 600 workers and occupied a complex of buildings on the banks of the Merrimack River near Manchester, N.H.

Coincidentally, tests on the mill workers for anthrax infection, sponsored by the Biological Warfare Laboratories of the U.S. Chemical Corps based at Fort Detrick, Maryland had begun in 1955. It was considered that their was a slim possibility that these workers exposed to this goat hair might contract a mild form of anthrax and the Military wanted to study it. A prototype vaccine to anthrax had also been developed and it was felt that this was too good an opportunity to pass up. This vaccine, developed in 1955 is basically the same serum administered to soldiers and others at risk for anthrax.

However, in spite of the deaths of four workers, the mill continued to operate as if nothing had happened, and little, if any, thought seems to have been given to trying to disinfect the facilities. In fact after the deaths, though it was kept rather quiet, between 1946 and 1958, 63 other workers came down with cutaneous anthrax, the most common form of this disease. Cutaneous anthrax is a naturally occurring type of infection, normally caused by skin contact with infected meat or leather from infected animals.

Finally, in 1958, the mill finally shut down due to financial reasons. There were no further reports made available about additional infections from anthrax, but in 1966, eight years after the mill closed and the buildings were abandoned, a worker at a machine shop across from the mill died of inhalation anthrax. New Hampshire Health Officials speculated that this infection was due to lethal spores remaining from the 1957 epidemic that migrated from the Arms buildings through a shared ventilation system between the two businesses. So anthrax is a gift that keeps on giving long after the initial attack. Had the weapons grade anthrax sent to the Senators gotten a foothold in the buildings, there is no question that the buildings would probably be unusable for many years to come, at a minimum, the disinfecting process would cost a large sum of money.

Based on this information alone, there is no doubt that anthrax is a deadly disease that can strike without warning and lingers long after it is forgotten. To make matters worse, hospital staffs do not generally recognize the symptoms of the agents that are used in these types of attacks. Thomas Morris, one of the postal workers infected by the anthrax attack had his condition diagnosed as a common chest infection, even though he very clearly informed the treating physician that he had been exposed to anthrax[111]. He was forced to call his own ambulance to be transported to the hospital and then after being told he

---

[111] Mr. Morris' detailed description was a textbook case of anthrax infection.

did not have anthrax infection, he died in the emergency room. Sadly, the only person who believed that Mr. Morris had been infected with anthrax was the EMS dispatcher who had been trained to recognize anthrax symptoms.

WAR GAMES

What is the most unnerving is that Mr. Morris' fate may not be the exception, but rather the rule. In June of 2001, the John Hopkins University Center for Civilian Bio-defense, the Center for Strategic Studies and other organizations conducted a large-scale exercise designed to test the bio-terrorism readiness system in the United States. This exercise was called Dark Winter and on June 22 and 23, 2001 this senior level war game was undertaken in order to examine the national security, intergovernmental and information challenges relating to a biological attack on the continental United States[112].

Under the scenario upon which Dark Winter was based, with tensions rising in the Straits of Taiwan and a major crisis developing in Southwest Asia, a smallpox outbreak was confirmed by the Center for Disease Control (CDC) in Oklahoma City. During the thirteen days of the game, the disease spread to 25 states and 15 other countries.

The most important issues that developed from this role playing were the adequacy of the public health response, roles and missions of the federal and state governments, the abridgement of civil liberties that were associated with quarantine and isolation of those infected as well as the role of the Department of Defense and potential military responses to those responsible for the attack.

In essence, the findings of this War Game were as follows:

- An attack on the United States with biological weapons could threaten vital national security interests. Among the ways that US national security interests could be compromised are by massive civilian casualties, a breakdown in essential institutions, violations of the democratic processes, civil disorder, loss of confidence in government by the population and reduced US strategic flexibility abroad.

  A loss of confidence in the government by the populace is the very essence of the terrorist act. By overwhelming the essential institutions of the nation with mass casualties, the system can be brought to a screeching halt.

---

[112] A more complete report on the many lessons learned from this timely War Game can be found at the website of the ANSER Institute for Homeland Security at http://www.home;landsecurity.org/darkwinter/index.cfm for those who would like to see the full script and the outcome.

- The current organizational structures and capabilities are not well suited for the management of a bio-warfare attack.

  This country has never been the victim of such a devastating attack and for the most part, each state tends to act independently of each other.

- There are major "fault lines" between different levels of government, between government and private sector, among different institutions and private agencies and with the public and private sectors. These disconnects could impede situational awareness and compromise the ability to limit loss of life, suffering and economic damage.

- There is no surge capacity[113] in the US health care and public health care systems, or the pharmaceutical and vaccine industries. This inability to increase productivity on the part of the medical profession could result in hospitals being overwhelmed and becoming inoperable; could impede public health agencies in their analysis of the scope, source and progress of the epidemic and in their ability to educate and reassure the public and also limit the ability to limit casualties and the spread of the disease.

- Dealing with the media will be a major immediate challenge for all levels of government. Information management will be a critical element in crisis/consequence management.

- Should a contagious bio-weapon pathogen be used, containing the spread of the disease will present significant ethical, political, cultural, operational and legal challenges.

ONE POSSIBLE SCENARIO

In the plot of *Manhattan Conspiracy: Angel of Death*[114], terrorists conduct a chemical attack on this country by having a well dressed individual walk through the airport with a small plant sprayer in his briefcase leaving a trail of aerolized smallpox in his wake. However, as part of his preparation, he had allowed his handlers to also infect him so that during the infectious period of the disease he would be a walking weapon himself. Through the use of his own body as a weapon and through the process of infecting others with his sprayer, this one man has created hundreds of new vectors for the disease. Then each of these people that have been unwittingly infected meet others and infect them and so on

---

[113] Surge capacity is the ability to increase production during a time of national emergency.
[114] Hudnall, Ken, <u>Manhattan Conspiracy: Angel of Death</u>, Omega Press, EL Paso, Texas 79912. 2003

and so forth. It has been estimated that one person could infect hundreds if not thousands of unsuspecting victims before becoming too ill to continue.

It is only a matter of time before the terrorist organizations move from suicide bombers to suicide Human Biological Weapon Systems. It has been estimated that the greatest non-nuclear threat to the Untied States would be the deliberate use of humans carrying contagious diseases. Rather than pay teens to blow themselves up, they just infect them, either knowingly or unknowingly, and then turn them lose to wander around the town, infecting person after person.

Such a scenario, if launched against the US, could in a matter of just a few weeks, kill hundreds of thousands of people and infect millions. World trade would come to a halt; there would be a boycott of US products for fear of infection. Every other country would close its borders to American trying to flee the disease stalking every American in the country.

Lest someone thinks this scenario is too far fetched to be believed, in the late 1950s Fort Detrick[115]'s Special Operations Division ran vulnerability tests in which operatives walked around Washington D.C. and San Francisco with suitcases holding a bacteria called Serratia marcescenes. Tiny holes had been punctured in the suitcases that allowed the bacteria's release so that the agency could trace the flow of the germs through airports and bus terminals. Shortly thereafter, eleven elderly men and women were checked into area hospitals with a never before seen Serratia marcescens infection. One patient died from the infection[116]. The Army has clearly overstepped the bounds of safety and sanity, but this experiment did show how vulnerable this country was to a chemical attack of this nature. Unfortunately, with the rise of the metropolitan centers such as Houston and Chicago, we are even more vulnerable to such attacks.

In the summer of 1966, agents of the Special Operations Division entered three New York City Subway Stations and tossed light bulbs filled with Bacillus subtilis, a benign bacteria, onto the subway tracks to determine how a chemical agent could be spread through the subway system. The movement of the subway trains pushed the germs through the entire system and theoretically killed over a million passengers.

POTENTIAL BIOLOGICAL WEAPONS

Of course, smallpox is not the only disease that can be converted into a useable weapon, or is known to have been modified for use as a weapon by the world of science. Of course, smallpox is the disease of choice as it is highly contagious and sometimes fatal. There is no specific treatment for smallpox and the only prevention seems to be vaccination. However, the vaccination program

---

[115] Fort Detrick was formerly the U.S. Army's biowarfare center.
[116] Carroll, Michael Christopher, Lab 257: The Disturbing Story of the Government's Secret Plum Island Germ Laboratory, William Morrow, New York. 2004.

ended when the World Health Organization declared that the disease was eradicated.

Unfortunately, when this disease was declared eradicated, there were still samples left for use in scientific research. By international agreement, these deadly samples were housed in only two locations, at the Centers for disease control in Atlanta, Georgia and at a Russian virology institute in Siberia called Vector. In spite of the supposedly rigid security, it is now known that Iraq, North Korea, and possibly Iran, have samples of this deadly disease[117]. The smallpox incubation period is from seven to seventeen days and the person that has been exposed to the disease becomes contagious when the telltale rash appears. In unvaccinated people, the lethality factor is in excess of 30%.

Other well known potential bio-weapons include:

- **Anthrax**, which has already been discussed;

- **Brucellosis** is an agent that incapacitates rather than kills. The fatality factor is generally five percent or less. The agent has an incubation period of from five to sixty days and symptoms of fever, headache, weakness, fatigue, anorexia, nausea, constipation, diarrhea, and osteoarticular complications. There is no vaccine.

- **Cholera** has long been studied for use as a bioweapon but it is not yet known to have been actually used as a weapon. This agent would most likely be spread through the contamination of drinking water, otherwise it would be very difficult to use as a weapon. Cholera has an incubation period of from four or five hours to five days with symptoms which include vomiting, headache, intestinal cramping, and "voluminous" diarrhea. The lethality factor of cholera is 50% if left untreated and death may result from severe dehydration, hypovolemmia and/or shock. There is a vaccine that provides 50% protection.

- **Glanders** has been used as a bioweapon and is almost always fatal without treatment. The incubation period is ten to fourteen days after inhalation and the symptoms include fever, rigors, sweats, myalgia, pleuritic chest pain, cervical adenopathy, headaches, splenomegaly and generalized pustular eruptions. There is no known vaccine.

- **Pneumonic Plague** has been used as a weapon historically and is known to have been weaponized on more than one occasion. During World War II, the Japanese Army pioneered the modern use of this disease as a weapon, using fleas to disperse the disease in China. The Soviet Union is known to have prepared large quantities for aerial disbursal in

---

[117] Preston, Richard, The Demon in the Freezer, Random House, New York. 2002

intercontinental ballistic missiles. The incubation period is one to ten days and the symptoms are acute onset of flu-like symptoms. Pneumonic Plague is almost 100 percent lethal if left untreated and 20 to 60% if treated within eighteen to twenty-four hours of the onset of the symptoms. There is a vaccine.

- **Q Fever** is another agent that incapacitates rather than kills. The incubation period is two to fourteen days and the symptoms include chills, cough, weakness, fatigue, chest pain and pneumonia. The lethality factor is only one to three percent, but the survivors may have relapses once they are thought to be cured of the disease.

- **Pneumonic Tularemia** is another agent that is known to have been weaponized by several countries. The incubation period is one to twenty days and the symptoms include the sudden onset of acute febrile illness, weakness, chills, headache, body aches, dry cough and chest pain. Thirty to sixty percent of those who contract this disease will die if left untreated. There is a vaccine.

- **Viral Hemorrhagic Fevers** such as Congo-Crimean hemorrhagic fever, Ebola, Hanta Virus, Lassa Fever, Marburg Virus, Rift Valley Fever, and yellow fever are some among a large group of naturally occurring potentially deadly ailments that have been studied as possible weapons to incapacitate or kill an enemy. Even with treatment, the lethality rate for Ebola, as an example, can run as high as 90%.

- **Botulinum toxin** has been used as a weapon in the past. It is considered to be the most lethal substance known to man and has been used as early as World War II. It is one of the many agents that are known to have been prepared, or used, as a weapon by Iraq under Saddam Hussein. The incubation period is one to five days and the symptoms include blurred vision, diploplia, dry mouth, ptosis and fatigue. The disease is considered to be lethal to 60% of those who contract this ailment.

- **Ricin** is an agent that has been in the news lately as one of the agents found in the Senate Office Buildings. This particular bioweapon has historically been used as both an assassination as well as a murder weapon by agents of the KGB and Bulgarian Intelligence Services. The Al-Qaeda terrorist camp at Darunta is known to have developed and trained its agents to make small quantities of this agent for use in the field. The incubation period is eighteen to twenty-four hours and the symptoms include weakness, tightness in the chest, fever, cough, pulmonary edema, respiratory failure, circulatory failure, and hypoxemia resulting in day with seventy-two hours. There is no vaccine and this agent is highly lethal, especially with continued exposure.

The list of potential bioweapons is growing each year as scientific breakthroughs make it possible to transfer diseases from the animal kingdom to the human species. A disease to which we a have no natural immunity would kill hundreds of thousands before we could even begin to create an effective, safe vaccine. Look at the number of deaths that are attributed each year to the AIDS Virus; even after years of research and billions of dollars in research there is no cure.

AND SO

The fact that terrorist will use chemical and biological weapons against us should not shock anyone. Our own government has pioneered the effective methods of dispersing any number of chemical agents among us, using our own transportation systems against us to spread chemical agents far and wide for the purpose of studying the effect. Our fumbling attempts to pierce the secrets of nature have created some of the most lethal weapons ever seen and we have never hesitated in using our discoveries for military purposes.

The number of potential bioweapons available to an enemy is growing by the day. In fact, it is not even necessary for a potential terrorist to bring his own weapons of mass destruction as we have so many here in the United States that he or she can choose from. One tempting prize for a terrorist is located near the Hamptons, the playground of the wealthy. I am, of course referring to the laboratory complex located on Plum Island, just a short drive from New York City. The biological agents experimented with on that Island are highly dangerous and highly contagious. This may well be the proving ground for the development of what we now know as Lyme Disease. Should the containment facility be breached, there is no telling what agents might be released on one of the largest cities in the world.

CHAPTER TWENTY-SIX

THE MOST DANGEROUS WEAPON OF ALL

In God we trust, all others we monitor[118]

As if the danger of terrorist attacks using chemical and biological weapons is not enough, there is one weapon in the arsenal of the terrorist that is by far the most dangerous of all. With this weapon, the enterprising terrorist has no need to even leave home; with a computer and a modem he can use this weapon to inflict unbelievable terror, death and destruction in this country. This weapon of such incredible destructive power is the innocuous Internet.

MODERN COMMUNICATIONS

The goal of the terrorists is to attack the infrastructure of this country[119]. That is to say, utilities, hospitals and the medical system as a whole, food distribution points to name but a few. To achieve their goals, modern terrorists are increasingly turning to sophisticated computer systems and high technology communications systems to coordinate their activities. With the level of sophistication of today's technology, secure communications can be set up virtually anywhere.

---

[118] This is the intercept operator's motto, from the NSA study, Deadly Transmissions, December 1970.
[119] In fact, Osama Bin Laden had given these very instructions in an interview by Arab Newspapers on December 27, 2991 wherein he said that "*It is very important to concentrate on hitting the US economy through all possible means. . .*"

304\ROBERT K. HUDNALL, JD

Terrorists need secure communication systems, without which, they cannot operate effectively. Codes have been used by every government and clandestine organization for centuries, in order to communicate secret information. It is assumed that manual electronic communications are often intercepted, so a secure system is needed. With the ability of the U.S. National Security Agency to monitor all communications, finding such a secure communications system has become an increasing more difficult task. However, with advances in technology, there are news communications methods being developed almost daily.

In 1960, there were five thousand stand alone computers, no fax machines, and no cellular phones. If someone wished to make a telephone call, they used a landline, which could be easily monitored. Today, according to Lieutenant General Hayden, the NSA Director[120], there are over 180 million computers, most of which are networked, fourteen million fax machines and over forty million cellular phones. Even with the aid of computers, how does one find a terrorist communication needle in a global telecommunications haystack?

Methods that terrorists have used to communicate include:

- **Written codes and ciphers** – this is still a favorite of the groups that were trained by the KGB or other intelligence agencies and the less sophisticated groups such as the Mujahideen of Afghanistan. The strength of this method is the necessity of an adversary capturing the encrypted message and then decoding it.

- **Internet encryption** – there are a large number of commercial programs that encode e-mail communications as a way to ensure the security of their communications. Some of these programs are actually downloadable as freeware or shareware. Messages can even be hidden inside of digital photographs sent over the Internet.

- **Secure Voice Communication** – digital encryption and other security modules can be purchased on the open market and attacked to communications equipment to make them secure. These attachments can render messages incomprehensible to listeners, though not to individuals with the proper decryption equipment.

- **Telephones** – there are now so many telephone systems, companies and networks, that it is sometimes difficult to gather information through wiretaps and other legal methods. The use of throwaway global phone cards for cell and public telephones has simply compounded the problem.

---

[120] Bamford, James, Body of Secrets, Anchor Books, New York, New York. 2002.

- **Satellite Telephones** – satellite phones have made it easy for a caller to talk to someone on the other side of the world without the necessity of going through operators or other connecting links. In order for a terrorist group to have instant worldwide communication, they only have to subscribe to one of the satellite phone systems.

- **VHF/UHF Handheld Radios** – Commercially available secure radio systems such as those manufactured by Motorola have made it easier for terrorists to coordinate their activities during the conduct of an operation.

WEAPONS OF MASS DESTRUCTION REVISITED

Though it may be hard to believe, in addition to a very rapid method of communication, the personal computer sitting on the edge of most desks in this country can actually be a weapon of mass destruction. These computers are actual doorways into the very heart of our infrastructure.

The unimaginable might of this great country lies not in its buildings or in its standing military or its trappings of wealth but rather in its systems. Beneath our feet are hundreds of thousands of miles of cabling connecting vast arrays of computers that control almost everything in our world. Computers control the electrical power grids, the water supply systems, the transportation systems, the communication systems, and most importantly the financial system. Adding to the vulnerability, many of these infrastructure systems are linked to the Internet making them open to attack from afar. Without these all important computer systems to coordinate the operation of these life support systems, our world would come to a stop.

This dependency on our computerized life support systems has been fully recognized by government. In her first major policy address on the topic of cyber security on March 22, 2001, National Security Advisor Condoleezza Rice said that "Today, the cyber-economy is the economy. Corrupt these networks and you disrupt this nation[121]." Clearly, the goal of a terrorist organization is to disrupt this nation, so one target would be the cyber-economy.

To combat this possibility, the average American looks to government. However, more than 85% of the national's most critical computer networks and infrastructure is in the hands of private corporations[122]. No longer is it the responsibility of government to protect the millions of Americans who depend on

---

[121] Policy Address of National Security Advisor Condoleezza Rice, given March 22, 2001

[122] Verton, Dan, Black Ice: The Invisible Threat of Cyber-Terrorism, McGraw Hill, New York, New York. 2003

the infrastructure support systems of this nation, it is now the responsibility of faceless corporate employees.

Historically, we in America have been able to depend on the barrier created by two oceans and two relatively peaceful countries (Canada and Mexico) to keep us safe from would be invaders. Now, with the advent of wireless Internet connections, even while sitting in a cave in Afghanistan, terrorists can launch attacks at the very heart of this country. These attacks could be launched to coincide with physical attacks on facilities in the Untied States.

Frankly, in this country there are so many targets that it would almost be a bigger problem to choose which one to attack than it would to carry out the attack. One way to disrupt the Internet would be to attack the 13 core domain name servers that direct traffic over the Internet. Or one potential physical target might be the building in San Francisco that houses one of the two largest and most critical Internet nodes in the world. The building is known simply as MAE-West (Mae stands for Metropolitan Area Ethernet) and the Internet node housed there handles over 45% of the Internet traffic in the United States. If it should be shut down or destroyed, think of the chaos and disruption to e-commerce.

Cyber attacks launched against the Supervisory Control and Data Acquisition (SCADA) systems that control the electric grid and natural gas pipelines could disrupt normal operations and endanger the entire distribution system. If the control mechanisms can be altered, then critical functions such as valves opening and closing in the natural gas pipelines can be altered. This can create unstable pressures in the system that can cause tremendous damage. Critical junctions can be affected in the electrical grid that can cause overloads and shut downs in the nation's power grid system.

Using the Internet, hackers can conduct a reign of terror unequaled in world history. As an example, many hospitals are linked by computer systems that give doctors access to individual medical records. These records are crucial to proper treatment. Suppose in conjunction with a chemical or biological attack on a city such as Washington DC, a hacker accesses the medical records data base and corrupts the files or alters the blood type on the records of those citizens living in the area to be attacked or removes notations regarding specific drug allergies. In the past few years more and more hospitals have been placing medical records on computers to allow quick and easy access by treating physicians and the interaction of treating physicians and specialists or pharmacists. If these records are hacked and vital data changed such as blood type, when survivors arrive at area hospitals for treatment, those needing transfusions will be given the wrong type of blood or administered drugs to which they are allergic. The death toll can be staggering.

The attacks on the national power grid, the natural gas pipelines, and perhaps water distribution systems, if not addressed quickly, can lead to shut downs. These shutdowns lead to denial of service to the civilian population of the affected areas. The shutting down of any part of the overall system then put an added strain on the remainder of the system. The added strain can cause other portions of the system to fail and before long a domino effect has happened and the entire system is shut down. Almost all waste water treatment plants, water distribution systems, chemical, and oil refineries have computerized command and control systems. The failure of these systems can have a tremendous impact on operations.

A consistent denial of service attack against the Internet infrastructure can cause major Internet Service Providers (ISPs) to lose connectivity. Some of these ISPs will revert to peering agreements, but even these agreements are not sufficient to handle the volume of traffic moving between Internet links. Many transactions will fail and as each link fails, increased strain is placed on the others.

Much of the telephone traffic in this country is handled by computerized systems. With the failure of the power grid and an overload of the Internet systems that connect one critical element to another within the communications system, these computerized routing systems will fail, cutting off communications for extended periods. Most people who are able will switch their communications to cellular phones, which will also soon overwhelm the routing systems available to the cellular service companies.

WHAT HAPPENS IF 911 IS BUSY?

In this country, most citizens are used to calling 911 in an emergency and medical treatment or law enforcement personnel arrive in only a few minutes. However, in the event of an overloading or failure of the electrical and communications systems, this rapid first response capability can be serious eroded or non-existent. We as a nation are so dependant on our communications and utilities that the failure of these systems alone can cause panic to set in. We have almost forgotten how to fend for ourselves.

There is no question that each level of government has superb response plans to deal with problems in their areas. The problem is that each level of government writes their plans in a vacuum without taking into consideration the immediate impact on others systems of the failure of the particular subsystem for which they have responsibility. Not even the infrastructure system providers really understand how each system is dependant on other systems.

One of the major barriers to effective response planning is that even some of those who do the planning do not really understand the computer and how vulnerable it is to a cyber attack. It was only a few years ago that the very concept of the personal computer was looked at as some space age device. Now almost every home in America either has one or access tone. Look at each one of these devices as a loaded weapon pointed at the heads of the American public.

There are two groups of individuals coming onto the scene in response to the threat of Cyber terrorism. There are the traditionalists, consisting mainly of pseudo-experts[123], industry analysts, media commentators and "paper warrior" point men who view terrorism as we did in the past. Then there are the new breed who understand that there is a connection between the virtual world of the computer and the problems of real world security. The new breed has a nothing is impossible outlook and thus are better able to deal with the unique problems offered by asymmetrical warfare.

The traditionalists, on the other hand, (look at them as the Doctrine Generals) believe that a terrorist has to plant a bomb, blow up a building, or hijack an airliner. These attacks we understand, there is a concrete result that can be investigated and dealt with in the traditional manner. To them computer attacks are not terrorist attacks. These are the people who laugh at wild and crazy notions such as airplanes being used as "field expedient" missiles.

The new breed, however, (look at them as the proponents of small unit operations) have been trained to look at the big picture and how the Internet interacts with real world security concerns. It is primarily as a result of these newcomers that a definition of Cyberterrorism was created. According to the FBI, *Cyber terrorism is the premeditated, politically motivated attack against information, computer systems, computer programs, and data which results in violence against noncombatant targets by sub-national groups or clandestine agents[124]*. This definition had the benefit of having been designed based upon actual events that have happened.

In November 2001, an Australian man used the Internet and stolen control software to release up to one million liters of raw sewerage into public parks and creeks throughout Queensland in Australia. The culprit was enraged that, even though he had been a consultant on the water project, he had not been given a job by the company that installed a computerized sewerage system for a local government council. He used the very system installed by this company to carry out his dirty deed. However, this could have been avoided if the system manager had been made aware of any of the previous 44 failed attempts by this man to hack into the system.

In February 1998, the U.S. Congress was made aware of attempts by Islamic extremist organizations to development a hacker network to not only support their efforts, but also to engage in offensive information warfare. This is certainly not science fiction, but an organized attempt to infiltrate the very

---

[123] A pseudo-expert is someone that received his training in a classroom and spent his entire career behind a desk shuffling papers regarding terrorism.

[124] Pollitt, Mark A., *Cyberterrorism: Fact or Fancy?*, Proceedings of the 20th National Information Systems Security Conference, October 1997.

infrastructure that makes out society run. The talent is available on the open market for hire. After the fall of the Soviet Union, just as there were thousands of unemployed scientists that would work for the highest bidder, there were also unemployed world class programmers who could very easily turn their talents to hacking for the right price.

So how vulnerable are the computer systems in this country? Probably the benchmark of our cyber security would be the security of our military computers. With this thought in mind, in 1997, the Joint Chiefs of Staff organized an exercise to test the security systems in place to protect critical computer networks. The exercise was called "Eligible Receiver[125]" and the results sent shock waves through the entire military.

ELIGIBLE RECEIVER

Thirty-five NSA[126] computer hackers were chosen at random to be the "bad guys" in this operation. Using only software tools and other hacking utilities that could be downloaded freely from the Internet, they were tasked to try and hack into the computer networks of the U.S. Pacific Command in Hawaii. The Pacific Command is responsible for all military contingencies and operations conducted in the Pacific theater, including Korea. A number of secondary targets were also chosen, to include the National Military Command Center (NMCC) at the Pentagon, the U.S. Space Command, the U.S. Transportation Command, and the U.S. Special Operations Command. All of these commands should have the best security systems available to the United States Military.

To everyone's shock and surprise, except the hackers, the NSA hackers had very little trouble accessing military computer networks. They mapped critical networks, determined passwords through trial and error, and also through a technique called social engineering. BY social engineering, it is meant that they simply called up people that did have access, pretend to be a technician or a high ranking individual and ask them for their passwords. More often than not, they received what they asked for. Once the hackers had achieved access to the systems, they simply created their own accounts on the servers, deleted accounts belonging to authorized users, reformatted hard drives, shut down systems and generally raised merry hell.

The final result of the exercise was that using only freely downloadable tools and hacking utilities, these government hackers could have crippled the U.S. military's command and control system for the Pacific theater. The resulting chaos and confusion would have been an open invitation for an attack by an enemy.

---

[125] Verton, Dan, Black Ice: The Invisible Threat of Cyber-Terrorism, McGraw-Hill, New York. 2003.
[126] National Security Agency.

THE WIRELESS THREAT

As if things are not bad enough, along comes wireless Internet, a boon to the traveler. No longer must you connect to a telephone system, but you can access the Internet from literally almost anywhere. This is a fantastic idea whose day has come and it is also an open invitation to the terrorist.

In an effort to be more user friendly, American Airlines installed wireless roving agent[127] and curbside check-in systems, at more than 250 airports across the nation. These systems allowed agents to check in passengers for flights from anywhere in the terminal, including out in the street. The concept was to allow frequent flyers and first class passengers to avoid long ticket counter lines. It was a great concept, but there were a few flaws.

These systems were not encrypted, that means that anyone who could access the systems could read information in the clear. Additionally, both systems were integrated with the baggage check system, reservation system, aircraft maintenance databases, and a number of other critical systems. This naturally placed the daily operations of the airlines as well as passenger safety, were now compromised. Terrorists could use what is called a sniffer program loaded on a laptop computer that had wireless Internet capability, to be able to pluck this information out of the air, as well as user names and passwords. With this access, it would be possible for a terrorist to ensure that a piece of luggage would be loaded on a specific flight without the owner being present, a strict security violation. Passenger names could also be changed to allow terrorists to board unimpeded. With access to the passenger reservation list, a hacker can even determine the identify of the federal sky marshal, his or her seat number and then disabled the marshal in flight and commandeer his or her weapon.

Wireless Internet depends on the utilization of nodes that are installed in a number of locations. I have even seen commercials for wireless terminals that entrepreneurs can purchase and install in locations with high traffic. Airports, naturally, and many of the major hotels have now installed wireless nodes for the use of their customers.

Returning to the American Airlines Roving Agent program for a moment, once a legitimate agent has logged into the system, someone with access to the wireless system can determine an Internet protocol address inside the network. Once this is accomplished, the hacker has access to the switches, routers, internal serves, web servers, Intranet, suppliers, and anything else interesting. This hacker could access the wireless system from a vehicle outside airline property. It is an open invitation for disaster.

---

[127] The Roving Agent is a hand held device that allows access to a number of airline systems, to include check in and baggage check systems.

PART V

SURVIVING THE TERROR

CHAPTER TWENTY-SEVEN
PLANNING TO SURVIVE

I have painted a rather bleak picture in the preceding pages, but I also painted a very real picture. Our government has gone so far to the extreme to make us feel safe that they have actually misled many of us into believing that while it is possible to have a major terrorist attack in this country, it is not likely. The unfortunate fact is that there is really no safe haven from a determined terrorist that is willing to risk his life to carry out his mission.

However, this does not mean that there is no hope or that we should stay locked up in our houses, weapons loaded, waiting for the attack. There are actually some very common sense steps that can be taken in order to ensure the safety of our families. First and foremost, the wise man, or woman, does not make himself or herself an easy target. Becoming alert to our surroundings is a good start to protecting yourself and your family from becoming a potential victim.

SOFT TARGETS

In an asymmetric war, the favorite target of a terrorist attack would be a soft target. A soft target is accessible, predictable and unaware of the danger. The soft target makes the job of the terrorist easy to access their private information, such as phone numbers, addresses, and schedules. A soft target follows a consistent routine at home and at work, allowing the terrorist to be able to predict the target's movement in advance. Soft targets are normally unaware of their surroundings and do not employ individual protective measures or use predictive equipment. This description certainly fits the majority of those who live in the larger cities. The desire not to get involved in the problems of others has led to a mind set where we do not even meet the eyes of those we pass on the street because they might ask something of us. This must change; we are all in this struggle together.

Weapons of mass destruction are easily employed against soft targets and there is really no need for a terrorist to seek them out. Picture, if you will, a nice enjoyable day at the mall; suddenly, those around you grab their throats and began to cough and wheeze. You may have just been a victim of a chemical attack. So how can you tell? The following is a list of indicators that there has been a chemical attack[128]:

- Numerous dead animals, domestic as well as wild, birds, and/or fish in the same area. This does not refer to "road kill", but rather large numbers of animals in a particular area that are found dead with no visible injuries. Chemical agents do not kill or sicken just humans but many affect the animal population as well;

- Lack of insect activity may also be a sign of a chemical attack. There are insects around is almost all of the time, though we are so accustomed to it that we rarely pay much attention. If this activity is missing, then it is very possible that there has been a chemical attack;

- Numerous people experiencing unexplained waterlike blisters, wheals similar to bee stings, pinpointed pupils, choking respiratory ailments and/or rashes. These symptoms would very clearly indicate exposure to some chemical;

- Numerous individuals exhibiting unexplained health problems ranging from nausea to disorientation, difficulty breathing, convulsions or dying;

- A pattern of casualties that may indicate a possible chemical or biological dissemination method;

- The illnesses seem to be limited to a confined geographical area;

- Numerous surfaces have oily droplets or film, or the surfaces of standing water seems to be covered by an oily film;

- Areas appear different from the surrounding environs, such as a patch of trees, shrubs, bushes, crops and/or lawns that are dead, discolored or withered;

---

[128] This list of possible indicators of a chemical attack came from the Chemical/Biological/Radiological Handbook, Director of Central Intelligence, Interagency Intelligence Committee on Terrorism, Community Counterterrorism Board. October 1998.

- Unexplained odors that range from fruity to flowery, sharp or pungent, garlic or similar to horseradish, bitter almonds or peach pits, or the smell of new mown hay. The most telltale sign is that the odor is completely out of character with the surroundings;

- There may be low lying clouds or patches of fog that are not in keeping with the surroundings;

- There may be unexplained or unusual metal debris lying in the area. The unexplained or unusual metal debris might be remnants of the shell casing that contained the chemical or biological agent.

Should you find yourself in a situation where these indicators are present, it is best to leave the area, contact authorities and then seek medical assistance. With some chemical and biological agents it is possible to become contaminated, but not show any signs for some period of time, so it is always wise to play it safe and seek quick medical care.

The indicators of an attack using biological agents rather than chemical agents are similar, but there are some additional indicators that should be watched for as outlined below[129].

- An unusual number of sick or dying people and/or animals in a given area is a very clear indication of a biological attack. The symptoms of these illnesses can be many and varied. Casualties from a biological attack can also come days or weeks after the actual event as the time required for the first symptoms to appear are dependent on the agent used and the dose received. Some of the symptoms are likely to include unexplained gastrointestinal illnesses and respiratory problems that are most likely to be mistaken for flu or colds.

- The sight of unscheduled or unusual spraying being conducted especially if at unusual times such as during pe4riods of darkness.

- The sight of abandoned spray devices that do not have a distinct odor.

HARD TARGETS

If you are caught in a chemical or biological attack, it will not matter what kind of target you are, as such an attack is very widespread. However, short of such a broad based attack, there are precautions that you can take to place

---

[129] Ibid

yourself and your family at the bottom of the list of potential terrorist targets. This process is known as making yourself a hard target.

A hard target is inaccessible, unpredictable, and aware, and makes it difficult for terrorists to gain access to themselves or their families. Someone who does not wish to become an easy target for a potential terrorist varies their routines and does not set patterns in their daily lives. Such an individual becomes security conscious and is always very much aware of their surroundings. Just as terrorists are unpredictable, you too much become somewhat unpredictable. This inability to pin down your movements or anticipate your activities will cause a potential attacker to go choose an easier target.

To become a hard target, there are certain don'ts that must be observed.

- Do not put your name or other information on your mailbox;

- Do not run or walk at the same time each day along the same route or to the same destination;

- Do not take part in outdoor activities such as yard work at the same time each day;

- Do not shop at the same stores on the same day of each week;

- Do not follow the same routes at the same time each day;

- Do not attend the same service at the same church on the same day each week;

- Do not sit at the same spot either in your vehicle (this of course, is difficult if you are alone and driving the car), at a restaurant or at any public gathering;

- Do not arrive at work, go to lunch, run errands, or depart work at the same time each day and always by the same entrances and exits;

- Do not go to the same restaurants or bars whenever you go out;

- If traveling in a foreign country, do not always go to only American restaurants or other establishments;

- Do not always park your vehicle at the same location or in an area where it cannot be seen.

BE SECURITY CONSCIOUS

The need to on guard at all times is not something that has been historically a requirement in this country. But with the continuing threat of international terrorism as well as the increasing incidence of domestic terrorism, becoming more security conscious is certainly a good idea. Becoming more security conscious does not require the expenditure of a large sum of money or radically changing your life style. Unlike many parts of the world, the likelihood of your home being invaded by masked terrorists is somewhat remote, but in outlying areas, such a possibility is not completely out of the question. Short of living in a fortress and surrounding yourself with armed guards, there are a number of steps that can be taken that only require becoming aware and taking some basic precautions.

For example, don't provide information to potential terrorists or anyone else, for that matter, via the telephone, mail, computer or in your trashcan. Always shred documents before placing them in the garbage or, if possible, incinerate them. Look into what you need to do in order to make both your phones as well as your computers secure.

Do not place your name and address in the local telephone directory. Use caller ID or call blocking if available and if you receive an unusual number of hang up calls or wrong numbers, report this to your local law enforcement. When you answer your telephone don't give personal information and especially do not given out personal information over the Internet. Should you have any interruption of service on your telephone system or unusual interference with either your phone, electrical or computer service report this to both the phone company as well as local law enforcement. These are the first signs that perhaps your phone line has been bugged. Always have an operational cellular phone available as a backup in case your normal service is interrupted.

Terrorists normally stake out a potential target and conduct surveillance to determine schedules and plot the best times and locations for an attack. To counter this you might consider forming a neighborhood watch organization to keep track of strange cars in your neighborhood. Stress to family members and any domestic employees that you might have the importance of noticing and reporting strange callers or vehicles in the area. Around your office, make the acquaintance of the local store owners who might be counted upon to notice anything out of the ordinary.

At home, consider getting a pet, if you do not already own one. A watch dog can be a major deterrent to common criminals and a first line of both warning and defense in the event of an intruder. In addition you might consider installing an alarm system with motion detectors. Additionally, consider putting up fences and walls to block off direct avenues of egress to your property. Always lock your doors and windows, perhaps turn an inside room into a secure room or a panic room where you, or your family, can go in the event of an emergency.

It is not wise to place the security and safety of yourself or your family completely in the hands of others. If your plan is to summon the police in the event of an emergency, consider alternatives in the event that terrorists disable local emergency communications through the use of a rather inexpensive EMP bomb. Police help might be hours in arriving. What will you and your family do in the meantime? Though the idea is abhorrent to many of our liberal citizens, your might want to consider purchasing a firearm and taking instructional classes. Once you become proficient with a firearm, if called upon to use it in a life or death situation, do not hesitate. It is the instinctive hesitation to use a weapon against another human being that usually gives the intruder time to disarm the owner or results in the death of many gun owners in such situations. With a serviceable weapon, the knowledge and determination to use it, you at least have a fighting chance to protect your life and the lives of your loved ones in the event that your home is invaded by terrorists.

Finally, make sure that you have a first class communications system and that it is operational and secure. If your house is large, install an intercom system and consider handheld radios for communications between family members. Install an audible alarm system that is monitored by your local law enforcement or a private security firm.

BE PREPARED

I hate to use such a trite heading as "Be Prepared" but it is true that if you are prepared for the worst, that generally you never have to use it. In the event of a major disaster it is unreasoning fear and the lack of basic preparedness that endangers the lives of many. Those with serious medical problems become so worried that they cannot get medical help that this sometimes triggers the very attack they are worried about having. Perhaps someone with a known illness could obtain a backup supply of medication, just in case he or she cannot get to medical help or the drug store to have prescriptions refilled.

If a terrorist attack knocks out the local electricity most of us would just shrug and dig out the candles. However, what if the attack disabled the regional electrical grid for an indefinite period of time? How many of us could survive for an indefinite period of time without television or all of the many labor saving devices that work on electricity? Lack of electricity would disabled the telephone system, as well as the water distribution system. How many of us are prepared for an indefinite period of time with no water service? It would turn the inner cities into deserts. So let us look at some things that can be done to prepare for a terrorist event.

THE BASICS

In the event of a terrorist attack in the United States, experts believe it will most likely be an attack using some type of weapon of mass destruction. No one individual or group of individuals will be singled out, but it will be an attack against a broad range of people. Such an attack will normally find many of us at or near our homes or able to get to our homes within a short period of time. Therefore, logically, we should have out homes prepared to enable us to survive not only the attack but also the aftermath of such an attack.

The government generally recommends that each family be able to be self sufficient for at least three days. Though this sounds like a short period of time, the unfortunate fact is that most families are able to be self sufficient for any appreciable length of time. This might be due to lack of funds, illness, age, or infirmity. But even individuals in this situation can take certain basic steps to prepare.

We are a nation that likes its comforts, but in an emergency situation, there are certain necessities that rank higher than comfort items. The following is a list of those things that should be obtained and kept on hand in the event of an emergency[130]:

- Flashlights – The importance of a good flashlight(s) goes without saying, but I want to stress that in the event of long term power outage, a bright light, in addition to making movement easier can also have a positive effect on morale. Also being a firm believer in the validity of Murphy's Law[131], I recommend having more than one flashlight available;

- Battery or solar powered radio – During a period of emergency, one of the most important things to have available will be a radio. This will be your new lifeline where the local, state, or national governments will be issuing bulletins regarding the current situation. With the distinct possibility that electrical power will be interrupted for some appreciable period of time, you should look at a good solid portable radio that had the ability to operate on batteries. There are even a large number of portable radios on the market that can operate on solar power, making the necessity of keeping a supply of spare batteries on hand unnecessary. I would also recommend that a radio be obtained that has one or more short wave bands. Quite often, foreign broadcast stations have more concrete information about events taking place in this country that is reported on our news broadcasts.

---

[130] The U.S. Government Guide to Surviving Terrorism, Barnes & Nobles, New York. 2003

[131] Murphy's Law says that whatever can go wrong, will go wrong and it will be at the worst possible time.

I would also recommend that a radio capable of monitoring local emergency communications be obtained if it is at all possible. The information available to you from monitoring these calls will be much more up to date than on news broadcasts. It is often possible that these broadcasts can be monitored with a multi-band radio such as the Zenith Transoceanic, as the band upon which most of them operate is within the short wave spectrum. Monitoring these broadcasts can, however, be a problem in larger jurisdictions where the police and fire departments use automated trunking systems where the specific frequency used for a call is selected at random by a central computer. To be able to monitor these calls, a receiver such as a dual trunking scanner is necessary. One model that is suitable for this purpose is the Radio Shack PRO-94, a reasonably priced, 1,000-channel dual trunking scanner.

Finally, under the topic of radios, I would also suggest, should you have immediate family members that are living in other areas, that you consider purchasing a battery operated citizens band radio or an Amateur (Ham) radio. Radio Shack makes a mini handheld amateur transceiver that is very reasonably priced and can cover the 2-meter band as well as the 438-450 MHZ band. I cannot stress too strongly that dependable communications during an emergency is an excellent way to reduce stress.

- Extra Batteries for each battery powered item are a necessity.

- A complete first aid kit is also a necessity during a period of emergency. It may not be possible for you to rush to the emergency room or your doctor's office for any number of reasons. As a result, you may be forced to be your own doctor for anything but the worst medical problems. The US Army has developed some very complete first aid kits for field medics that can give you what you need to deal with most problems short of surgery. You might check your local military surplus stores to try and obtain such a kit. If you need to rely on commercially prepared kits, make sure that the kits contains as a minimum;
Two pairs of sterile gloves,
Sterile dressings,
Cleansing agent and antibiotic towelettes for disinfecting wounds,
Antibiotic ointment,
Burn ointment;
Aspirin or non-aspirin substitute
Various sizes of adhesive bandages,
Anti-diarrhea medication
Antacids
Diaper rash ointment if babies will be present

Laxatives
Thermometer;
Medicine dropper
Eye wash solution
Prescription medications
Prescribed medical supplies such as glucose and blood pressure monitoring equipment
Scissors
Tweezers
Petroleum jelly

- A strong, sharp, utility knife should also be included in your survival kit. Having spent many years in the U.S. Army, I prefer the survival knife made by the Gerber Corporation, though the cost of this particular knife can be very pricey. As a backup for my more expensive blade, I also like the various models of the Swiss Army knife manufactured by the Victorinox Corporation[132]. Some of their knives have more tools than a mechanics tool chest. The most versatile knife that I possess is the Swiss Army Knife called the Cybertool. This particular model is designed for working on computers, and I have yet to find a situation where one of the tools on this handy little knife has not filled the bill.

    In addition to a knife, I would also suggest a fire extinguisher, pliers, a selection of wrenches such as you might use to shut off gas lines, a compass, several waterproof containers of matches, as well as paper and pencils or pens;

- Foods that take little preparation or storage such as freeze dried foods or prepackaged military meals[133]. I would also make mention that some of the larger grocery stores carry selections of foods that are nutritious, taste good and do not take a lot of preparation. It is important to keep in mind that during periods of stress, food consumption may increase, so think ahead and purchase more than you would normally consume in any given three day period. The foods selected should require no refrigeration, preparation or cooking and little or no water.

    As a suggestion for types of foods, you might think about purchasing ready to eat canned meats, fruits, and vegetables; fruit bars or granola; peanut butter and crackers; dried fruit; nuts; canned juices as well as non-pasteurized milk. This menu could also be supplemented by high energy foods or candy bars. You should also make sure that you do

---

[132] Victorinox, Ibach, Switzerland.

[133] Many Army surplus stores and sporting goods stores have prepackaged survival foods at relatively inexpensive prices.

not forget special needs such as baby foods, or easily digested foods for any elderly members of your family. Some individuals with high blood pressure or diabetes also control their conditions through diet, if you have a person in your family group, be sure to obtain foods that meet these criteria.

Along with the foods, do not forget those items necessary for dining or storage of foods. I am referring to mess kits that are easily cleaned and do not require much water (back to the military surplus store), paper cups, plastic utensils, aluminum foil and storage containers. Especially do not forget a manual can opener. Many households have handy electric can openers which may not be too effective in the absence of electricity.

- Water – Government recommendations calls for a three-day supply of water per person. Normally, it is estimated that there should be a gallon of water per day per person for dinking and sanitation purposes. Depending on the climate, however, such as in the hot summer months, substantially more water per person per day may be required. Children, nursing mothers and those that are ill may also require more than a gallon of water per day. The water should be stored in clean, reusable plastic containers.;

- Toilet articles;

- Feminine hygiene products;

- Garbage bags and other sanitation supplies are a must. Do not assume that conditions will be normal, so lay in a large supply of paper products such as toilet paper, paper towels, and moist towelettes. A field expedient toilet can be manufactured from a garbage bag, a five gallon plastic bucket and a gallon of water. Also do not forget to include household chlorine bleach;

- Prescription medicine or any other special items needed by any family member;

- A supply of cash[134] and picture identification;

---

[134] A friend made mention that in case of emergency he would use his credit cards for all purchases he needed to make for his family. However, remember credit cards are approved through a national computer network and if the credit card terminal is a wireless such as I use, it requires connection to a cellular telephone network. In the event

Once you have gathered your emergency supplies, place them in one area so that if needed you are not searching high and low for where you put the flashlight batteries. Consider obtaining one or more duffle bags and packing your emergency supplies into these bags. This way, if you are forced to leave your home, you can carry your emergency supplies with you. You might even consider preparing a smaller one day supply emergency kit and storing it in your car in case you are on the road when you are forced to deal with such an emergency.

AERIAL DEFENSES

By this title, I am not referring to anti-aircraft guns, but rather the fact that many potential terrorist attacks involve the use of microscopic particles that are released into the air such as aerolized smallpox that could be sprayed in an area. Many of these particles must enter your lungs in order to cause injury. The goal in regard to these dangers is to keep the microscopic particles from entering your body. This can be achieved through personal protection as well as environmental barriers.

One of the quickest and most basic barriers available might be a mask that you would place over your nose, mouth, eyes and any open cuts your might have. These masks or coverings should be made of a dense weave cotton material. This might consist of two or three layers of cotton t-shirt, handkerchiefs or towels. Insure that the air that you breath comes through the mask and not around it. You can get ready made masks in various sizes at your hardware stores or paint stores. Given the many and varied type of attacks that terrorists could launch there is no single mask that could be a perfect fix for this problem. However, anything you can use to place over your nose and mouth to filter the air that you breath is better than nothing and may be the difference between life and death.

In the event that a terrorist has released a biological or chemical spray in your area, you may want to seek shelter and create a barrier between yourself and the potentially contaminated air. If you have them available, consider using plastic garbage bags or plastic sheeting to cover the doors, windows, and air ducts of whatever room you have chosen as your shelter. These "field expedient" barriers can be held in place with duct tape. The key is to ensure that you have sealed every open airway into the space you have chosen. As a precaution, you might also have on hand several large rolls of duct tape and a large supply of garbage bags or plastic sheeting that you do not plan to use for sanitation that can be used for creating barriers.

---

of a major terrorist event that knocks out communications or the Internet, credit cards are useless.

If you plan on riding out any potential terrorist attack in your home, you might also consider investing in a portable air purifier with a High Efficiency Particulate Air Filtration (HEPA) filter. The HEPA filer can help remove contaminants in the air of the room in which you are sheltering. Of course you need to remember that while these filters can remove dander, dust, molds, smoke, some biological agents and many other contaminants from the air, they are useless against chemical gases.

WHAT TO WEAR

Though it sounds a little silly, what to wear during a chemical or biological attack can become rather important. Some of the nerve agents can kill if a drop falls on your hand and is absorbed through your skin. For this reason, the clothing that you use during a terrorist event should be carefully considered.

You might want to wear or have handy a jacket or a coat; rather than stylish shorts, wear long pants, perhaps you should consider sturdy denim jeans. You should wear long sleeved shirts, and sturdy shoes that can take a lot of hard wear and always wear a hat and gloves. If you live in cooler climates, depending on the time of year, if the power is out, then the heat may well be out. In this case, you need to dress for warmth.

MAN'S BEST FRIEND

I could write a book on how to prepare for various emergencies, but in this volume I am giving only an overview, covering the basics of preparation for chemical and biological attacks. My intent is to show that while a terrorist attack using a weapon of mass destruction such as chemical or biological weapons is almost a certainty, that it is easily survived with the use of common sense. However, I do not want to leave this chapter without stressing the need to consider what to do with your pets.

Our dogs and cats give us a lifetime of love and loyalty and expect, in return, that we take care of them. To many of us, our pets are an integral part of our daily lives, so in preparing for our survival, we need to prepare for their survival as well. If your pets need medication, make sure you have a large supply on hand for the foreseeable future.

Just as you prepare a safe room for yourself and your family, either plan on taking your pets into the room with you or prepare them their own safe haven such as a utility closet, or some other secure, easily cleaned room. Do not plan on putting your cats in the same room as your dogs. Even the friendliest of animals may show their claws during stressful periods. Make sure that the room prepared for them has access to a supply of clean drinking water. Consider what to do to insure your pet's safety if the room should flood or catch fire.

Purchase a larger than normal supply of dog food and bottled water for their use. Make sure that can openers are available for opening those cans. Stock up on the most common medications for pets, even consider making a pet first aid kit. Look at your pets as you would your children and look out for their welfare.

CHAPTER TWENTY-EIGHT
DEALING WITH A JIHAD

There is no doubt that the various Islamic terrorist groups are our enemies. We cannot look at them as we would the inhabitants of a hostile country. They are not motivated by nationalism, patriotism, or some other noble emotion. These people are motivated by the belief that killing us is what their God wants them to do. Their hatred of us, and everything we stand for, is basic to their very nature. We cannot reason with them or negotiate with them like any other enemy we have ever dealt with.

We must take the war to them in the same fashion that they bring it to us. We cannot fight a polite war and crucify our military in the press for treating the enemy in an impolite fashion. The Islamic fundamentalists only understand force; they look at attempts to make peace as weakness. Our homeland has been attacked and yet the liberals have made efforts to defend their assaults. Only when we show the world a unified will to win will the terrorists turn their attention to other weaker enemies.

PROFILING IS NOT A CRIME

This country is so civil rights sensitive that to look at someone from the Middle East as a potential terrorist is considered racial profiling and illegal. In the days after 9/11 I had cause to fly across the country. Even though I always set off the metal detectors due to my metal leg braces, I was never searched. At Chicago's O'Hare Airport I was behind a group of four Middle Eastern men. These Middle Eastern men who met every profile for terrorist members that I have ever seen, were waved onto the plane without any search whatsoever, while an elderly white lady and two teenage girls were searched not once but twice before being allowed to board.

I asked the senior member of the security officers at the gate why the four Middle Eastern gentlemen had not been searched and was told that if they had searched them that they (the security officers) would have been accused of profiling by their own superiors. As a result of complaints form the American Civil Liberties Union and Middle Eastern special interest groups about the alleged singling out of Middle Eastern men for searches, strict orders had been issued by Air Port Security officials to the security officers at the gates to avoid even the appearance of profiling or lose their jobs. So it was easier and safer for them to search the old ladies and the teenage girls rather than those who were very probably terrorists.

It is stupidity such as this that is the terrorists' best ally. Had the Middle Eastern that hijacked those planes on 9/11 been searched prior to boarding perhaps they would not have been able to get their box cutters on board those planes. However, for Airport Security to have singled them out under our "politically correct" racial laws for searching would have been illegal. This mind set is going to get a lot of Americans killed before we wake up and realize that we are really in a war and political correctness is one of our greatest enemies. I had rather be alive than have my friends all gather over my casket to praise how politically correct I was.

Even a fanatic learns not to stick his hand in a fire or his head in a hornets' nest. When we make it too difficult and costly in terms of dead terrorists for these extremist groups to launch their terrorist attacks in this country, the war on terror will be over. Until then, we have to listen to the defeatist rhetoric of the politically correct group and hope we are not in the crosshairs.

INDEX

www.ingramcontent.com/pod-product-compliance
Lightning Source LLC
Chambersburg PA
CBHW021850020426

42334CB00013B/259